JOHN RINGO

DAVID JOHNSON

Barbed Wire Press

PO BOX 2107, STILLWATER, OK 74076
A WESTERN PUBLICATIONS COMPANY

Library of Congress Cataloging-in-Publication Data

Johnson, David D., 1950-
        John Ringo / David D. Johnson.
            p. cm.
        Includes bibliographical references and index.
        ISBN 0-935269-23-1
        1. Ringo, John. 2. Outlaws—Southwest., New—Biography, 3.
Frontier and pioneer life—Southwest, New. 4. Southwest, New—Biography.
I. Title.
F786.R57J64 1996
979'.02'092—dc20   96-44951
    [B]   CIP

First Edition
Cover design by Marcus J. Huff
Copyright © 1996 by David D. Johnson
All rights reserved.

Published by Barbed Wire Press, P.O. Box 2107, Stillwater, Oklahoma
74076. 1-800-749-3369.

Manufactured in the United States of America. First Edition.

CONTENTS

LIST OF ILLUSTRATIONS

FOREWORD

A compelling irony infuses the relationship between gunfighter John Ringo and his most famous adversary—Wyatt Earp. Earp has been elevated to the heights of a Sir Galahad by numerous writers, especially Stuart N. Lake. Earp produced his own version of historical events within a few decades after the famed "O.K. Corral" gunfight which has fascinated historians and the general public for more than a century.

John Ringo, whose life ended in its prime, had neither the benefit of providing an autobiography nor of being subject to a biographer's talents. Rather, Ringo's career is known essentially through the work of writers focusing on his adversaries. As such he has emerged as a Hamlet-like figure (Walter Noble Burns), the black sheep of an aristocratic family (Eugene Cunningham), and a man remembered merely for the gunfighter tonality of his name (Jack Burrows).

Ringo had his faults, but being a cold-blooded murderer wandering the West with no redeeming virtues was not one of them. He deserves more from history. The tragic guerrilla atrocities of the Civil War must have played deadly havoc on his own personality, but he was man enough to avoid sinking to the level of the guerrilla. Witnessing his father's accidental death might have caused a weaker person to wallow in self-pity. But the young John Ringo, in spite of those hardships, grew to a reasonably well-adjusted manhood. He later contributed to the family's earnings and well-being. He provided support to his mother and sisters. He did not abandon himself to dissolution, as some writers have blatantly asserted.

John Ringo, in spite of the hardships and tragedies of his youth, became a man, willing to risk his life and well-being to fight for what he believed to be right. The blood feud turbulence of the mid-1870s nearly engulfed him, and his name became a household word in central Texas.

That reputation preceded Ringo's arrival in Arizona Territory, where history has become best acquainted with him, and where he was nearly always at odds with the Earps. Therein lies the ultimate irony: Ringo destroyed himself, but Wyatt Earp later claimed him as a victim. The legend that Earp killed Ringo to avenge his brother's murder has become embedded in the Earp myth. Recent books and movies seem to consider Ringo's being killed by Earp or his sidekick, Doc Holliday, *de rigueur.*

John Ringo may not have been a paragon of virtue, but he deserves much better. Through the research of Dave Johnson, Ringo has received his proper due, and he will stand as a historical figure alone against the elements, rather than in the shadow of a lawman certainly no better than himself.

Chuck Parsons
Smiley, Texas 1995

ACKNOWLEDGMENTS

A number of people over the years have helped in this research project. Chief among them are David L. Ringo, May Ringo King, and Dr. William Hall, who patiently answered questions on the Ringo family. They and other members of the Ringo family were consistently gracious, helpful and generous with their assistance. Special thanks also to Dave Stark of Gallatin, Missouri, who helped tremendously in tracking the Ringo family in Missouri and to Randy Brown who not only shared his knowledge of Martin Ringo's grave site but kindly furnished photographs of it. He and Jim Browning, who traveled to the grave site independently to help out a friend, provided service "above and beyond."

Special thanks are also due to Jane Hoerster, County Historical Commissioner of Mason County, Texas, who provided numerous insights and a wealth of information on the Mason County War and its participants—not to mention a lasting friendship. Beatrice Langehennig, Linda Phillips, and Diane Pence of the Mason County clerk's office were particularly helpful and generous with their time. Marley Brant, the preeminent authority on the Younger family, was always gracious and supportive. Special thanks to Donaly Brice, who helped tremendously, and to his wife, Clare, who suffered through it all. Chuck and Marjorie Parsons, Sue C. Van Slyke, Janaloo Hill, Gary Fitterer, Jack DeMattos, Phil Rasch, Ed Bartholomew, Pete Rose, and Rick Miller provided help in many ways. My friend Steve Gatto provided help and inspiration.

I would like to acknowledge the help of many librarians and county and district clerks in numerous states. Beyond this the Olney family provided information and photographs of their ancestors and answered innumerable questions. My gratitude also to the families of the Farris brothers, Tim Williamson, George Gladden, the Bairds, Hoersters, Jordans, John Clark, and numerous others.

Special thanks are also due to J. Marvin Hunter, Joe Small, and John Joerschke who served not only as inspirational models for western researchers but as keepers of the flame for truthful western history.

Last, but hardly least, my eternal thanks to my grandparents, who encouraged me to have a curious mind, and to my parents, Charles and Ruth Fergus Johnson, who always had complete faith in me—also, to my daughter, Kristina, who has grown up with John Ringo, and to my wife, Ieva, who suffered through all of it with no complaints but lots of love and support. Most of all, I thank my Maker for all of the blessings I have received, not only throughout this search but through my entire life.

Thank you all.

PREFACE
"A Hamlet among outlaws"

Walter Noble Burns can be credited with creating almost single-handed the John Ringo of legend. In 1927 Burns wrote, "John Ringo stalks through the stories of old Tombstone days like a Hamlet among outlaws, an introspective, tragic figure darkly handsome, splendidly brave, a man born for better things, who, having thrown his life recklessly away, drowned his memories in cards and drink and drifted without definite purpose or destination."[1] With that single, emotional sentence, Burns set the stage for the romantic myth of John Ringo.

Unfortunately for history, Burns allowed his desire to write a marketable book to interfere with reality. His book, *Tombstone*, mingled folklore with fact to the point that the two are indistinguishable and the entire volume is suspect. Characterizing Burns' work as "seriously flawed," author Jeff Morey commented, "When Walter Noble Burns wrote *Tombstone* in the style of his time, the question followed: 'Is this history or is it a novel?'"[2] In creating the mythical John Ringo, Burns also created a target for later historians and writers to assault or glorify as their natures dictate. Author Gary L. Roberts termed such writers "rocking chair historians," adding, "Past writers, particularly [Stuart N.] Lake and [William E.] Connelly, were bitterly attacked by men who had neither the talent nor the research ability nor the understanding of the West's history of these early writers."[3]

Roberts' criticism is not entirely unwarranted, but neither is it entirely valid. Certainly criticism based on primary documents and contemporary accounts is justified. That is the correction of historical fiction rather than debunking or "bashing." A case in point is Ed Bartholomew's two-volume biography of Wyatt Earp. In it Bartholomew thoroughly destroyed a fictitious account of Earp's disarming gunfighter Ben Thompson after Ben's brother, Billy, shot Chauncey B. Whitney.[4] Lake first presented that concoction as fact in his fictionalized *Wyatt Earp, Frontier Marshal.* Bartholomew's disclosure is neither pointless debunking nor uninformed attack. Quite the contrary. It exposes a fiction foisted on the public to glorify Wyatt Earp.

For better or for worse, John Ringo has become inextricably linked to Tombstone folklore. Yet without writers such as Burns and Lake, Ringo's notoriety would be in doubt. Certainly he did not have the "kill" record of a John Wesley Hardin, the foremost gunman of the time. Cullen Baker, considered by some to be the first real gunfighter, successfully battled Reconstruction forces in Texas for some time before being killed. Six-Shooter Smith, whose real name was John Henry Hankins, a member of the loosely knit Dodge City Gang, operated in several states before being killed in La Salle County, Texas. His death was front page news in several states. Today, however, few recognize their names.

Biographer Jack Burrows believed Ringo's attraction lies in his name and speculated that it has a built-in gunfighter sound.[5] Perhaps, but if that were the case, the Ringo family as a group would be better known than it is. The family was far flung, and many of them made their way west. Yet, other than John, none of them has gained any notoriety or fame.

Burns' book might help explain Ringo's fascination. A zesty blend of fact and fiction, it established Tombstone as the archetypical frontier town. Whatever his faults as a historian, Burns was a highly talented storyteller. From his pen emerged John Ringo, a tarnished knight errant who rode out of nowhere and died mysteriously. That skillfully drawn portrait certainly contributed to the legendary Ringo's popularity, but the factual Ringo was a man of legendary potential even before Burns began to write.

John Ringo was far more than a creation of Walter Noble Burns. He was a recognized and respected figure of the pre-*Tombstone* gunfighting West. John Wesley Hardin, Texas killer par excellence and veteran of blood feuds, made Ringo's acquaintance in the Travis County jail in Austin. Hardin apparently liked the man. William Preston Longley, a gunman of equal notoriety though much shorter life span, also knew Ringo but disliked him. Any number of men tried to enhance their own reputations by boasting that they killed Ringo. Little glory attaches to killing a reputed drunkard, however, so the historian asks why so many have made that claim.

Part of the answer lies in Ringo's Texas years. He fought in the Mason County War and arrived in Arizona with garbled accounts of that feud dragging at his heels. In his abbreviated account of the feud,

Burns confused Ringo's actions with those of fellow feudist John Baird: "While he was little more than a boy, he became involved in a war between sheep and cattle men. His only brother was killed in the feud, and Ringo hunted down the three murderers and killed them."[6] Burns doubtless drew that succinct and over-simplified version from one of his informants. Inaccurate though his reputation was, Ringo could not escape it. He was the feudist who destroyed his enemies, the remorseless gunman who killed savagely and emerged unscathed.

In contrast, the men who knew Ringo generally liked him. Writer Grace McCool, an Arizona native who interviewed Ringo's acquaintances, asserted, "All the old timers, who knew him, liked him, and spoke well of him."[7] Some men hated him. Most feared him. We may never know exactly what quirk of fate cast him into the limelight of history, but it is likely to have been a combination of factors.

In recent years three authors have published significant work on John Ringo. Jack Burrows, a member of the faculty of San Jose City College, published two articles about him and a book, *John Ringo— The Gunfighter Who Never Was.* Burrows was the first to publicize the existence of the diary of Mary Ringo, John's mother. Critical of earlier authors, Burrows concluded that Ringo was simply "a vicious and dangerous drunk."[8] Another writer, Ben Traywick, published a forty-page pamphlet, *John Ringo—Mythical Gunfighter,* in 1987 and produced copies of some documents drawn, apparently, from the collection of the late Al Turner.[9] Traywick generally followed Burrows' portrait of John Ringo as a teenage alcoholic and high school dropout who abandoned his family.

The best contemporary work on Ringo has been done by historian Jack DeMattos. DeMattos, a thorough and painstaking researcher and author of such books as *The Earp Decision* and *Mysterious Gunfighter: The Story of Dave Mather,* wrote several articles on Ringo basing logical conclusions on the materials available. As he located new information, DeMattos corrected his previous mistakes, and his articles, while not definitive, are a valuable contribution to Ringo studies.

Beyond those authors a number of researchers and historians have contributed to our knowledge of John Ringo and the Ringo family. Chief among them is historian David Leer Ringo, who has authored several excellent books on the Ringo family. More recently, Steve Gatto has contributed significantly regarding Ringo's activities in New Mexico.[10] Last, but not least, was researcher Allen Erwin. Erwin, who had planned a biography of Ringo, disseminated a great deal of misinformation about the Ringo family; many of his actions were less than creditable.

As for John Ringo, the polarized opinions are clear. The man, of course, lies somewhere in between.

CHAPTER ONE

"...the first ancestor of John Ringo..."

In his brief biography of John Ringo, Ben Traywick says Ringo's family descended from Burtis Ringo, a soldier of the American Revolution, and "the first ancestor of John Ringo to appear clearly in History."[1] Burtis, whose full name was Alburtis, was born in 1763, the son of Cornelius Ringo by Margaret Switcher. He was married to Hannah Rector in 1790, and the couple had thirteen children.[2] None of those children, however, was an ancestor of John Ringo, although they were distant relatives. John's great-grandfather was Major Ringo, one of Burtis' many cousins. Major's parents were Henry Ringo, Cornelius' brother, and Margaret Major. Both Burtis and Major were the grandsons of Judge Philip Ringo, who in turn was named for his own grandfather, Philip Janszen Ringo.[3]

At this writing, the earliest known document that mentions the Ringo name is dated April 1, 988, when Count Baudouin IX and his wife Suzanne gave their estates at Alverghem to the abbey of St. Pierre at Ghent. Among the court officials witnessing the transaction was a member of the court in Flanders who signed his name as Reingodus

(Ringo) and was nicknamed *Le Calve* (the Bald).[4]

Between 1040 and 1106 the Ringo name appears frequently on documents due to the prominence of two men, Reingot I and Reingot II.[5] Reingot I styled himself of Ghent and flourished from about 1037 to 1067. It was undoubtedly he who was killed in the battle of Cassel in 1072 while fighting the forces of Richildis (Richelde), countess of Hainaut.

The second prominent Ringo of this time was Reingot II, Lord of Dendermonde, who was probably the son of Reingot I. Reingot was noted as a Crusader in 1096 and was at the capture of Jerusalem on June 15, 1099. He died on October 5, 1106, without any male heirs. The Reingot name appears in various forms on documents of the time: Ringotus, Ringoti, Ringoto, and Ringotum in the declension; Raingotus, Reingodus, Raingotus, Rengotus and Reingotus in the nominative.[6] All are early variants of the Ringo name. In 1072, for example, a noble named Eggebertus gave a villa to the Church of Saint Salvatoris dedicated to the soul of his father Raingoti. The following year Walter of Avesnes gave land at Liezle to the abbey of St. Pierre. Witnesses included Reingodi (Reingodus) and his brother Apri (Aprus). The name appears to have become more popular from this time, eventually becoming a patronymic surname.

There is no evidence that the family of John Ringo was descended from these early lords. Philip Janszen Ringo, the founder of the Ringo family in America, is the first ancestor of John Ringo to emerge clearly in history, but his antecedents are vague. Philip appears to have been born about 1618 in Vlissingen (Flushing) on the Island of Walcheren, Province of Zeeland, in the Netherlands.[7] His name indicates that his father's Christian name was either Jan or Jean, probably the latter, and he appears to have been of Walloon stock.[8] Quite probably Philip Ringo's grandfather fled France in the wake of the infamous St. Bartholomew's Day massacre of August 24, 1572. On that date Catherine de Médicis had some 50,000 Huguenots killed. No records shedding any light on Jean Ringo have been located in France.

One tale, probably apocryphal, recounts that Jean was born around 1590 and was a descendant of Jacques Ringo of Bruges. According to this story, the Ringo family, sailing merchants at the time, received forewarning of the intended massacre and "fled to the water with their gold and belongings." One of the younger Ringos refused to leave his pregnant wife and carried her through the marshes. The young couple reached safety where Jean Ringo's father was born. Dramatically, none of the other Ringo family survived. "Far in the distance he could see the fiery glow of his kinsmen's ships, where every ship had been plundered and mutilated and finally set afire."[9] Beyond this nothing has been determined about Philip's ancestry due to the destruction of Vlissingen's town hall in 1809.[10] David L. Ringo, however, reached some general conclusions as to the family's origins. He summarized his findings in a 1970 letter to Charles Ringo. "The area within a 25 to 50 mile radius of the western section of the French-Belgian border is obviously the original home of our Ringos and still remains so today."[11]

As a young seaman, Philip Ringo appears to have arrived in New Amsterdam (New York City) around 1637 or 1638. A declaration dated October 13, 1643, links him to the privateer *La Garce* (the Wench) in which he was a partner with Anthoni Crol.[12] Crol and Ringo had a traditional business arrangement and on November 18, 1644, made a joint will naming each other as their heirs. Philip Ringo specified that in the event of his death 200 guilders were to go to the poor. In 1645 or 1646 they captured the *St. Antonio of Havanna* and seized its cargo of sugar and tobacco following an engagement in Campeachy Bay. Among Philip's share of the spoils was a captive named Manuel.[13]

On October 18, 1646, Philip made out a new will, and sometime afterwards sold his interest in the *La Garce*. Philip was soon to wed, and perhaps he, his future bride, or both feared the life of a privateer left too much to chance. A short entry in the early records of the Dutch Reformed Church recorded the nuptials: "August 11, 1647, Philip Janszen Ringo, young man from Vlissingen, was married to Geertje Cornelis, widow of Jan Philipszen from Amsterdam."[14] While marriage brought significant changes, Philip remained attached to the sea for the rest of his life. Records indicate that Philip became the owner of the *New Netherland Indian* under contract to the West India Company. On May 3, 1657, he took the Burgher's Oath of citizenship. Perhaps he considered retiring from the sea. If so, it was a short retirement. By October 26, 1659, he was back on the Delaware River. It proved a fateful decision. During the winter of 1661–62, while outbound for the Netherlands, he "fell overboard, perished and was drowned."[15] He was survived by his widow and five children: Janneken, Cornelis, Jan, Albertus, and Pieter.

Albertus Philipszen Ringo was born in 1656 and baptized in the Dutch Reformed Church on July 9. In his youth he was apprenticed to a shoemaker. On August 13, 1679, he wed Jannetje Stoutenburg, a daughter of Pieter Stoutenburg and Aefje van Tienhaven. Records indicate that Albertus was working as a shoemaker in New York City in 1686. On August 30, 1699, he took the freeman's oath and was appointed to the board of deacons for the Collegiate School of the Reformed Dutch Church. The Census of 1702 shows the family living on Broad Street, but in 1707 Albertus moved to Burlington County, New Jersey. There on September 29 he obtained a deed for twelve acres of land along Assunpink Creek. Albertus served two terms as a justice of the peace in 1716 and 1719. He died in 1734. Of his children, only Philip and Aefje are known to have left descendants.[16]

Philip Ringo, second child and eldest son of Albertus Ringo, was born November 2, 1682, in New York City and baptized into the Dutch Reformed Church by Domine Hendricus Selyns on November 15.[17] Philip had the benefit of a good education, probably at the Collegiate School of the Dutch Reformed Church where both his father and grandfather had served on the ruling board. On July 28, 1704, Philip volunteered for service against a French privateer which was harassing English shipping; the results of that expedition are unknown.[18]

By 1706 Philip's father was planning a move to New Jersey due to an overabundance of shoemakers in New York City. Records indicate that Philip was working at the gristmill of Mahlon Stacy in New Jersey during that year. Here, on January 11, 1712, he was named treasurer for a committee seeking to organize a new county.[19] By 1717 he was assessor for Maidenhead Township, and on November 3, 1718, he purchased thirty acres of land from James Harpon (or Harpin) for five pounds and erected a gristmill.[20] The tax roll of 1722 shows him owning the mill and fifty acres of land.

Philip married Jane Cook on May 13, 1721.[21] Their first child, Albertus, was born on October 3 of the next year. In 1723 Philip was appointed captain of the Hopewell Militia under Colonel Daniel Coxe. The same year he received an appointment as justice of the peace for Hunterdon County.[22] Philip served in that capacity until 1730, when he sold his mill and moved to Amwell Township and purchased a tavern. During that time two more children were born to the family: Henry on December 14, 1724, and Peter on June 1, 1730.

Philip was appointed collector for Amwell Township in 1734. Over the next few years Jane and Philip Ringo had two more sons: John, born March 18, 1736, and Cornelius, born April 28, 1739. In March 1749, Philip was appointed judge of the court of common pleas for

Hunterdon County.[23]

Tragedy struck the Philip Ringo family in 1750. On December 22, their youngest son, Peter, died. Eight days later, on December 30, Jane followed her son to the grave. During the same period one of their grandchildren also died. The triple tragedy must have affected the old man deeply, and at sixty-eight years old the possibility that he might need someone to care for him was very real. Following a period of mourning, he married a woman named Catherine.[24] Philip died on May 10, 1757.[25]

Henry Ringo was thirty-three years old when his father died. A blacksmith, Henry had married Margaret Major on March 29, 1749.[26] Unlike his father, Henry had little interest in politics. On March 8, 1763, he was appointed overseer for Rock Road in Amwell Township, but by 1766 the family's resources were overextended. On July 31, 1766, the *Pennsylvania Gazette* published an announcement that his 220-acre "plantation" was to be sold to cover his debts. The plantation was sold, but not until April 8, 1767, to his brother John. At the same time Cornelius Ringo was experiencing similar problems, and by 1769 the two brothers had moved their families to Loudoun County, Virginia.[27]

Virginia proved kinder to Henry's family. On November 13, 1769, Henry was named "Overseer of the Road." He was reappointed to that position on June 10, 1771, to handle the road between Piney Creek and Little Creek. In 1772 the family moved to Prince William County, where they lived for some time. On April 16, 1788, he sold his holdings to Moses Cocke of Pennsylvania and moved to Kentucky.[28] There, at dawn on January 20, 1795, Margaret died following an illness. Henry died on May 12, 1803.

Six of Henry and Margaret's children survived them.[29] Of those, Major Ringo, their fourth son, proves one of the most elusive. Born August 15, 1755, Major is known to have worked as a laborer in New Jersey for a time during 1783. By 1787 he had returned to Virginia, where he married Elizabeth Hazelrigg on September 10.[30]

Major Ringo moved his family to Kentucky in mid-1789, ultimately settling in Montgomery County no later than 1797. In 1819 he and his brother Samuel were designated by their older brother Peter to run his plantation. Five years later Major purchased two slaves.[31] Beyond that, Major Ringo's life is obscure. He died in Montgomery County, Kentucky, on July 15, 1838.

Major Ringo fathered eleven children. Of them, Peter Ringo, the grandfather of John Ringo, was born on June 29, 1791. Peter married Margaret Henderson[32] on October 6, 1813, and at least two children were born to them in Kentucky: Joel on September 27, 1814, and Elvira on April 5, 1816. Family records indicate that the couple's next two children also were born in Kentucky, William H. on November 24, 1817, and John Ringo's father, Martin, on October 1, 1819. That may, however, be in error, for a deed recorded in Wayne County, Indiana, in 1817 indicates that the family already may have settled there.

Why Peter Ringo decided to move to Indiana is unknown. As noted, the earliest record located with his name is a deed bearing the date of October 7, 1817. At that time John and Sarah Jones sold him a plot of land in Centerville for $130. Sarah Jones relinquished "all her Right of Dower" to the property. The deed was witnessed by William Black and Ruth Jones. Justice of the Peace Isaac Julian recorded it on October 13, 1817.[33]

This land transaction implies a move by Peter Ringo's family to Indiana before William's birth. Allowing for the fact that Margaret was in an advanced state of pregnancy at the time, she might have remained with the children in Kentucky while Peter acquired their new home. That would place the family's arrival in Indiana no later than the spring of 1818. Yet Martin consistently listed his place of birth as Kentucky. That could possibly be accounted for by the family's desire to be near kinsmen during Martin's birth. Whatever the case, the 1820 census places the Ringo family in Wayne County. The records note four white males and two white females in the household and list Peter's occupation as "manufacturing."[34] The next year a fourth son, Albert H., was born on November 22.

Records indicate that the Ringos were founding members of the Centerville Methodist Episcopal church in 1823.[35] In 1824 Peter served as county treasurer.[36] On February 28, 1825, Peter again purchased land in Wayne County, about eighty acres, from Samuel and Sally Lough.[37] Peter further expanded his holdings at a sheriff's sale on April 10 of the same year.[38]

The remainder of the Ringo children would be born in Wayne County: Hamilton on February 3, 1824; Melissa Jane on January 1, 1826; Pugh on February 27, 1828; Waldo P. on May 18, 1830; John on March 19, 1832; Martha Elizabeth on July 9, 1834, and Marshall C. on December 27, 1838.[39]

The 1830 Census for Wayne County notes the Ringos' presence but reveals little beyond their ages.[40] The Census for 1840, enumerated by

W.F. Brown, lists seven children of varying ages and states that three of the family were engaged in agriculture, undoubtedly Peter, Martin, and Hamilton.[41] The eldest Ringo children had moved on. Joel Ringo was in Arkansas, probably engaged in his medical practice, and certainly living in close proximity to his uncle, Daniel Ringo, who was then serving as the first chief justice of the Arkansas Supreme Court.[42] Joel and Daniel remained very close during their lifetimes, and Daniel's will refers to him as his "esteemed nephew" in whom he had "full and implicit confidence."[43] Elvira had married John R. Funk on December 6, 1832, and by 1840 had three children of her own.[44] William Ringo also had moved to Arkansas, where he was practicing law.[45]

Peter Ringo prospered in Indiana. A description of his farm four miles northwest of Centerville noted, "It consists of One Hundred and Sixty Acres of Land, of good quality, and in a good state of repair. The improvements comprise a very good Barn, Dwelling and Outhouses, large Orchard, & c. There are a good Spring and Well near the house, and never failing stock water in almost every part of the farm. It is also very well timbered."[46]

But if Indiana brought prosperity to the Ringos it also brought its share of tragedy. Pugh Ringo died in infancy in 1828, and the winter of 1841 brought new grief when Peter's youngest sister, Lucinda, died on February 6. She was buried in the Centerville Cemetery.[47]

During the early 1840s Martin Ringo also left home. Possibly he went first to Arkansas to visit his brothers but, perhaps on the recommendation of his uncle, Daniel, he ultimately went to Missouri, where his cousins, descendants of Samuel H. Ringo, were well established.[48]

Samuel H. Ringo, a younger brother of Major Ringo, was born March 16, 1761, in Hunterdon County, New Jersey. The family moved to Virginia where, on November 12, 1785, he witnessed his brother Peter's purchase of a slave named Easter from Anthony Buckner.[49] Peter later freed the woman in Kentucky.[50] Around 1795 Samuel moved his family to Montgomery County, Kentucky, where they remained until 1820. Late in that year or early in 1821 the family moved west again, this time settling in Howard County, Missouri. The date of Samuel's death has not been determined with certainty but it probably was around 1827.[51]

Martin apparently worked for his cousin, Samuel Ringo, for a time. Martin later engaged in the mercantile trade, which he may have learned at the firm of S. & A.H. Ringo. Certainly Martin and his cousins remained close throughout their lives. That business association may also have led to a more pleasurable one, for it was in Liberty, Missouri, that Martin met Mary Peters.

Traywick notes that Mary and her sister Augusta, who married Coleman Younger, were twins.[52] Burrows, aware that Mary had sisters, mentions only Augusta by name, noting that she was an older sister of Mary.[53] Neither writer discusses the Peters family in any depth, but Mary Peters linked John Ringo to the Younger, James, and Dalton families. John's obituary makes a slightly garbled allusion to the kinship, calling him a "grandson" of Colonel Coleman Younger.[54]

John R. Peters, Mary's father, was born in Woodford County, Kentucky, on February 15, 1797.[55] In 1821 Peters married Frances A. Simms, moving to Liberty four years later. When Liberty was incorporated on May 4, 1829, Peters served on the first Board of Trustees.[56] With him on the board was Samuel Ringo, his nephew by marriage.[57] The Peters family was well thought of in the community. John served for a time as sheriff of Clay County[58] and justice of the peace.[59]

Frances Simms, John's wife, was born on August 24, 1796, to Richard Simms and Elizabeth Ashby.[60] Like the Peters family, the Simmses were well respected in the community. John and Frances had seven children: Vienna Strother, born May 22, 1822; Augusta, born September 26, 1823; Mary and Martha, twins, born November 13, 1826; Enfield S., born October 15, 1830; Ashby, born circa 1838; and William, born circa 1840.[61] Through this family John Ringo was related by marriage to some of the most famous families in outlaw history.

The best known of those ties was through his aunt, Augusta Peters. On July 21, 1842, Augusta married a Presbyterian minister named James M. Inskeep, who was born in Virginia around 1809. The couple had two children, Florence, born about 1846, and a second child that died young.[62] Later, Augusta wed Coleman Younger, an uncle of the Younger brothers.[63] Less commonly known is that Younger's half-sister, Adeline Lee, was the mother of the Dalton brothers.[64]

Through Mary's uncle, Benjamin A. Simms, the Ringos were linked briefly to the James family. Benjamin was born around 1800 in Virginia and served as a youth in the War of 1812 in the Regiment of Virginia Militia under Captain Elijah Harding.[65] Simms married Mary Ann George on December 11, 1823, in Woodford County, Kentucky, before moving to Missouri. After Mary Ann's death, he married a second time, about 1851, to Zerelda Cole James.[66] The marriage was short lived. The 1885 *History of Clay and Platte Counties, Missouri*, notes, "...the chief trouble arose from the fact that her three little children, Frank, Jesse, and Susie, whom she had always humored and indulged, gave their old step-father no end of annoyance." Benjamin demanded that the children be sent away, and when Zerelda refused the couple separated. One historian notes that the "tradition in the James family is that Zerelda left Simms because he was mean to her sons."[67] Simms lived in Clinton County, Missouri, but died January 2, 1854, in Clay County.[68]

In the spring of 1846 Mexico declared war on the United States. Martin Ringo enlisted on June 7, 1846, in Company C, First Regiment, Doniphan's Missouri Mounted Infantry, for a term of one year. He was mustered into service at Fort Leavenworth, Kansas, and his mount was valued at forty-five dollars.[69] According to family sources, Martin went to Sacramento before moving into Mexico.[70] His record indicates that his horse failed at El Gardo, Mexico, for want of forage and was abandoned on October 30, 1846. On June 21, 1847, he was honorably discharged at New Orleans.[71] On June 22 he appeared in the First District Court of New Orleans and filed for 160 acres of "Bounty Land." He requested that the certificate be sent to him at Liberty, Clay County, Missouri. On September 9 of the same year he was issued his certificate.[72]

Martin returned to Missouri and renewed his courtship of Mary Peters. The romance was marred by the death of Mary's mother on January 20, 1848, but on September 5 of that year the young couple were wed in Clay County, Missouri.[73] The *Liberty Tribune* announced, "In this county, on Tuesday evening the 5th inst., by Rev. J. M. C. Inskeep, MARTIN RINGO, Esq., of Washington, Indiana, to Miss MARY, daughter of John R. Peters, Esq., of this county."[74] It was truly a family wedding with Augusta's husband performing the service. The Ringos then headed for Indiana, where they planned to establish their home.

CHAPTER TWO

―――◈◈◈―――

"...passionate, domineering, and dangerous..."

During the mid-1800s Indiana was largely a rural, agricultural state. In 1850 it ranked seventh in population of the United States. Its people were concentrated in the southern part of the state and had strong ties to the South, whence the bulk of them had come. As the decade wore on, immigration to the better farmland available in the central part of the state increased. Madison was the largest city, with a population of 9,000. Indianapolis was second with 8,000.

By 1850 the fires that would ignite the Civil War were already lit. During the crisis before the Compromise of 1850, the overriding issue for Indiana's growing population had been whether to remain in the Union. The strongly unionist citizenry were resolved to stay in the Union, even if they had to swallow some unpalatable conditions. The state selected a middle course, evidenced in part by Governor Joseph A. Wright's denunciation of both the Northeast and the South. Amid widespread feelings that eastern interests dominated Congress, in 1850 a Convention for the Protection of Western Interests met in Evansville.

Two major issues commanded Indiana politics during the period. The Ordinance of 1787 prohibited slavery, but while Indiana remained a territory a strong pro-slavery element successfully contravened the ordinance. The practice was not actually abolished until 1816 when a strong anti-slavery majority drafted the state constitution. Not only did the constitution prohibit slavery and involuntary servitude, but it further declared, "No alteration of this Constitution shall ever take place so as to introduce slavery or involuntary servitude." The state supreme court ruled that the constitution effectively outlawed the practice, and by 1820 slavery in Indiana had ceased.[1]

The abolition of slavery did not end racial prejudice. The dominant attitude of the 1850s was neither for nor against slavery but anti-negro.[2] The severe racial prejudice resulted in a set of infamous "Black Laws," despite the fact that before 1850 residents of African descent comprised less than one percent of the state's population. State law defined a "Negro" as anyone having more than one-eighth African heritage, and the constitutions of 1816 and 1851 limited voting privileges to white men.

The intensity of the prejudice is evident in the Black Laws' origins among the strict codes of the slave-holding South. A law passed in 1831 required all residents of African descent to post a bond that would be forfeited if they were convicted of a crime or became a public charge. In 1850 the state supreme court ruled that only whites were allowed to attend school, and during the constitutional convention of 1850–51 sentiment favored denying African-Americans the right to own property. That prohibition was not enacted, but African-Americans were barred from entering the state, and residents of African heritage were "encouraged" to move on. Worse still, free blacks were often kidnapped in Indiana and sold into slavery across the Ohio River.

Chief among the opponents of those despicable conditions were the Quakers of Wayne, Randolph, and Henry counties who worked to repeal the Black Laws. In September 1838, the Anti-Slavery Society was organized in Wayne County at Milton. It was followed in 1841 by the Wesleyan Anti-Slavery Society, which also originated in Wayne County.

Temperance was the second major issue of the day. The majority of Indiana's citizens favored temperance, and as early as 1829 a state temperance society had been organized. It was followed in 1845 by the founding of the Sons of Temperance. School children commonly debated whether slavery or intemperance was the greater evil.

Women's suffrage, an unpopular movement which had little impact on Indiana politics, also had its advocates. As with the Anti-Slavery Society, suffragists first organized in Wayne County. Meeting at Dublin in 1851, a group of militant women formed the Women's Rights Association, declaring "that unless women demand their rights politically, socially and financially, they will continue in the future as in the past, to be classed with negroes, criminals, insane persons, idiots and infants."[3]

Politics in Indiana was a serious affair in 1850. Methodist clergyman Frederick J. Jobsson in 1857 recalled a visit to Indianapolis: "Though moderate and temperate men in other matters, in politics they are most resolute and determined." Jobsson noted further that the citizens had "no forbearance" towards anyone with a diverging view.[4]

Clay Township, the area surrounding John Ringo's birthplace, was officially created in May 1831, on petition from Thomas Hatfield and others.[5] James Martindale, from North Carolina, was the first settler on Green's Fork bottom. He was followed by Jonas Hatfield, Sr.[6] One of Jonas' sons, Thomas, laid out the town where Ringo was born.

Ringo's birthplace has proved troubling to his biographers. Burrows calls the town Greenfork.[7] Traywick states that Ringo was born at Green Fork on March 3, 1850, noting further that the town had previously been known as Washington Village.[8] Erwin also gives the date of John's birth as March 3 and places it at Greensfork.[9] The confusion is understandable, for the town has had many names in its nearly two centuries of existence. Even today the name is routinely misspelled.

The original settlers designated the settlement as Westfield, but when the town was officially platted in 1818 it was renamed Washington in honor of the first president. When citizens learned in the late 1860s that another Washington already existed in Daviess County, Indiana, they again had to change their town's name. They chose "Green's Fork." In time the name was shortened to Greens Fork, which it officially remains today.[10] It may well be the only town in America that once had the name of a distinguished president but was "renamed in honor of a reputed murderer."[11]

Green's Fork took its name from John Green, a controversial figure in early Wayne County history. Of Native-American descent, Green was allegedly an accessory to the murders of Charles Morgan and his two half-brothers in 1813.[12] The brothers were working in their maple sugar camp when Indians attacked and killed them.[13] Authorities had no proof of Green's involvement and never took action against him.[14]

The killing of John Shortridge that same year proved a different matter. Shortridge and Isaiah Drury, early residents of Wayne County, were on their way to Germantown on a cold, rainy day. After some persuasion, the thinly-clad Shortridge had donned Drury's overcoat. Shortridge was riding ahead of Drury when he was suddenly shot from the saddle. He died the next day.

Suspicion fell on Green, who had quarreled with Drury. People believed he had mistaken Shortridge for Drury, but his guilt was never proven. Hearing that a large number of settlers planned retribution, Green fled and was never captured.[15]

John Peters Ringo was born at Washington, Wayne County, Indiana, May 3, 1850.[16] He was named for his maternal grandfather, and his birth went unheralded by the local press. The earliest known public record of John Ringo is in William Russey's September 26, 1850, enumeration of the "Free Inhabitants of Washington, Clay Township." Russey noted the Ringos as family 665 in dwelling 665. He listed Martin Ringo, age thirty-one, male, born in Kentucky; Mary Ringo, age twenty-four, female, born in Missouri; John P. Ringo, age "2/12," male, born in Indiana; and Sarah Singer, age twenty-six, female, born in Ohio. Russey placed the value of Martin's property at $200.[17] Details of Sarah Singer's identity are lacking. Nor is any occupation listed for Martin. Although contemporary records are far from enlightening, they reveal that Martin had only one milk cow, valued at $12.[18] Equally uninformative is the Production of Industry Schedule, which names neither Martin nor any other Ringo in Wayne County.[19] Martin apparently rented his home or lived with family members, for no deeds of property in his name have been located in the county.[20] That evidence and his later life suggest that Martin worked as either a laborer or, more likely, some sort of store clerk.

John's birth came just as gold fever swept the nation. Following the discovery of gold in California, a mass of immigrants headed west. Wayne County was no exception, and by late 1848 Samuel C. Meredith had closed the *Wayne County Record* and given word of his imminent departure.

> Pay your debts—so I can Pay Mine.
>
> The subscriber respectfully and earnestly requests all persons indebted to him for subscriptions to the late "Wayne County Record," and for *Job Work* and *Advertising*, to come forward and make settlement immediately, if not by

CASH, to give their NOTES.

I expect to leave this place in November next, to be absent several months. All who do not comply with this notice, by the first day of November ensuing, may expect to have their Accounts left with an officer for collection—*No mistake!*

Those who have contracted to pay in Trade, are requested to bring it on, I am now ready to receive it, or make arrangements about it.

SAMUEL C. MEREDITH[21]

Meredith's departure was but one of many. The *Free Territorial Sentinel* of March 28, 1849, noted that Dr. John Pritchet, Daniel T. Woods, David B. Woods (editor of the *Whig*), John Bloomfield, Henry R. Hannah, John Frazier, Nathan Gibson, William Young, — Simmers, John M. Williams, and Isaac Suffrins had left for the goldfields "on Monday last."

In 1850, another gold strike rocked the state—this one far closer to home. On April 25, the *Richmond* (Indiana) *Palladium* reprinted an article from the *Bloomington Tribune*:

Gold Mines of Indiana

This may sound rather strangely to some of our readers, who have been in the habit of looking upon Hoosierdom as entirely destitute of the precious metals, but it is nevertheless true; gold in abundance is now being found in Brown county, as well as Morgan.

A Mr. Walker from Kentucky, (brother to Capt. Walker, of the Texas Rangers), who has been to California, and fully examined her mineral wealth, has examined the "Placer of Brown," and declared it ample, perhaps equal to the California mines.

So far as discovered, Bear Creek and its tributaries contain the richest specimens. It is said that the gold dust is abundant on the premises of Messrs. 'Stump, David, Richards, Tomey and others; and also upon the lot of ground upon which the Bear Creek Meeting house stands. This will of course enable the church to build a better house on another lot. Extensive arrangements are being made to work these mines in the spring.

The *Palladium* noted that Walker had purchased land in the area and commenced work.

Martin and Mary Ringo's immunity to the gold fever sweeping Indiana and the nation at the time indicates their character. One man who knew Martin described him as a "very mild, pleasant and unassuming gentleman" who was highly esteemed by those who knew him.[22] Martin's decision to move to Indiana, a free state, rather than remain in Missouri, implies that he favored the Union, although he apparently was not against slavery. Contemporary records indicate that he sometimes handled slaves on a limited scale. Almost certainly he was a religious man, based on his upbringing, and probably a temperate one as well. His lack of interest in the goldfields demonstrates a practical nature.

Mary Ringo appears to have been a good match for Martin. She was certainly a religious woman, proof of which lies in one contemporary newspaper's statement that four of John Peters' daughters were "professors of religion."[23] That Mary was temperate is beyond doubt. The *Liberty* (Missouri) *Tribune* noted that Peters had raised "five pleasant, sensible, amiable daughters."[24] While the Ringos held strong beliefs, practicality was their overriding trait.

Both Traywick and Erwin erroneously say that John's grandfather, Peter, moved to Franklin County, Texas, in his later years.[25] Their confusion, however, has a logical explanation. A Peter Ringo did, in fact, live in Texas at that time, but he was John's grandfather's cousin. The family of that second Peter Ringo would influence John Ringo in later years.

The Peter Ringo of Texas was a son of Samuel H. and Catherine Ringo, born February 19, 1800, near Mt. Sterling, Kentucky.[26] His twin brother, Cornelius, apparently died young for no later records on him have been located.[27] In 1821 Peter accompanied his father to Howard County, Missouri. There, on January 8, 1822, he married Edy (or "Ede") Jones, a daughter of James and Grace Jones, born around 1804. By 1830 he had moved to Cooper County, where the family remained until 1839. On March 26, 1839, Peter sold his farm to James English and headed for Texas. On March 7, 1842, he received a land grant for 640 acres in Red River County based upon his three-year residency in Texas.[28] Census records for 1840 indicate that Peter had also purchased extensive holdings, for at that time he owned 5,800 acres.[29]

Peter Ringo appears intermittently in the chronicles of Red River County. During 1845 he was on the arrangements committee for

Clarksville's July Fourth celebration.[30] The next year he ran unsuccessfully for county commissioner.[31] Edy died around 1849, and some time after 1850 Peter remarried.[32]

Peter Ringo of Texas gave every appearance of a hardworking, quiet citizen. Yet contemporary records indicate he had legal problems. On September 18, 1848, Andrew Barnes of Missouri sued him for the use of one Reuben Harvey on the grounds that Peter owed him $800 on a promissory note dated April 26, 1845. Ringo countercharged that he had made full settlement on May 16, 1846, and that Barnes had owed him $75. The case eventually went to the Texas Court of Appeals.[33]

Peter Ringo apparently had some land problems as well, although the relevant file is now missing from the courthouse. Era Fay Huff, a descendant of Peter Ringo of Texas alleged, "The file in Clarksville, Texas, courthouse concerning Peter Ringo (mine) [i.e., my ancestor] is missing—you can vouch [Allen] Erwin stole it when he thought it was John P. Ringo's grandfather."[34]

Not until 1854 did indications of Peter's troubles begin to appear. In an item headed "Stealing Mules," the *Northern Standard* on October 7 of that year reported, "Green Caudle was committed to the County jail on Thursday last, on a charge of stealing two mules from the range, near Wm. Humphries in this County, and of offering them for sale for $60.—The low price raised suspicion and led to his arrest."

What the paper did not report until two weeks later was that in pursuing Caudle the sheriff had taken along warrants for the arrest of both Elias Ringo and a second son of Peter Ringo. When the posse stopped at Ringo's and inquired after Elias, Peter Ringo became excited and told the sheriff that "he and his sons would all shoot had the best sort of tools always in the best sort of order, and warned him that if he came to take any of them, he had better come well prepared and bring a large force—that they would die before they would be taken."[35]

Peter Ringo's threats to Sheriff Edward West did not go unheeded. West, an experienced lawman, had served as sheriff of Red River County from 1837 to 1850. He had been reelected sheriff on August 7, 1854, and served continuously until August 2, 1858. His term of service was the longest of any sheriff in Red River County. Forewarned of possible trouble, West led a posse of fourteen men to the Ringo home on October 17. Finding no men at the house, West detailed William Powers, James Ward, Marion Stanley, and a man named Simmons to watch the home while the rest of the posse went on.

West was scarcely out of sight when Peter Ringo rode up and shook hands with Powers. He then continued to the fence, where one of his daughters met him with his double-barrelled shotgun and exclaimed, "Pa—there is Bill Powers—he is the first one who set foot on the place—shoot him."[36]

According to the *Northern Standard*, "As Ringo reached forward for the gun, Powers told him not to take it, or he would shoot. The reply was that it was his own gun, and that he would take it at the hazard of his life; he took it, cocked it, (the barrel of it being near Powers' breast) and as he cocked it, after hearing the click of the lock, Powers shot him near the neck, the load of buck shot probably ranging toward the heart."[37]

The Ringos were a tough lot. West and his party heard the shot and hurried back. As they did one of Peter's daughters leaped the fence and seized the weapon from her mortally wounded father, leveling it on the posse. Further violence, however, was averted. The *Northern Standard* editorialized that in Peter Ringo's neighborhood "there has been for a long time a dread of the family as passionate, domineering, and dangerous."[38] Peter Ringo died that night, but both his family and the kinsmen of Green Caudle would have an impact on John Ringo's later years.

John's grandfather, Peter Ringo, was in Wayne County in 1850. John B. Still entered him as the head of household 380 in Centre Township on September 21. The household included the fifty-nine-year-old Peter, a farmer born in Kentucky; Waldo Ringo, a twenty-year-old male student; John Ringo, a nineteen-year-old male farmer; Martha Ringo, a seventeen-year-old female; and Marshall Ringo, an eleven-year-old male, all born in Indiana. Peter's holdings were valued at $4000.[39] Notably absent from the census was Margaret Ringo. She had died on May 15, 1849, while visiting their son William, who was studying law in Helena, Arkansas.[40] Her body was brought back to Indiana and interred in the old Centerville Cemetery.[41]

The 1850s were a decade of grief for the Ringo family. On July 23, 1851, Martin's twenty-nine-year-old brother, Albert, died of "bilious fever" in Helena, Arkansas, where he was studying law with William.[42] Albert's untimely death was but an omen of things to come. On January 12, 1852, Hamilton Ringo died in Wayne County, Indiana, leaving a wife and five children.[43] Nine months later, on October 13, William Ringo died at Helena, Arkansas, where he had become Recorder of Public Money.[44] Yet another of Peter's sons, Waldo, died in Wayne County, Indiana, on December 29, 1853.[45] The deaths in rapid succession of his wife and four sons must have shattered Peter Ringo. His grief may have been tempered somewhat by the birth of Martin and Mary's second son, Martin Albert, on January 28, 1854.[46]

Burrows attempts a psychological analysis of "what made Johnny run."[47] That analysis is based largely upon Mary Ringo's journal of the family's trip to California in 1864 and on letters from distant family members. It totally ignores John's most impressionable period, the first twelve years of his life. In so doing, Burrows, to whom the Ringo family "simply materialized on the date and place of departure" (Liberty, Missouri, May 18, 1864), overlooks what may have been a critical part of John's psyche.[48] That may well have been an aversion to mobs, imparted to him by his parents during his youth.

In the 1850s a "spirit of lawlessness" infested Indiana.[49] In response, vigilante groups and mobs became common. In 1852 the state passed the Horse Thief Law, which sanctioned the formation of companies "for the detection and apprehension of horse thieves and other felons." In effect, the law gave private individuals the rights and privileges of constables.[50]

That well intended but poorly thought through law had dire consequences. Mob activity rose throughout the state. Secret societies began regulating not only the laws but the morals of their communities. Lawmen were intimidated and feared to restrain the vigilantes. That the 1852 legislation effectively legalized mob justice became quickly apparent. By 1859 Governor Ashbel P. Willard was feebly insisting that people arrested by the mobs should be tried in courts of law. An attempt to repeal the law failed, and vigilante activity continued well into the 1870s.

Wayne County's vigilantes were brazenly regulating the community's morals by 1850. On April 25, the *Richmond Palladium* announced, "The Vigilante Committee"

> Will meet to-morrow (Thursday) night in the S.T. Hall, at early candle-lighting, for the purpose attending to the business entrusted to them by their fellow-citizens. It will be seen, by reference to the preceedings of the City Council, that our law-makers have responded to the resolutions of the people, who elected a Prosecuting Attorney, who, together with the Mayor and Marshal, have been busily engaged the past week dispensing equal and exact justice to the liquor-selling law-breaker. As long as the nefarious traffic is continued in our city, the committee will have

some work to do in furnishing the powers that be with capital to do business on. We are convinced that a large majority of the people of this city, will sustain all lawful means to abolish the liquor traffic, and it only requires a united, zealous and firm effort to accomplish this result. It is hoped the committee will all be present.[51]

Why the Ringos decided to leave Wayne County is unknown. Perhaps they were at odds with the principles of vigilante justice. Perhaps they left for economic reasons or to find a milder climate for Martin, who had contracted tuberculosis at Sacramento during the war.[52] Or their departure might have been linked to the politics of the 1850s, which toppled the Democratic party from power in Indiana.

In the face of the Union's collapse, Indianans, who generally disliked southern agitators and distrusted eastern interests, favored conciliation and compromise. Following the death of John C. Calhoun, one citizen wrote, "The great southern agitator is no more, and I hope the doctrine that slavery is a divine right & political blessing will end with him....I think we shall hear less hereafter about disunion, and in view of this desireable end, Mr. Calhoun can well be spared."[53]

By 1856 it was apparent that the Kansas-Nebraska Act—which the Democratic party had supported—had created an untenable situation in Kansas. Newspapers were filled with accounts of border ruffians spreading terror in their wake. In Indiana, James H. Lane, a former lieutenant governor who had split with the Democratic party, agitated to equip forces for fighting in Kansas. The Indianapolis *Daily Journal* quoted Judge John W. Wright as saying, "If a contest with arms come off in Kansas hundreds of Hoosiers Will be there, and money can be furnished in any amount."[54]

Martin Ringo was one man who had no intention of being in Kansas. In 1856 the family headed west. Their destination was Liberty, Missouri.

CHAPTER THREE

——⟐⟐⟐——

"Ringo & Pryor"

Martin Ringo and his family arrived in Liberty, Missouri, during September 1856. The *Liberty Tribune* reported, "THANKS—We are under obligations to Madison Miller, Chas. De Spada, Geo. W. Morris, and Martin Ringo, Esqrs, for late St. Louis and other eastern papers."[1] The Ringos' third child, Fannie Fern, was born in Liberty on July 20, 1857.[2]

The many Peters, Simms, and Ringo relations in Liberty and surrounding Clay County made it an obvious destination for Martin's family. Among the first relatives they saw were Mary's sister, Enfield, and her husband, Robert Miller. Miller, who founded the *Tribune* in 1846, was one of the city's leading citizens. Another was Elizabeth Ringo, the widow of Martin's father's cousin Samuel. Samuel had been part owner of the firm of Ringo, Wirt and Ringo, and Martin probably worked briefly for the firm during his previous stay in Missouri, hoping to become involved in the business.

Ringo, Wirt and Ringo began as S. & A.H. Ringo. Its founders were Samuel and Andrew Hodge Ringo, sons of Samuel H. Ringo and brothers of the Peter Ringo who had been killed in Texas. Samuel Ringo was born April 22, 1798, near Mt. Sterling, Kentucky. In the early 1820s he had come with his father to Howard County, Missouri. In 1824 he moved to Liberty, where he married Elizabeth Ashby Wirt on April 6, 1826. He established a general store in Liberty and when the town was incorporated on May 4, 1829, he was a member of the first board of trustees along with John R. Peters.[3] By 1850 he owned some $10,000 in property, and his fortune was assured.[4] Samuel Ringo, known for his "sterling integrity and consumate [sic] ability in business," died July 1, 1854.[5]

Andrew Hodge Ringo was born March 14, 1806, in Kentucky. Like his brother Samuel, Andrew came to Missouri with his father. When the firm of S. & A.H. Ringo was established, Andrew had a store in Richmond, Missouri. On September 2, 1830, he married Margaret Simms Wirt, Elizabeth Wirt Ringo's sister, in Liberty.[6] Like Samuel, Andrew prospered in the business. By 1850 his property was valued at $5,000.[7] Ten years later his total worth was a staggering $54,650.[8]

John Ringo was related on both sides of his family to these Ringos. Elizabeth Wirt, born in Scott County, Kentucky, on October 10, 1810, had come to Missouri with her uncle, John R. Peters. Margaret, also born in Kentucky, on April 18, 1815, moved to Ray County with Andrew in 1832.[9] Elizabeth and Margaret were the daughters of John R. Wirt and Mary Augusta Simms. Their brother, Philip Wirt, was born April 6, 1814. In due course, he became a partner with his brothers-in-law, and the firm was renamed. Philip held the general merchandise store in Gallatin, Missouri.

On March 3, 1858, Elizabeth Wirt Ringo sold her remaining interests in the Gallatin business to her brother Philip for $700.[10] As Elizabeth was a resident of Clay County at the time, Martin may have accompanied her to Gallatin so that she could execute the papers. He must have liked what he saw. In addition, some members of his old military regiment were living there. Animosity between the Simms family and the Wirt and Peters families also may have influenced Martin's decision to leave Liberty. After Mary's grandfather, Richard Simms, died on October 21, 1850, John, Benjamin, Joseph S., Margaret, and Terissa Simms sued a number of the heirs, among them Mary Ringo.[11]

Whatever his reasons, in 1858 Martin moved his family to Gallatin, where he became part owner of Clendenen & Ringo, dealers in groceries and general merchandise. His store was only a few blocks from Wirt's, but the competition does not seem to have damaged the family's closeness. Martin's partner, Adam Clendenen, was a wealthy farmer who had settled in the county as early as 1837. Clendenen engaged in many real estate transactions before turning his business over to Sheriff J.J. Minor in September 1858.

On November 26, 1858, Martin Ringo appeared for Clendenen & Ringo before Justice of the Peace Hanley Webb and obtained a judgment against Thomas B. Sabins for $48.79 in debts plus $1.60 in damages.[12] By December Martin had apparently acquired a new partner, Bennett B. Pryor. On December 29, the pair leased a stone house from John W. Sheets for $200. The lease was to run until April 1, 1861. Sheets reserved for his father's use half of the building's back room, "so long as it is occupied for a Gunsmith Shop by Henry Sheets who now occupies it for that purpose." The building was to be used as "a store house and no other purpose," except with Sheets' consent. The lease was terminated December 3, 1859.[13] Historian David Stark has speculated that John Ringo may have had his first lesson in guns from Henry Sheets.[14] That is quite possible, for in that time and place learning to handle a gun was as essential to a boy's education as learning to ride a horse.

In his biographical letter, Allen Erwin writes, "This same Captain Sheets was at one time a business partner of Martin Ringo Sr."[15] That bit of misinformation is not confirmed by the deeds available. Martin's real partner, Bennett Pryor, was a son of James Pryor. Sheets, a landlord rather than a partner of Martin Ringo, was later shot to death by the James brothers.[16]

Martin Ringo's father died in 1859. He had gone to Texas to visit his daughter, Martha Elizabeth, and her husband, Albert H. Black, and died at their home in Hopkins County on August 8. The *Indiana True Republican* noted his death on September 8 and printed his obituary on September 15, 1859:

> Died, at the residence of his son-in-law, in Texas, August 8th, PETER RINGO, of this vicinity, aged sixty-eight years.
>
> The fact of Mr. Ringo's death was mentioned in our last, but, as an old and estimable citizen, something more seems due to his memory. He came to Wayne County from Kentucky about 40 years since.—We knew him long and intimately as a friend and neighbor and can testify to his many exemplary qualities. He was a man of more than ordi-

nary intelligence, and in his manners was a kind and courteous gentleman. In faith and practice he was a Christian, living a life of unobtrusive usefulness, following the paths of peace, and universally respected. The worthy companion of his youth, with whom he lived so long and happily, like him was fated to die in the far South. Her remains were returned to this place for interment, and we learn that his are to take their appropriate place beside her.—There sweet be their sleep till the dawn of that resurrection morn, in whose advent they believed and trusted.

The *Indiana True Republican* of February 23, 1860, confirmed his body's return: "The remains of the late Peter Ringo arrived here from Texas and were deposited by the side of his late wife last week. His funeral was preached at the M.E. Church on Sunday by Rev. Mr. Bushong."

Martin Ringo's name again appears in the Daviess County, Missouri, court records on October 15, 1859. The judgment against Thomas Sabins had not been satisfied, and on September 13, 1859, Sheriff James J. Minor seized "all the right title interest and estate" of Sabins. On October 24 Minor sold the land, some 120 acres near Gallatin, to Martin Ringo for twenty-seven dollars at public auction.[17]

On May 2, 1860, another child, Mary Enna, was born in Gallatin. Daviess County census taker E. Washington failed to note her when he listed the family on June 2, 1860, in dwelling 68:

Martin Ringo	36 M W	Merchant	Kentucky
Mary "	30 F W		Missouri
John "	10 M W		Indiana
Martin	6 M W		"
Fannie	3 F W		Missouri[18]

The Ringos' immediate neighbors included J.S. Agnew, a marble cutter, and Peter Booth, a Baptist minister. The Booth family had two boys, Nathaniel and Silas Booth, aged twelve and nine respectively, who would have been ready companions for the Ringo children. Beyond the Booth home lived J.J. Minor, the county sheriff

At the outbreak of the Civil War, Union forces swiftly seized Missouri. Its status as a slave state within the Union divided populace, causing local troubles which in turn led to the guerrilla warfare that finally spawned such outlaws as Frank and Jesse James and the Younger brothers. Daviess County contributed some 900 men to the Union and 300 to the Confederacy.

Despite Mattie Ringo's confused recollection that her mother had confederate money,[19] contemporary documents indicate that Martin had accumulated a considerable amount of United States funds. He did not, however, oppose slavery. In 1862 Martin was party to a property transfer involving slaves:

> This Indenture made and entered into on this 7th day of February 1862 by and between Silas H. Pryor party of the first part Martin Ringo party of the second part and Lavinia Pryor wife of the party of the first part, party of the third part, all of the County of Daviess and State of Missouri. Witnesseth That, whereas said Lavinia Pryor party of the third part, did since her intermarriage with the party of the first part, become by inheritance and of her own right to certain Real & personal estate lying and being in the State of Ohio county of Ross, which said Estate personal and Real has since been sold by the party of the first part, and the proceed of said sale appropriated to his own use amounting inclusive of legal interest up to this time to Twelve Hundred dollars. And whereas the said party of the first part is now desirous and intends by this deed to restore to the party of the third part and to her own esparto use and benefit an amount of property Equivalent in value to the amount of the proceeds of the sale aforesaid. Now therefore know all men that I Silas H. Pryor party of the first part for and in consideration of the premises and of the love and affection I bear to my said wife Lavinia Pryor party of the third part and of the sum of one dollar to me in hand paid by the said party of the second part the receipt whereof is hereby acknowledged have this day given, granted, bargained, sold and delivered unto Martin Ringo, party of the second part and to his successor, or legal representative, all my right title, interest and claim in and to the following described Negroes slaves for life to wit Henry, Elva, Taylor, George & Frank, in trust however for the sole and separate use and benefit of the said Lavinia Pryor party of the third part to have and to hold the same to the entire exclusion of the claim of the party of the first part or his creditors and the said party of the third part shall have power to retain

the said Slaves in her possession or by & through her trustee to hire out or sell said slaves the proceed to be given to the party of the third part or applied to her use by her direction and the said party of the second part hereby agree to accept and execute this trust.

In testimony whereof we the parties of the first, second, and third parts have hereunto set our hands and seals on this the 7th day of February 1862.

Silas H. Pryor

Lavinia Pryor

Martin Ringo[20]

That Martin Ringo would accept responsibility for the slaves indicates a firm friendship between his family and the Pryors. Quite obviously he was acting as a front so that Silas Pryor's intent could be carried out. Of a certainty he did not benefit from the transaction. In any event, the Ringo family had more personal things on their minds, for on April 28, 1862, another child, Mattie Bell Ringo, was born.[21]

Although John Ringo's first encounters with violence may have taken place in Indiana, the first recorded incident of violence that he was likely to have witnessed was an 1862 skirmish at Cravensville, a town only a few miles from Gallatin, and subsequent actions near the Martin Ringo farm. In 1862, with most of the Union forces east of the Mississippi River, General John M. Schofield was assigned to raise troops for Missouri's defense, and he ordered every town to raise cavalry regiments and companies. Gallatin raised three units: Company A, under Captain Joseph H. McGee, the county clerk; Company B, captained by William H. Folmsbee, a local physician; and Company G under Captain John Ballinger, a hotel proprietor. All three companies were under the overall command of Colonel James H.B. McFerran, a lawyer from Gallatin.[22] Another group, Company C, was formed from the men who lived between Gallatin and Mirchile in Colfax and Sheriden townships under Aaron B. Vickers, a forty-two-year-old farmer from Illinois.

On August 5, 1862, Vickers received orders to move his men to old Camp Everly. After resting his mounts at Gallatin, Vickers moved on to a ford south of Cravensville. Unknown to Vickers, Confederate General Sterling Price had sent orders to his recruiters to march on Independence and Lexington during the second week of August, and Confederate sympathizers were moving south to join the planned attack. On the afternoon of August 5, Captain Jesse Clark had hidden his men in the brush south of Cravensville in preparation for a night move.

As Vickers approached the ford he sighted Clark's camp. The bulk of Clark's men were unarmed and untrained recruits. They broke and fled. Vickers dismounted his men, and in the ensuing skirmish six rebel soldiers were killed and nine others wounded and captured along with their mounts. During the night two more companies joined Vickers and Colonel McFerran took command.[23] The troops managed to capture three more men, but the search ended on August 7.

Two of the prisoners, Thomas Hicklin and Daniel Hole, were identified as previously paroled rebels. The pair were executed by a firing squad as nightriders and bushwackers. Both executions took place near the Ringo farm, and John Ringo may have witnessed them.[24]

John was certainly aware of the bushwhackers who "pillaged and terrorized the country." They killed David Lockwood during 1864 and attempted to kill John Meadows but were thwarted by the courage of his wife, Nancy, who sat in their home's doorway holding a candle in one hand and a butcher knife in the other.[25] Such acts increased his revulsion to mobs.

The Cravensville skirmish, exciting as it must have been, had little effect on the Ringo family. Martin continued in business with no hint of disruption throughout 1862 and 1863. On March 4, 1863, his name was recorded in Daviess County for the last time. That day Bennett B. Pryor appeared in court and acknowledged the sale of land to Martin on November 23, 1859, for the amount of $300.[26] As 1864 dawned the Ringos made ready for another move. Martin had contracted tuberculosis during the Mexican War, and the disease apparently became more pronounced in Missouri. The family hoped that the climate of California would provide relief.

CHAPTER FOUR

―――⟫●⟪―――

"I pray God we may get along safely."

By 1864 Martin's health was deteriorating due to his tuberculosis, and he resolved to move his family to California, "where he thought it would be better for him in a milder climate."[1] Mattie Bell Ringo, John's sister, later recalled, "We had two large covered wagons, one drawn by oxen and one by mules, we brought a lot of things, a large bed and dresser, a number of heavy books besides all the things necessary for a long trip."[2] Clearly the family was not poor.

Mary Ringo's journal is the best source of information on the family during this time. Mattie transcribed the journal in 1942, when she was eighty years old. She died three months later, and another fourteen years would pass before her children published a printed version of her transcription.

Burrows suggests that the journal indicates Mary was neither "given to thoughtful observations and effusions" nor prone to either introspection or analysis. He states further that her "lack of grammatical skills leads to the conclusion that she lacked the skills necessary for clarification of her thoughts."[3] Judged solely on the merits of the printed journal, that assertion might have some validity. But is the journal alone, so carefully printed by Mary's grandson, Frank Cushing, adequate basis for so harsh a judgment? Dr. William K. Hall, a family researcher and author, had access to the diary in 1970. Hall insightfully writes, "I find the diary quite interesting although a bit laconic. But when you think back to the conditions under which it was written—the extreme hardships and the intense fatigue the poor woman must have suffered you are amazed she had the courage at the end of the day to write anything at all."[4]

A note in the printed journal provides further insight. "The contents of this '*Journal of Mrs. Mary Ringo*' was taken from a copy of the original manuscript which has become quite illegible over the past ninety-two years. We have followed the original spelling, punctuation and capitalization."[5] If the original journal, written in pencil, was "quite illegible" in 1956, it doubtless was already quite faded when Mattie transcribed it. Might not the faded writing and Mattie's fading eyesight have contributed to the irregularities of grammar?

Moreover, it is obvious that Mary kept the journal for her own pleasure. She did not intend it for publication, but rather as a memory jogger for her more expansive letters home. Given the fact that Mary had five children, two of them less than five years old, was pregnant with a sixth, and had to maintain a family on the trail, it is a wonder that she managed to keep a journal at all.

The family left Liberty, Missouri, on Wednesday, May 18. In her initial journal entry, Mary recorded the event with an obvious twinge of pain. "Left my family and started on my long trip across the plains, went 10 miles, had some trouble with the oxen and camped for the night and here I took my first lesson in camp life, cooked my supper and went to bed but couldn't sleep until after the chickens crowed for day and after a short nap I awoke."[6]

On May 19, the Ringos reached Leavenworth, where "the children have the pleasure of seeing a steamboat." After taking the ferry across the Missouri River, the family purchased supplies in town. John, assigned to driving the oxen, received some help from his father while a "gentleman by the name of Owen drives the mules up in the city for me while Mr. Ringo helps Johnny with the oxen here."

At Leavenworth on May 20, the Tipton, "Cirby," and "Dr. Moors" families joined the Ringos. [7] One of Tipton's wheels broke and the party laid over on the twenty-first to repair it. Mary's entries for the next several days record little more than the weather and distance traveled. Following a storm on May 23, the group waited at Clear Creek for "D. Gatty" on the twenty-fifth. On June 1, rain forced the train to stop. Mary noted that the "gentlemen went fishing and caught a great many fish." The company spent a pleasant evening listening to some of the travelers playing on their violins.

Six days later, on June 7, the wagon train experienced its initial brush with sudden, violent death: "Today Johnnie got his foot hurt quite badly by the wheels running over it…a little boy was run over by a wagon and killed and a wagon master by the name of Hase [Hays?] killed one of his teamsters, shot him through the head. The murdered man leaves a wife and children."[8]

The company remained in camp on the eighth to hunt for fresh meat: "We lay over for the gentlemen to go buffalo hunting, they stay all day and until one o'clock at night, they came back very much elated having killed a nice buffalo…Johnnie goes along not withstanding his foot is very sore, he says they saw a great many Elk and Antelopes."

As June progressed Mary's entries grew longer. On the twelfth she posted letters to her sisters, Vienna and Enna.[9] On the thirteenth they reached Fort Kearny, where their hopes for letters from home were disappointed. Due to rain they made little progress the next day, and Mary noted that John was ill: "Johnnie has a chill when we stop and now seems quite sick. I hope it may not be anything serious. Johnnie remains quite sick tonight."

John's illness appears to have been no more than the chill described, perhaps giving way to a cold. It did not prevent the company from moving the following day. On June 18 Mary noted that they "passed fewer ranches than any day yet." They also found an Indian scaffold which they observed but did not molest. Mary found it of interest, noting that the body was "not straightened as we straighten our dead but the feet are doubled found most to its head and it is tied up in blankets." At camp that night the ladies went to the river for some impromptu recreation.

John Ringo appears again on the twenty-first when the company stopped to gather wood. "Mr. Ringo, John and Allie [Martin Albert Ringo] take the wagon and go up a canyon some 2 1/2 mi. and get plenty of good dry Cedar, they tell me it is the most beautiful place in these mountains, every variety of flowers. We hitch up and noon and travel 10 miles and camp on a lake called Fremont—it is a beautiful place." Such is the writing of a woman "not given to thoughtful observations." The journal itself belies that assessment of Mary. Her entries clearly note what she found interesting. Of Lake Fremont, she wrote, "To look at it you would not think it any ways deep but it was over the cattles back, we had a laughable time driving them across the lake, some of them would jump in and go under as though they enjoyed it very much."

Similar journal entries follow:

> To day for the first time I see some Antelope, they are beautiful [June 22, 1864].

> We see some Indian Wigwams and two Indians came and offer two ponies [June 23, 1864].

> I walked with Mr. Ringo down to the river, the water does look so swift, they are crossing wagons quite fast. Several Indians came to camp this morning, one of them had a saber, we asked him where he got it, he said he killed a soldier and took it [June 29, 1864].

> I had such a nice walk over the bluffs and through the canyon and gathered mountain currants and we saw some beautiful flowers [July 9, 1864].

> This morning we have to mend the wagon and I take a long walk and climb to the top of the highest bluff, on one of them is the grave of W. Craner who was shot by accident. We have several Indians to come in our camps and trade for buffalo robes and antelope skins....In the night the wolves come in and howl and scares me a good deal at first [July 11, 1864].

> ...today we pass the great Courthouse rock...I would have been delighted to have gone up close to it [July 13, 1864].

> ...Today we pass Chimney Rock this is another grand edifice, you can see it for some 20 miles, it is a 150 feet high, the chimney being some 70 feet in height. The young ladies walked up to see it and brought me some specimens of the plants [July 14, 1864].

These entries, and others like them, illustrate Mary's natural curiosity and humor. Far from being the relatively uneducated and somewhat shallow woman portrayed in Burrows, a more human Mary emerges who took delight in the beauty of nature and the differences of cultures. She also noted more mundane matters. On the night of July 13–14 one of the Ringos' mules, Kate, ran off with a horse belonging to the Tipton family. Martin spent most of the day hunting for the errant animals before finding them eight miles from camp. The following day, July 15, the train had a brush with an Indian war party. They had traveled about ten miles to a "telegraph office," where they were warned of war parties attacking wagon trains. Mary recalled, "We did not think much of it and had gone on some 2 miles when they attacted two of our wagons." The wagons in question had taken the wrong road but the main group moved on, "knowing that they could see us and would cross the prarie and come to us."

At that moment of vulnerability, the Indians attacked. The two wagons were lucky. Firing from the wagons forced the raiders to flee across the river where they killed a man on another train. The Ringos' train turned back, and that same day another train led by a Mr. Morris joined them, swelling their number to sixty-two wagons.

The party passed Scott's Bluff on July 16. On the nineteenth Mary recorded another near tragic encounter with Indians. Though the party had traveled some ten miles by noon, they formed a defensive corral twice, "thinking the Indians were going to attack us but we mistook friendly Indians and one of our train fired at them…" Fortunately no one was injured; however, Mary anticipated trouble, "as the Indian has gone to the Fort to inform against us." Her premonition was correct, for the immigrants were detained until they made peace with the Indians by paying them flour, bacon, sugar, and coffee. At Fort Laramie Mary also received a letter from her twin sister, Mattie.

The train left the fort on July 21. On the twenty-fourth they split up again, and on the twenty-fifth came news of more hostilities. "This morning early some emigrants came to camp who had a man killed by the Indians last night…I pray God we may get along safely. The same day one of their oxen died. Two days later, July 27, Mary wrote, "We find posted on a tree a notice that the Indians have killed six men near here. We hear they had a fight ahead of us."

Tension on the train ran high. On the twenty-eighth Mary noted that three miles from their camp a raiding party killed some men and took the women prisoner. On the twenty-ninth the party passed "the

MARY PETERS RINGO

MARTIN RINGO'S GRAVE SITE

corpse of a man lying by the side of the road, scalped." They moved on without burying him. That same night a man named Davis went out to gather his horses and was shot through the arm.[10] The wagon train spent some tense moments awaiting an attack, and the men guarded the train through the night.

Then tragedy struck the Ringo family. William H. Davenport, a member of the train, recounted the event:

> The shooting of Mr. Davis created considerable excitement in camp, as we expected to be attacked by Indians in force. The whole company stood guard during the night so as to be prepared in case we were attacked. Just after daylight on the morning of the 30th ult. Mr. Ringo stepped outside of the wagons, as I suppose for the purpose of looking around to see if Indians were in sight, and his shot gun went off accidentally in his own hands, the load entering at his right eye and coming out at the top of his head. At the report of his gun I saw his hat blown up twenty feet in the air and his brains were scattered all directions....He was buried near the place he was shot in as decent a manner as was possible with the facilities on the plains.[11]

The shock of Martin's death to Mary is clearly evident:

> And now Oh God comes the saddest record of my life for this day my husband accidentally shot himself and was buried by the wayside and oh, my heart is breaking, if I had no children how gladly would I lay me down with my dead—but now Oh God I pray for strength to raise our precious children and oh—may no one ever suffer the anguish that is breaking my heart, my little children are crying all the time and I—oh what am I to do. Every one in camp is kind to us but God alone can heal the breaking heart. After burying my darling husband we hitch up and drive some 5 miles. Mr. Davenport drove my mules for me and Oh, the agony of parting from that grave, to go and leave him on that hillside where I shall never see it more but thank God tis only the body lying there and may we only meet in Heaven where there is no more death but only life eternally.

Traywick describes a quick burial in a hidden grave, ostensibly to prevent Indians from desecrating it.[12] That is at wide variance with Davenport's eyewitness account, which must be accepted. Nor was the grave carefully hidden. In 1982 Ed Bartholomew, who had researched Ringo for years, located the grave. Bartholomew described the discovery succinctly: "...in 1982 I worked hundreds of miles of the Oregon Trail and finally walked up to two lonely graves. I knelt down in the brush and inspected a flat gravestone which evidently had lain there over a century....I made out a faint inscription on the nearly buried headstone. It read simply, 'M. RINGO.'"[13]

Mattie Ringo later wrote of the accident that her father was killed while raising his gun. It got "caught in his boot strap as the boots were worn over his pants."[14] His death was a brutal blow to the family, and sympathetic government officials offered Mary an escort of soldiers to go back to Missouri. She declined because it "wouldn't seem like home without father."[15]

The train moved onward on July 31. Mary wrote in her journal, "I and Allie drive our mules they are very gentle and go so nicely." Burrows points out that young Martin was helping drive the mules and questions where John was.[16] The answer is simply that John was driving the second wagon as he had done since leaving Liberty, Missouri.[17] Erwin would add what he learned from John's family. "Young John was 14 years old. A young man, doing a man[']s work. It was his duty and obligation to see the family through to San Jose." In that, John was certainly capable, and Erwin noted further, "Young John was a crack shot at 14 years of age. He provided much of the caravan with birds and game along the way."[18] For all practical purposes John Ringo left his childhood behind that tragic day in Wyoming.

Mary's journal entries over the ensuing days reflect not only her natural grief and faith in God, but her continued interest in her surroundings as well.

> August 1—Monday—We travel 10 miles and cross Platte River bridge, it is a nice bridge. There is a company of soldiers here who seem to be very fearful of an attack from the Indians.

> August 2—Tuesday—...I am so anxious to be moving, time seems so long to me. This morning quite early a good many of the Rappahoes [Arapaho] tribe came in to camp but seemed quite friendly....every one is very kind but I am so lonely and tonight Fanny has an attack of cholremorbus

and after she gets easy I rest better than I have any night since the death of my dear husband. Oh God help me to bear this hard trial.

August 4—Thursday—We are detained in camp waiting for some young men who got their wagon wheel broke....we start and go about 200 yards and break another wagon.

Mary Ringo and her daughters have been portrayed as "humorless," "lacking in introspective powers," and having a "strong religious background."[19] While Mary certainly was a religious woman, such harsh judgments of her mental ability based on her diary and distant cousins are untenable, particularly as the journal itself refutes them. Between May 18 and October 8, 1864, there were twenty Sundays; Mary wrote a journal entry on every one, and of those twenty entries only four mention religion. On June 19 she wrote of hearing a good sermon, and on the twenty-sixth she noted her hopes of hearing another. She wrote the other two entries August 21 and 28, after Martin's death. So, while Mary was religious, it was not the dominant factor in her life. What appears to have most occupied her was nature's beauty:

August 8—Monday—...There is a great deal of alkalie through this section, many places the water is crusted all over with beautiful white crust....We passed Independence Rock and it is a grand sight, many names are carved there, some few of whom I knew.

August 9—Tuesday—We...drive to a point called Hell's Gate (I do not think it an appropriate name for the grand and sublime scenery). The pass is very narrow and perpendicular walls on either side. We heard that a gentleman had fallen from the top of them and was killed instantly.

August 11—Thursday—...We...camp near three crossing at a beautiful place...

August 14—Sunday—...the night is beautiful. We pass several trains and their campfires look so cheerful.

August 21—Sunday—...This is the most beautiful river I ever saw—tis very rapid and the water looks green and is very clear. I have not spent my Sabbath as I would like to…

August 24—Wednesday—…I walk several miles pass Church Buttes, the sand hills are grand looking domes.

On August 26 the train reached Fort Bridger. John, driving the slower ox wagon, arrived later. Mary did not appear overly concerned, so the delay cannot have been unanticipated. Two days later, Sunday, August 28, Mary noted that the company was laying over. "I am glad that we do. I do not think it is right to travel on the Sabbath."

The journal mentions John one last time on September 2: "I sent Johnny to see if he could buy some potatoes and he has not caught up with us yet, he does not get any potatoes but gets some nice turnips."

The family reached Salt Lake City on September 6 and remained through the ninth. There Mary was poignantly reminded of how far they were from home. On the sixth she found two letters, both written to Martin before he had been killed, one from her sister, Mattie, and one from a Mr. Halliday. Mary toyed with the idea of selling her outfit but was advised that the people were too poor to buy it. Instead, she hired one John Donly to drive the oxen, and son John began driving the mules.

The journal entries after September 8 become shorter. Mary recorded layovers and grass conditions and other small talk. On the twenty-first she noted that their mule, Bet, was sick. The next main entry, dated October 6, hints obliquely that something may have gone wrong with her pregnancy. "October 6—Thursday—…had a very bad hill to climb and a worse one to descend. I walk down which brings on a spell of sickness for tonight I am very poorly."

On October 7 the family reached Austin, Nevada, where Mary had "the pleasure of seeing cousin Charley Peters and my old acquaintance Mr. Ford from Liberty, Mo. They are very kind and assist me to dispose of my oxen and wagon." On October 8 Mary Ringo wrote her final journal entry: "We remain in Austin, Nev."

CHAPTER FIVE

"Mrs. Mary Ringo, Proprietress"

At Austin, Nevada, Mary Ringo falls silent. Her final, terse journal entry gives no hint of the tragedy that befell her there. It was left to her daughter, Mattie, to provide the details. "In Austin she had a son born, fortunately it was still-born for he was horribly disfigured from seeing father after he was shot. Even my brother [John] who was fourteen years old noticed it and said he looked just like father did."[1] That loss is undoubtedly why Mary abandoned her journal.

The family remained in Austin long enough for Mary to recover. Considering that she was incapacitated for some time, a week or ten days, logic dictates they stayed with Mary's cousin, Charley Peters.

According to Traywick, the family had to sell most of their possessions for a pittance in Austin, and Mary used the money to buy stagecoach tickets to San Jose, California. John supposedly followed, driving the mules and one wagon.[2] Erwin also contends that the family sold their belongings. "The Mormons treated her and family rather shabby. They had sold much of their belongings they had valued and had brought from Missouri, for practically nothing. Mary Ringo and the Children boarded a stage coach to San Jose, and John driving alone with a team of mules and wagon made the trip into San Jose which is quite a few hundred miles over rough country."3 The only family account of the journey, Mattie's, disagrees: "I don't know how long we stayed in Austin, probably a week or ten days and I don't know how we made the rest of the trip. We took the mules and one wagon to San Jose and she [Mary Ringo] told of stopping in San Francisco."4

Mattie's account, with John probably driving the team, appears more likely. That Mary, in the wake of all her trials on the trail, would allow her fourteen-year-old son to make the long and dangerous trek to California alone seems improbable. Still, Erwin gathered information from John's family. If his and Traywick's version is correct, it tells us much about John Ringo. At fourteen he was a crack shot. He was also developing independence and self sufficiency. In time those qualities, combined with intelligence and toughness, would draw men to him as a leader. If Mary let him make the trip alone, she must have recognized those traits in her son.

The family probably arrived in California in December. Although San Francisco might have been their original destination, Mary had resolved to seek out her sister, Augusta Younger, in San Jose. Traywick contends that Colonel Coleman Younger gave them a "shack" to live in then left them to their own devices.5 This allegation of a parsimonious and uncaring Younger has no substance. Mattie remembered the "shack" well: "My aunt and her husband had a very large place and Mr. Younger raised blooded cattle. They had a small house on the place that had formerly been a carriage house made into a house. We lived there a year as mother was not able to do anything for some time."6

Based on what is known of Coleman Purcell Younger, this tarnishing of his name is unwarranted. The uncle of the outlaw Younger brothers, Coleman was born to Charles Lee Younger and his second wife, Sarah Sullivan Purcell, on April 18, 1809, at St. Charles, Missouri. He wed Elinor Murray on April 30, 1829; she died in 1845. In May 1846, he married Rebecca Smith; she died December 27, 1850. Younger served several terms in the Missouri legislature but in 1851 moved to Santa Clara County, California, where he began breeding Durham cattle as early as 1857. On March 17, 1851, Younger married Augusta Peters Inskeep. Augusta's first husband, the Reverend James M. Inskeep, had died in 1849.

Coleman Younger's career indicates that his contemporaries thought highly of him. In 1851, while visiting in Mexico, he was offered a high government position which he declined. He had been a member of the Whig and Know Nothing parties prior to becoming a Democrat in 1856, and he was one of the main organizers of the Santa Clara Valley Agricultural Society.[7] One modern family researcher summarized the family's opinion of the man: "The family always regarded Col. Coleman Younger as a very fine gentleman."[8] Without doubt, Younger assisted the Ringo family.

Equally certain, John had to abandon his formal education in California to help support his family. During that time he labored as a dairyman and a muleskinner, as well as a farmer and cowboy.[9] Quite probably he worked for Colonel Younger, learning the cattle business, while his mother and uncle encouraged him to continue studying in the less formal setting of his home.

Mary's ill health becomes apparent in her actions at San Jose. She was greatly concerned about providing guardians for the children, and on June 6, 1865, John Ringo made his first court appearance.

> In the matter of the estate and guardianship of John P. Ringo, Martin A. Ringo, Fannie F. Ringo, Mary E. Ringo Mattie B. Ringo, Minors
>
> In the Probate Court of the County of Santa Clara and State of California.
>
> To the Hon. Isaac N Reinir Probate Judge of the County Probate aforesaid.
>
> I the undersigned one of the minors above named above the age of fourteen years do hereby nominate and respectfully request your Honor to approve Mary Ringo (my mother) my guardian.
>
> John P. Ringo

Additional papers were filed concerning the guardianship of the Ringo children late in 1865. At that time Mary Ringo as principal and C.T. Ryland, J.C. Smith, and John F. Pyle as sureties bound themselves to the Ringo children in the "Estate of Martin Ringo deceased." The estate was valued at the sum of "Sixteen Hundred Dollars lawful money of the United States of America." The document was sworn to on November 20, 1865, and the bond was sworn before Court

Commissioner C.B. Younger on February 10, 1866.[10]

These documents reveal the family's finances at the time. That Martin's estate included $1,600 lawful money of the United States of America illustrates Mattie's confusion in 1942 when she wrote that her mother "had some money but it was confederate money and she lost 36 dollars on the hundred."[11] Frank Cushing, Mattie's son, later informed his distant cousin, Charles Ringo, that Mary was in serious financial shape when she reached California.[12] The undoubted source of the misperception was Mattie herself. The family, well off for the moment, had considerable but not inexhaustible funds. John worked to provide money for the family until the younger children could become self-sufficient without using their inheritance. Certainly the Ringos were not poor.

Charles Ringo alleged that Cushing also told him John had become a teenage alcoholic and left the family "in the lurch" in 1869.[13] Coming from John's nephew, that would be a serious charge, if it were not provably incorrect. John did not leave San Jose in 1869. The San Jose city directory for 1870 notes the presence of "Ringo, John, farmer, dwl 524 Santa Clara," along with "Ringo, Mary Mrs., dwl 524 Santa Clara."[14] Moreover, the federal census clearly places John in San Jose on July 25, 1870. Listed as member of family 435 are Mary Ringo, age forty-three, keeping house, born in Missouri; John, twenty, Indiana; Albert, sixteen, printer, Indiana; Fanny, thirteen, Missouri; Enna, ten, Missouri; and Mattie, eight, Missouri. Mary's personal estate was valued at $400, her real estate at $3,000. The girls had all attended school within the last year. Martin had left school, obviously to aid in supporting the family.[15]

John Ringo met Cole Younger during 1865. Thomas Coleman Younger, born January 15, 1844, to Henry Washington Younger and Bursheba Leighton Fristoe in Jackson County, Missouri, was a high spirited, impulsive man with a quick mind and a captivating personality.[16] Younger had joined Quantrill's guerrillas following an altercation with a Union soldier named Irvin Walley. In response, Missouri militiamen killed Younger's father on July 20, 1862. Cole Younger took part in the sack of Lawrence, Kansas, on August 21, 1863. Following an assignment in British Columbia, he arrived in California sometime during the spring of 1865, anxious to relieve his war-time traumas. He remained there through the fall and told John Ringo of the war in Missouri and of the jayhawkers' depredations.

In 1870 John was twenty years old, an age at which many men had already left home. That fall he finally set out on his own, but not without assurance that the family would have a steady income beyond his brother's wages. The San Jose City Directory for 1871-1872 shows Mary Ringo operating a boarding house at 268 and 270 Third, San Jose, and refers readers to an advertisement on the same page:

> BOARDING HOUSE,
> 268 and 270 Third Street
> First-Class Board with Good Airy Rooms.
> TERMS,...$ 7 PER WEEK
> MRS. MARY RINGO, Proprietress[17]

Contrary to both of his recent biographers, John's sisters saw nothing out of place in his departure. "He did not leave San Jose on account of any crime he had committed, he went to southern California with a harvesting outfit."[18]

Given the inaccuracy of his other assertions that John Ringo abandoned his family to poverty in 1869, Charles Ringo's claim that he was a teenage alcoholic is questionable. Indeed, either Cushing was deliberately misleading Charles or Charles was basing assumptions on what Cushing said and he himself had read. That Cushing would mislead Charles to his uncle's detriment is ludicrous. Burrows' belief that Cushing did not hold back with Charles is inconsistent with allegations that Cushing threatened legal action against anyone attempting to link John to the California Ringos.[19] For a man anxious to disassociate himself from his uncle to reveal all to a relative stranger is totally illogical. Nor would he repeat a tale that his mother had clearly denied.

More likely, Charles made sweeping assumptions based on Cushing's remarks and his own knowledge. One of the early family members to express an interest in John Ringo, Charles Randolph Ringo, was born September 16, 1899. On July 25, 1968, he sent Dr. William K. Hall a brief sketch of John Ringo's career.[20] David Leer Ringo, historian and author, revealed the source of Charles' information in 1981: "In the early 1930's his brother, Henry Raleigh Ringo, called his attention to mention of a John Ringo in the book 'Tombstone' by Walter Noble Burns....The story by Charles Randolph Ringo...was a direct quote from page 135 of the Burns book."[21]

Although Charles Ringo derived a great deal of misinformation from

Burns, he was nonetheless in a position to know much of the family genealogy. Thus his declarations were a superficially credible combination of fact and fancy. Hall recalled Charles Ringo with affection but cautioned, "Charlie Ringo was quite interested in the family history and read all the magazine and book accounts of Johnny Ringo so it is difficult to tell how much he knew from family accounts and how much he had learned from the fictionalized accounts."[22] Another early Ringo researcher, May Ringo King, similarly cautioned, "I would not rely on anything Charles gave in his letters. He was not a genealogist and he loved a good story....His interest in Johnny came out after Burns' book was published."[23]

Was John Ringo a teenage alcoholic? The descendants of men who had known him in Texas and who had fought with or against him in the Mason County War answered unanimously: no one had ever heard of Ringo's being a heavy drinker in Texas. Historian David Leer Ringo summarized succinctly, "...it is indeed unfortunate that [Burrows] concluded that Charles R. Ringo was a genealogist and historian, but did not make contact with those working in the Ringo family area who were....He [Charles] loved a good story whether factual or not."[24]

Charles Ringo died on December 21, 1974. He was a grand gentleman, and the sad irony is that in his desire to see a biography of John Ringo in print, he further contributed to the Ringo myths.

CHAPTER SIX

"...the people he fell in with were fighters."

John Ringo's whereabouts and activities in the years immediately after he left San Jose are obscure. Historian Jack DeMattos repeats Burrows' error of labeling Ringo a "teenaged drunkard and troublemaker who abandoned his family in 1869 and went to Texas," but then summarizes simply, "Ringo's activities during the next six years are still clouded by mystery."[1] Burrows places Ringo in Texas and asks rhetorically, "What did he do between 1869 and 1875 when he first appears in newsprint?"[2] He answers that Ringo was leading a life of "reckless prodigality" and implies without documentation that he had embarked on an outlaw career.[3] As one reviewer points out, however, "merely because there is no documentation for [Ringo's] actions does not automatically place him within outlaw gangs."[4] Traywick, citing the collection of Al Turner, contends that Ringo returned to Indiana where he lived for a time with his uncle and aunt, John R. and Elvira Funk.[5]

The general framework of Ringo's missing years can be reconstructed, nonetheless. Sometime after the federal census counted John in San Jose on July 25, 1870, he left home. His sisters recalled his going with a harvesting outfit, which would mean a fall departure.[6] John might reasonably have returned home after the harvest to spend the Christmas holiday with his family, probably departing again after the first of the year.

John's absence from the San Jose City Directory for 1871 confirms that he had left, and his whereabouts can be determined by knowing why he went. One family researcher wrote, "I understand that he went back to Missouri to 'settle some land problems.'"[7] Mary Ringo's will supports that possibility: "My son John Ringo having been here to fore provided for I bequeath the sum of one dollar."[8] John could have been provided for previously only by Martin's estate, probably consisting of debts owed to the family. John would have been of age in 1871, old enough to handle any necessary legal actions. He had no need to return to Indiana, for his grandfather's estate was long since settled.

According to historian Ed Bartholomew, John Ringo and Bruce Younger returned to Liberty, Missouri, arriving in the spring of 1871.[9] Younger, a brother of Coleman Younger, was family. That he and Ringo would travel together is logical.

The time John Ringo spent in Missouri remains obscure. One persistent tale maintains that he attended William Jewell College. That college, however, has no record of his presence.[10] The primary sources available nonetheless indicate that Ringo did, indeed, have a better than average education. He probably continued to acquire an education, albeit informally, through his Missouri kinsmen, among them Elizabeth Wirt Ringo. An inventory of Samuel Ringo's estate following his death in 1854 listed many books, including the *Life of Henry Clay*, the *Anabasis* of Xenophon, Dickens' *Pickwick Papers*, Draper's *Chemistry*, Doniphan's *Expedition*, three volumes of Oliver Cromwell's letters and speeches, Bunyan's *Pilgrim's Progress*, and Hitchcock's *Geology*.[11] In short, the library could provide any interested reader with a good education. People raised on the frontier, as most of John's later associates were, might naturally assume his education came from a college, not from his own studies, especially since he revealed little of his background.

Among his enterprising Missouri relations, John logically might have tried his hand at business, though no records confirm it. In any event, the life would not have suited the John Ringo who had spent most of his life outdoors since 1864.

John's brother, Martin, meanwhile had contracted tuberculosis and, on August 29, 1873, he died. The *Liberty Advance Tribune* reported his death "of consumption" on September 19, 1873. When John learned of Martin's death is unknown, but the news could not have come as a shock, for he undoubtedly knew of his brother's condition. The symptoms would have manifested themselves by 1872.

John had left his family well provided for in 1871, but by 1874 the San Jose City Directory no longer listed Mary as the proprietress of a boarding house, noting simply "Ringo Mrs. Mary, (widow) dwl 524 Santa Clara."[12] Moreover, Mary herself had contracted tuberculosis. John would have realized the burden of his brother's illness on the family's finances, and he would have wanted to earn money for the medical expenses. Ringo researcher Allen Erwin alluded to this in one of his letters: "His life purpose was in getting ahead, and returning to his own immediate family which he was attached to."[13] The only trade John truly knew was the one he had learned from his uncle Coleman Younger, that of a stockman. The growing cattle trade would have attracted him, and in the 1870s cattle were synonymous with two things: money and Texas.

John's first stop on his move to Texas was in Hopkins County, where Mary Wirt Ringo's nephews and nieces lived. Era Fay Huff wrote:

> My great-great grandfather Peter Ringo came to Texas when it was still a republic and settled in Red River County. He and his wife, Ede Jones Ringo came with all their children except the youngest daughter. They had six sons and four daughters. Peter was a minuteman, and as a first lieutenant was second in command under Capt. William Becknal!
>
> John P. Ringo visited these relatives when Samantha V. Ringo was a young girl. She did not remember much about the visit. I have always maintained that he spent a longer time in Texas than is thought by writers; most of it was probably spent in Burnet County...[14]

Samantha V. Ringo was a granddaughter of Peter Ringo by his son, Robert William, who had married Mary Jane Walker. The oldest of six children, Samantha was born on June 9, 1857. The Ringos no doubt told John their version of Peter Ringo's death in 1854.

John also would have formed contacts with the Jones family, through Edy (or Ede) Jones Ringo. Edy, a daughter of James and Grace Jones, was related to Andrew Jones who, with three of his brothers, had come to Missouri from Hardeman County, Tennessee, around 1831.[15] The brothers were "coarse, rough mannered, illiterate men given to horse racing and gambling," and Andy appears to have been the worst of the lot. Rumored to be a horse thief, Andy was also a veteran of the Slicker War which spanned Polk and Benton counties in Missouri.[16]

The Slicker War was started by the family of Hiram Kerr Turk, who reached Missouri in flight from a lawsuit. The Turks, violent and hot tempered, were overbearing neighbors. Hiram Turk was shot in July 1841, and died from his wound on August 10. Local authorities and the Turks believed Andy Jones was the killer, although others were also involved. To retaliate, Hiram's son, Thomas, organized a vigilante committee, the Slickers, so named after their first raid, in which they whipped, or "slicked," several men. [17] In the ensuing violence Jones fled to Texas in 1842.

Two years later a posse captured Jones and two of his anti-Slicker cronies, Loudrich (Loud) Ray and Harvey White, in Fannin County. They and several others had robbed and murdered some peaceful Indians, a crime that the Clarksville, Texas, *Northern Standard* termed "barbarous." The killers were speedily tried and hanged by their captors July 10, 1844.[18]

From the Jones and Ringo families John would have gained his first-hand knowledge of Texas. The northeast had largely been taken up, but the sparsely settled frontier counties offered more opportunities. Moreover, John had family ties in that area. Isaac Jones had settled in central Texas, and a William Ringo would take up land in Blanco County on November 6, 1874. [19]

John might have first settled in San Saba County in 1872. The tax rolls that year include a "John Ringer," possibly a misspelling of John Ringo. Ringer is listed as having 102 acres of land valued at $500, five horses valued at $300, twenty-five cattle valued at $125, $575 in personal estate, and $150 of "miscellaneous" property. The 1873 tax records again list Ringer for essentially the same amount. The next name listed in the 1872 poll tax is W.Z. Redding, who played a significant part in the Mason County War. If Ringer were, indeed, Ringo, settling in San Saba County was a fateful move.

Of John's Texas years, Erwin writes, "Ringo was caught up in history at the right time....The fact he was fearless, and known for coming to the heart of a situation without asking any favors, he won the respect of such men as John Wesley Hardin....

"The people he fell in with were fighters. He was loyal to his friends."[20]

Ringo now found himself in the vicinity of Burnet County, where he met the men who would shape his future. Many of them lived along the Colorado River, which forms the boundary between Burnet and Llano counties. Foremost among them was the family of Joseph Olney.

Joseph Olney was born in Virginia in 1811 to Joseph and Amelia Graves Olney. In 1836 he married Mary Katherine Tanner. Mary K., eight years her husband's junior, was the daughter of John A. Tanner by his first wife, Anne Kirkpatrick. Like the Ringos, the Olneys were an old family. Thomas Olney, the first member of the family in America, was one of the founders of Rhode Island with Roger Williams. A descendant of Thomas owned the Liberty Tree in Boston during the Revolutionary War. Other members of the family were prominent in New England as well.[21]

The Olney family came to Texas by way of Mississippi, where Joseph, a farmer, owned eleven slaves, four male and seven female.[22] Their first two children were born there, Minerva Catherine "Kate" on May 21, 1837, and John Tanner on April 3, 1841. Sometime between 1841 and 1845 the family resettled in Burleson County, Texas, the birthplace of most of their children: Samuel Young on September 9, 1845; Joseph Graves on October 9, 1849; Ann A. on March 4, 1853; William Wallace on February 3, 1854; Daniel Stirling on January 3, 1856, and Edward Thrower on June 1, 1859.[23] During the early 1860s the family moved to Burnet County, where their last two children were born: George Anderson on December 21, 1861, and Oscar Roberson on April 5, 1865.[24]

The Olneys were well off. A document Mary K. Olney executed on September 23, 1847, for reasons now unknown, shows a part of their holdings:

> A list of Mary K. Olney's separate property to wit one Negro boy Robert 17 years old one Negro woman Amey 60. Do. one Negro girl Louisa 9. Do. Seventy seven head of Cattle, one horse, 50 head of hogs, one waggon and three yokes of oxens 102 one hundred and two acres of land.

> I do solemnly swear that the within property is my own,
> to which I have a good and valid title to same.
> Mary K. Olney[25]

By 1850 their land alone was valued at $2,881.[26] Before arriving in Burnet County, the Olneys had sold their slaves.

Mary's family, the Tanners, were wealthier by far than the Olneys. They, too, had gone to Mississippi in the 1830s. The census for 1840 indicates that John A. Tanner had thirty-four slaves, twenty males and fourteen females. Like his son-in-law, Tanner was a farmer and had sold his slaves before arriving in Burnet County.[27] By 1850 the family was in Burleson County holding land valued at $1,870. The census lists John Taner [sic], a forty-year-old male farmer, born in Virginia; Angelina, thirty-two, female, born in North Carolina; Matilda, thirty, female, born in Tennessee; Harriet, twenty, female, born in Tennessee; Salley, eighteen, female, born in Alabama; Allis, four, female, born in Mississippi; John, two, male, born in Texas; and Johnathan, two months, male, born in Texas.[28]

The 1860 Census in Burleson County appears to have missed the Olneys, but it does enumerate the Tanners. Tanner's real estate was then valued at only $1,636, but his personal property was valued at $12,000. Moreover, Alice Gray (the "Allis" of the 1850 Census), then fourteen, held personal property in her own name valued at $1,100.[29]

Two of the Olney brothers served during the Civil War. In 1923 W.T. Linn recalled that the frontier counties of Burnet, Llano, Mason, and San Saba organized a joint company for frontier defense. The company first went into camp at the Hall ranch on Richland Creek before moving to old Camp San Saba.[30] The muster roll names a number of men from families that would eventually figure in John Ringo's fortunes, including Allen Roberts. John Olney later enlisted in Company A, Morgan's Texas Cavalry, on March 26, 1862.[31] Sam Olney remained with the Rangers until they were mustered into J.E. McCord's Company K, Mounted Volunteers, on July 2, 1863.[32] Joseph Graves Olney, best remembered as Joe Hill of the San Simon, was to become a lifelong friend of John Ringo.

The 1860 Census of Burleson County confirms the oral tradition that the Olneys had known the Baird brothers in their youth. It lists A.P. Baird, age twenty-nine, female, born Tennessee; John R., thirteen, male, born Missouri; Moses, eleven, male, Missouri; Marietta, eight, female, Missouri; and Laura, six, female, Missouri. All four of the children had attended school within the past year.[33] By 1868 the family had arrived in Burnet County.[34] The census of 1870 states that both Mary and Laura had attended school within the past year.[35] That indicates a reasonably well educated family. Laura Ann Baird later married Sam Olney. John Ringo would shed blood for the Bairds.

Also gathered along the Colorado were the Farris brothers.[36] Solomon Boone Farris, born December 2, 1823, married Laurinda Hinds in Marshall County, Alabama, on January 5, 1842. Laurinda, a daughter of Benjamin Hinds and Polly Mary Childress, was born in Blount County, Alabama, on February 20, 1823. The couple had two daughters, Mary Elizabeth and Laura Ann. They also had five sons, all of whom would be involved to some extent with John Ringo: John B., William Jasper and Champion Newton (twins), Benjamin A., and Robert Elihu (Bud). The older Farris died on May 12, 1857, leaving his wife to raise seven children. Laurinda's brothers provided help for the fatherless children. One descendant would write, "I understand she [Laurinda] served as a sort of practical nurse when families had illness, and that she was aided by her brothers Ben and William, and possibly one named Levi Hinds."[37] Uncle Ben Hinds would teach them far more than the cattle trade.

Benjamin J. Hinds was born in Alabama on April 27, 1818. Hinds had seen service in both the Mexican and Civil wars. By the end of the Civil War he was widely recognized in gaming circles, and John Wesley Hardin knew him.[38] He was also a noted mankiller, having admitted to slaying one man in Little Rock, Arkansas, and another in Lockhart, Texas. His contemporaries openly charged him with still more killings. Hinds preferred a knife to a gun, and in that skill his nephew, Champ, was also noted. Hinds transmitted his personal philosophy—"when they called him, he was always there"—to his nephews.[39] Through the marriage of E.E. Casner to their aunt, Margery Hinds, the Farris boys were also tied to the Casner clan. T.P. Williamson, a kinsman of the Johnson family in Llano, had lived in the area but resettled in Mason County. His brother Frederick was in Burnet County, though, with Allen G. Roberts. During his time in Texas, Ringo knew all of these men. Without exception, each of them was in the cattle industry.

Court records reveal much about the Baird, Farris, and Olney families. Charges against them during Reconstruction range from gaming to assault with intent to kill and murder. They were hot tempered men. That not withstanding, little contemporary evidence supports any theory that they were other than cattlemen at the time. Neither Roberts nor either of the Williamson brothers had any charges against them.

By 1874 John was working in the area and apparently sending what funds he could to help support his family. On December 25, 1874, he was celebrating Christmas in Burnet. Possibly he had been drinking, for in his revelries he fired a pistol across the town square. On April 5, 1875, he was charged with disturbing the peace. M.B. Thomas and John W. Calvert provided bond.[40] John Ringo had braved his first brush with the law. Considering the time and place, it was relatively innocent.

All that would soon change. Within a year he would be charged with murder and his friends would be involved in serious trouble.

Some of them would be dead.

CHAPTER SEVEN

"...back-shooting border scum and thieves."

The Mason County War, also called the Hoo-Doo War, is best known for the violence which swept the county in 1875.[1] DeMattos, who was concerned only with Ringo's role in the fighting, correctly attributes that phase's beginnings to the May 1875 murder of Tim Williamson.[2] Williamson's death and, subsequently, that of Moses Baird, mark distinct turning points in the war. The first brought in Scott Cooley, the latter John Ringo.

Traywick ascribes the feud's origins simply to Civil War animosities. Concerning John Ringo, he offers the sweeping statement that Ringo joined the Scott Cooley "gang which operated with the Americans when it suited their purpose."[3] Burrows, also referencing the Cooley gang, adds that organized outlaw gangs took "advantage of the German-American feud."[4] Elsewhere he is more explicit, noting that John Ringo joined the Cooley gang, "a gaggle of back-shooting border scum and thieves." He maintains that the Cooley gang "intruded" into a range war which "became a complex and bloody three-way struggle with the Cooley gang preying on both sides."[5]

These views diverge significantly from the primary sources on which C.L. Sonnichsen based his account of the feud. Sonnichsen understood clearly many of the conflict's underlying causes: lingering Civil War animosities, racial hatred, cattle, and greed.[6] Family alliances, intra-family animosities, and the ultimate cause of all blood feuds, revenge, further fueled the violence.

The Hill Country's German immigrants arrived in the mid-1840s. From the first they faced cholera, hostile Indians, and a harsh land totally unlike that of their birth. Yet with spirited determination they spread to New Braunfels, Fredericksburg, and Mason. Those families, composed mainly of Germany's poor and unemployed, survived the hardships and established lasting homes.[7] Their success was due in part to their own stubborn determination, but without visionary leaders such as John O. Meusebach, the whole effort could well have failed.

John Meusebach was born Otfried Hans Freiherr von Meusebach on May 26, 1812, to Baron Carl Hartwig Gregor von Meusebach and Ernestine von Witzleben in Dillenberg, Nassau, Germany.[8] Raised an aristocrat, in 1844 he accepted a contract as commissioner-general for the Society for the Protection of German Immigrants in Texas. The society was founded on March 25, 1844, with the avowed goals of improving the conditions of the working classes and decreasing pau-perism; opening new markets for the products of German industry; and developing maritime commerce.

Trouble began almost immediately when the outbreak of the war with Mexico prevented the immigrants' transportation to the promised land. Stranded in New Braunfels, a stopping-off point along the route, Rudolph Iwonski incited disgruntled colonists to riot on December 31, 1846. Meusebach narrowly avoided being lynched.[9] Little more than two weeks later a man named Schubbert tried to organize a second revolt. The attempt failed, and on January 17, 1847, a number of immigrants signed a petition supporting Meusebach. Among the sign-ers was Gottfried Bader, two of whose sons were later involved in the Mason County War. Among those who did not sign were Heinrich Hoerster, Ernst Jordan, and Heinrich Kothmann, all of whom were later accused of organizing the mob in Mason County.[10] Their sons would join ranks against Ringo during the feud.

The Germany that the colonists had left behind in the 1840s was an ununited collection of small states often at war with one another. The colonists thus understood quite well that in union lay strength. When secession loomed, Mason County's settlers voted against leaving the Union, and during the war they tried to remain neutral. The far more vocal settlers in Gillespie County to the immediate south formed the Union Loyal League. The Texas government considered the league a subversive organization and in 1862 dispatched forces under the command of James Duff to suppress it.

Realizing the seriousness of their situation, sixty-one members of the league fled toward Mexico under the command of Major Fritz Tegener. Duff's command surprised Tegener's camp on the Nueces River on August 10. They killed nineteen members of the league outright and captured and subsequently executed another nine. Duff's command pursued the remaining fugitives to the Rio Grande and killed nine more of them there on October 18.[11] The Germans never forgot or forgave the massacre. As late as 1925 German historian Don H. Biggers wrote that it was "a crime unjustifed by even the rules of savage warfare."[12]

The differences between the German colonists and their American counterparts went far beyond simple politics. The colonists clung tenaciously to their language and culture, speaking German in church and school even into the early 1900s. One historian noted, "Children learned English by mingling with the English speaking families as they grew up."[13] Discussing the "anti-Dutch" antagonisms of the post-war years, historian Julius E. DeVos notes, "The difference in languages virtually eliminated any clarification of each group's thoughts and reasons."[14] In effect, two countries lay superimposed over one another.

Moreover the Germans in Mason County differed from their counterparts elsewhere. Gilbert Jordan, Mason-born educator and scholar, recalled the contrast: "The Fredericksburg German element was and still is more fun-loving, more easy going than the Mason County Methodists. The Fredericksburgers love their Gemütlichkeit, their easygoing disposition and geniality, as much as the Mason County Methodists love their piety."[15]

These differences are clear in the words of "Dreux," an obvious German partisan. Writing to the *Austin Statesman* in 1875, Dreux charged that the outrages had been "perpetrated almost exclusively on Germans as a class, by a numerous and bloody band of outlaws gathered from all the surrounding frontier counties."[16] Dreux's charges summarize the feeling in Mason at the time. Locals were quick to accuse their neighbors of complicity in cattle theft and murder, often without any evidence.

That siege mentality still exists. Inevitably the American participants are referred to as outlaws, while the Germans "tried to reach a peaceful and legal solution to their problems."[17] DeVos ascribes the war's main cause to "penniless" Americans who arrived in Mason County from the South after the war. They "saw the German families with large land holdings, big herds of cattle and good substantial holdings. They saw the smaller, poorer houses of Americans here....Greed and envy undoubtedly appeared."[18] However, the majority of the "American" fighters came from outside Mason County, and most of them had either been born in Texas or lived there prior to the war. Contemporary records disagree. "Peter," a more objective correspondent on the feud, wrote, "The Germans, who as a class are farmers, and have small gentle stocks of cattle, accused the stock men of stealing their cattle."[19] Understandably the cattlemen denied the charges.

Max Krueger, a German pioneer who was involved peripherally in the feud, recalled of the Germans, "They kept true to their native virtues and faults...the worst was their discord and paltry jealousy of such of their countrymen as were more successful in business or unable to get used to their narrow way of thinking and acting."[20] Krueger found them "very clannish, and a newcomer was not welcomed."[21]

Cattle added to the trouble. Before the war cattle were essentially worthless, so the laws and traditions concerning them were mainly local. One such tradition was accommodation marketing. A man finding his neighbor's steer in his herd could sell the animal and then return the profits to the rightful owner.[22] One such transaction is recorded in the drive book of M.L. Hayes, an early cattleman from Mason. Entries from Hayes' book, written in about 1875, clearly illustrate the marketing system. The book names Bill Redding as the owner of one of the larger stocks of cattle, forty-four head; Ben Gooch, another cattleman, had nine head. Other entries were for only a single cow.[23] Of course, not every rancher was as scrupulous as Hayes.

Inadequate brand laws added to the problem. Because the brand laws were local, any individual in a county could use any brand not previously registered in that county. In theory three different men could record identical brands in adjoining counties.[24] On the open range that could lead to conflict. Consequently men engaged in the cattle trade often found themselves registering the same brand in many counties. Stock notices, such as one recorded by Roberts and Cavin, friends of John Ringo, were common:

STOCK NOTICE

ALL parties are hereby notified not to use, drive, or remove from the range either in Burnet or Lampasas counties, any STOCK owned by Roberts & Cavin, excepting parties legally authorized by us as agents. And for reference to the stock owned by the above firm, parties are hereby referred to the records of marks and brands in each county named.

Parties are hereby notified that the law will be enforced in regard to posting cattle in the county where the mark and brand is recorded.

A.H. CAVIN

A.G. ROBERTS

L.W. CAVIN[25]

In December 1873, Mason County voters elected John Clark sheriff. The Germans considered Clark "a good man and efficient officer." Their opponents charged that he used his office to persecute his personal enemies.[26] Texas Ranger Dan Roberts, who was present during the feud and knew Clark, referred to him as a "blue hen's chicken," a term often applied with contempt to former Union soldiers and Union sympathizers.[27]

Based on a family member's unsupported statements, Clark has tentatively been identified as John Rufus Clark.[28] John Rufus Clark was the son of Isaiah and Sarah Elizabeth Low, born in Missouri on May 24, 1849. The 1860 Census shows the family living in Burnet County, Texas.[29] On December 9, 1873, he enlisted in Company R of the Mason County Minute Men, serving through February 24, 1874.[30] Clark had been sheriff less than a year when violence struck Mason County.

On May 7, 1874, the *Houston Daily Telegraph* noted dryly, "Mr. Morrison, in Mason county, was shot to death a few days ago, by a party of unknown men." Morrison today remains unidentified, the motives for his killing unclear. No one was ever brought to trial for the murder. What is known is that a man was murdered and no arrests were made. That pattern would repeat itself during 1875.

During the summer of 1874, eleven Burnet and Llano county cattle-men rode cautiously into Mason County to gather their cattle. A letter to the *Burnet Bulletin* signed by six men, including the cattlemen's leader, M.B. Thomas of Burnet County, later recounted, "...knowing the animosity that some of the people of that county have toward non-resident stock men, and wishing to have no misunderstanding or trouble, Thomas hired two men from Mason County to stay continually with the herd that he was collecting and cut-out every animal that might get into the herd belonging to anyone in that county."[31] They gathered the herd and held it just across the line in Llano County. Learning of the drive, Sheriff Clark gathered a posse, rode into Llano County, and arrested the drovers. The herd was driven back into Mason County and scattered. Clark took the men to Mason and held them on the grounds that several of the beeves were not theirs.[32]

The Llano arrests created a sensation. The *San Antonio Daily Herald* reported, "A letter from Mason, dated on the 14th inst., states that 'great excitement exists at Quihi, on account of the Sheriff of Mason arresting 11 of the Llano cow boys. Some 40 of their friends came in and attempted a rescue but failed in the attempt.'

"This disturbance like many others is attributable to the confusion caused by the stock law."[33]

Ernst Jordan, an early settler in eastern Mason County, also recalled the attempted rescue. Some forty men had ridden past his home on their way to Mason. "Ernst Jordan knew what it meant; they were coming to release the prisoners or to make trouble."[34] Jordan took a different route to Mason, rounding up forces as he went. The two groups met in Mason, but there is no hint that the American cattlemen intended any violence. Following the hearing, during which Thomas and his men were released on a $2,500 bond, someone shot up the schoolhouse at the old Willow Creek settlement in eastern Mason County. The vandalism was blamed on Thomas and his men who, of course, denied any involvement. Thomas further denied that Jordan's alleged gang were outlaws, and he appears to have been correct.[35]

The men involved in this incident would be central to the violence of 1875. Marshall Brackston Thomas was a son of John Preston and Amanda Thomas, born around 1851 in Kentucky. The older Thomas was a schoolteacher. The family was living in Burnet County in 1860.[36] By 1863 Thomas was learning the cattle trade, and he was present on a cattle hunt in December of 1863 when his cousin, John Magill, was killed by Indians. The 1870 census listed him as a cattle drover along with his brothers James and Oliver.[37]

Thomas was not known as a troublemaker, but he had encountered the law previously in Burnet County. On February 4, 1868, he was indicted, along with Thomas Johnson, David Epley, and Ulysses Howard, for killing a dog. Bail was set at $200. The case was tried on October 23, 1868. Epley and Johnson were found not guilty. Thomas pleaded guilty and was fined one penny. The charges against Ulysses Howard were finally dismissed on April 20, 1870.[38] During the court terms of winter 1871 and spring 1872, Thomas served as a bailiff in Burnet.

The second leader of the cattlemen was Allen G. Roberts. Born around 1843 in Illinois, Roberts had arrived in Texas by the early 1860s. On July 2, 1863, he enlisted for three years or until the end of the war in Captain William G. O'Brien's Company K, Mounted Volunteers, of the Frontier Regiment.[39] The 1870 Census for Burnet County listed him with his wife, Louisa, and two young children, William and Kate. It gave his occupation as "driving stock" and valued his personal property at $1,000—a significant amount for the times.[40] Roberts served briefly in the state police during 1871, enlisting on September 8, 1871, and being discharged on October 31.[41] His name appears frequently in Hayes' drive book, associated with W.Z. Redding and others. Through 1874 no indictments of any kind were filed against him in Burnet County. Roberts would later serve as a deputy United States marshal.[42]

Also involved was William Z. "Bill" Redding. Far more controversial than either Thomas or Roberts, Redding was also a cattle dealer who had a considerable amount of stock in Mason County.[43] He appears to have been the son of William R. and J.M. Redding, born around 1848 into a wealthy Bastrop County, Texas, family.[44] Before his arrest in Mason, he was involved in a number of Burnet County lawsuits, both as a defendant and a plaintiff.

The remaining participants were all kinsmen of the Olney family by marriage: John and Moses Baird and A.T. Taylor. The Bairds' sister, Laura, had married Sam Olney, a brother of Joe Olney, who was, per-haps, John Ringo's closest friend. That connection would draw John Ringo into the Mason County War. Abraham Teal Taylor, son of David and Jemima Stanford Taylor, was born in Cherokee County, Alabama, in 1849.[45] Like the Reddings, the Taylors were wealthy. By the mid-

1850s the family had moved to Burnet County, where David Taylor engaged in ranching. The 1860 census listed the elder Taylor's wealth as $6,000 in real estate and $2,000 in personal property.[46] Taylor, a hot-tempered man according to family sources, was indicted at times for fighting in Burnet. Several times he was linked in those escapades to John Olney. At the time of his arrest he was also having problems with Mason County's brand inspector, Daniel Hoerster. Hoerster had sued Taylor in Burnet County, and the action was not resolved until August 4, when the men settled out of court and the case was dismissed. Taylor paid all of the costs. [47] Taylor and his wife, Ann Olney, would later shelter John Ringo and help significantly to clear him of cattle theft allegations.

Knowing those six men, we can speculate on the identities of the remaining five. One likely candidate was stockman Elijah Backus. Another may have been John Edward Cavin, an active participant in the feud who possibly participated in one of the later killings. The Cavin family were partners in the cattle trade with A.G. Roberts. Cavin would later be arrested on a charge of helping John Ringo to escape from the Lampasas jail. Jim Williams, a Llano County resident, is also a likely candidate. The mob targeted both Cavin and Williams for death. The last man may have been Joe Olney, also a mob target. Olney had been involved in a violent encounter during the spring of 1874 in Llano County during a dispute over cattle. Alternatively, one of the men may have been John Farris, an active feudist whose family and the Olneys would intermarry. Farris later fled Texas.[48] All of these men were linked to the cattle trade, and all of them were friends of John Ringo.

The two Mason County men involved are easier to identify. Thomas had hired men whom he knew to guard and register the cattle during the 1874 roundup. One appears to have been Tim Williamson. Williamson had lived in Burnet during the late 1860s and early 1870s. The other was likely to have been George W. Gladden, a Missouri-born wrangler who had been in Mason since 1872. Both men were then living in Loyal Valley, and both were later targets of mob violence. Gladden and Ringo would later ride together during the feud.

Enraged by their treatment in Mason, Thomas and his men sought justice. As soon as they crossed the line into Llano County, they hurried to the office of Sheriff W.W. Saxon and swore out complaints against Clark and twenty-seven other men. All twenty-eight of them were indicted for robbery and false imprisonment.[49] Thomas, however, remained apprehensive, noting, "It is true the sheriff and his posse have each of them been indicted by the grand jury of Llano County...but this will not afford us protection in the future."[50]

Truer words were never written.

CHAPTER EIGHT

———◦◦◦———

"The mob has been operating some..."

Eighteen seventy-five dawned with deceptive calm. Texas Ranger Lieutenant Dan Roberts of Company D opened his January 15 report to Major John B. Jones, commander, "Nothing having transpired of much interest since my report of the 1st."[1] The new year might have seemed equally uneventful for John Ringo, despite the charges that he faced in Burnet. They were hardly serious, and Ringo was undoubtedly busy gathering cattle for the drive to Kansas.[2]

Scarcely a month later Lieutenant Roberts would have to write, "Nick Colston...was shot at his ranch when putting his horse in the stable—only slightly wounded in the hip—there was some moccasin track and shoe tracks found near by—but the sign was rather bogus— for Indians."[3] Authorities never determined a reason for the assault on Colston, nor is there any clear link between him and the Mason County War. What is known is that the attack, the first violence reported in the area in 1875, occurred only days before a pivotal event in the looming war.

On February 13, John Clark arrested Elijah and Pete Backus along with seven other men on Brady Creek in McCulloch County. The move was reminiscent of the arrests in 1874 of M.B. Thomas and his men. Among the drovers were Abe Wiggins, Tom Turley, and Charley Johnson. The remaining four men have not been identified. All were charged with illegally driving a herd of cattle. Clark lodged his prisoners in the Mason jail on February 13 to await a preliminary hearing.[4] All of the men made bond and were released. Four immediately left town. The remainder stayed and were promptly rearrested after Mason County cattlemen reexamined the herd.

The Backus brothers' identities have puzzled historians over the years. They are so obscure that little about them can be stated with any certainty. Naomi Cox Miller, an early Mason resident, recalled in 1929, "I knew the Backus boys quite well and often danced with them."[5] The only contemporary document yet located is a tax roll of 1875 showing that "Elija Backus" owned 600 cattle valued at $3,000 and 47 horses and mules valued at $1,175.[6] Backus was not a poor man, but the absence of land and other personal property from the tax roll indicates that he was a nonresidential stockman. Without additional evidence, Burrows' reference to the "notorious Backus brothers" appears unwarranted.[7]

Of the other men only Charley Johnson has been identified with certainty. Born February 17, 1859, to Frank and Elizabeth Townsend Johnson in Llano County, Texas, Charles Walker Johnson and his family had already suffered a full measure of tragedy.[8] The family had moved to Kimble County in 1863, settling on Little Saline Creek.[9] There, Indians killed Frank Johnson on October 12, 1867. Charley's brother, Asa, later recalled, "My father was killed by Indians when he grew careless and one morning ventured out without his gun to hunt his horses. The Indians, who had concealed themselves in the tall grass, ran him down and killed him with their arrows and scalped him."[10]

After her husband's death, Elizabeth insisted on moving the family to the relative safety of Llano County. They went to Legion Valley, where they planned to winter at the home of Adam Bradford, an early settler. On the afternoon of February 5, 1868, Becky and Samantha Johnson, accompanied by Mandy Townsend and their youngest children went to the home of John Friend. Friend had asked them to stay with his pregnant wife Tilly while he went to Fredericksburg. That evening Indians raided the cabin. Tilly Friend, wounded and scalped, escaped doom by feigning her death. The others were less fortunate. The raiders left a trail of bodies—Fielty Johnson, three-year-old Nancy Elizabeth Johnson, Becky Johnson, Samantha Johnson, and Becky Townsend—to mark their passage. Only two of the captives were ever recovered: Malinda Caudle and Lee Temple Friend. Malinda Caudle was a daughter of Green Caudle, who years earlier had been linked to Peter Ringo's death. The others were killed. Texas had claimed a heavy price from the Johnsons. Charley was doing a man's work by age sixteen, but he was hardly old enough to be notorious.

The troubles of 1875 continued on February 17 when a man was found dead on the road between Mason and Menard. Lucia Homes, a thirty-five-year-old pioneer at the time, recorded, "A man found killed on the road with a card saying he wouldn't stop killing cattle so they killed him."[11] The victim appears to have been Allen Bolt, a son of William James and Lavinia Watts Bolt. One early resident recalled, "We had exciting times in those days...Among those who lost their lives [was]...a boy named Allen Bolt."[12] Bolt was only seventeen.

With Backus and the others still in jail, on February 18 Clark led a posse toward the James River where he had heard of cattle being gathered. Among his posse were county brand inspector Daniel Hoerster, rancher Tom Gamel, and Kale Hall, a friend of Clark and ally of the mob.[13] The chase proved futile, but on the way back Clark called Gamel aside and suggested that they lynch the jailed men. Gamel refused, and from Mason prudently rode on to the home of his father-in-law.

About eight o'clock that evening, Hall rode up to Gamel's father-in-law's place with the startling news "that a mob had taken the prisoners out of jail."[14] Hall told Gamel that he was wanted in Mason at once. Gamel refused to go, and Hall returned to town.

Sometime after ten o'clock—a full two hours after Hall had tried to fetch Gamel—the mob burst into the home of Deputy Sheriff John Wohrle, tied him to a chair, and attempted to seize the jailhouse keys. Wohrle's wife, pregnant at the time, went into hysterics and began screaming. One of these bravos snarled, "Hit her in the mouth and she'll shut up."[15] When the mob failed to locate the keys, they stormed the jail and hauled the prisoners down the road toward Fredericksburg. They hanged the Backus brothers first.

As the lynching progressed, Clark, evidently having had a change of heart, and Dan Roberts were leading a posse in pursuit. Clark, the only mounted man in the group hurried them along until they sighted the mob and opened fire. The panicked mob began shooting their prisoners, then fled. Wiggins was hit in the head. Johnson, whom the mob had put on a horse to await the noose, leaped from his mount and escaped. The posse arrived in time to save the dangling Tom Turley.[16] Wiggins died on the morning of the nineteenth.[17]

Kale Hall's role in the lynching is significant. That he served as a posseman is undisputed, but that the apparently clairvoyant Hall was sent to gather in Gamel two hours before the lynching clearly indicates not only that Gamel was marked for death but that Hall was a willing participant in the mob. Considering Hall's career, however, he was far more likely to be a victim of vigilante vengeance than a supporter.

Born June 15 (or 16), 1849, in Graves County, Kentucky, to Caleb and Lucy Hall, Caleb "Kale" Hall was a hardened cattle thief and outlaw by the time of the Mason County War. The 1878 *Fugitives from Justice* indicates that he was wanted for cattle theft in Kinney County. He later fled Texas to New Mexico, where he rode with John Selman's gang of thieves, killers, and rapists under the alias of Sam Collins during the Lincoln County War.[18] Nor was Hall the only outlaw to be associated with the mob. Brothers Dick, Dell, and "Roll" Dublin, notorious in their own right, also were involved.

The wily Gamel was no man's fool. Born November 28, 1846, to William and Catherine (Hixie) Gamel in Alabama, he had reached Texas with his family by 1850. In 1856 they settled in Legion Valley, later moving to Mason. During the Civil War he served in Company 1 of the Third Frontier Battalion.[19] He had also served on the state police, enlisting May 10, 1871.[20] A veteran of the frontier, he had correctly interpreted Hall's actions as a ploy to lead him to his death and prevent his revealing Clark's role in the mob. Now he clearly saw that his life was in danger, and he made haste to gather allies among his friends and kinsmen.

John Ringo no doubt learned of the lynching and its subsequent events from Charley Johnson. Johnson's kinsman, Green Caudle, had been among the friends of Peter Ringo's family. With John's mistrust of vigilante justice, hearing of the killings from a near victim would have made him a natural opponent of the mob.

While Gamel dodged the mob and gathered forces, Helene Wohrle, John Wohrle's wife, suffered a miscarriage on February 25. Lucia

Holmes would note, "Poor Mrs. Wordly [sic] had a miscarriage today the result of her fright the other night."[21] The tragic death of the war's youngest victim must be credited to the mob. That in itself discredits the local tradition that Wohrle knew beforehand of the planned lynching. As Sonnichsen points out, Wohrle would hardly have staged such a scene in his own home.[22] The charge undoubtedly arose because Wohrle did play a significant role in later events.

Johann Anton Wohrle was born in Wurtemberg, Germany, on November 14, 1845. His family immigrated to the United States and ultimately settled in Ohio. On January 27, 1864, Wohrle enlisted in the Third Regiment, Troop B, of the United States Army at Cleveland, Ohio. He was discharged with the rank of corporal at Fort Craig, New Mexico, on January 27, 1867.[23] He had arrived in Mason sometime before October 4, 1871, for on that date M.V. Bridges arrested "John Worley" on a miscellaneous charge.[24] Wohrle married Helene Geistweidt, and on October 22, 1873, she gave birth to twin sons, John Charles and Charles John. John Charles died in infancy.[25]

The mob struck again before the month was over. On March 1, Dan Roberts reported, "The mob has been operating some in Llano County lately. Killed one man named Wages—ordered several men to leave the country. As yet they've harmed no good man."[26] Whether Roberts truly believed what he wrote is irrelevant. Official tolerance of lynch law only encouraged the mob.

Or, in this case, mobs. In his memoirs, Miles Barler, an admitted mob member from Llano County, recalled that they had formed a second group to deal with cattle thieves. Most specifically, Barler charged A.G. Roberts (no relation to Dan Roberts) with being the leader of the outlaws.[27] More realistically, the group was not simply dealing with thieves but waging a cattle war to control the county's rangeland.

Tom Turley never stood trial. On March 6 Lucia Holmes noted a rumor had circulated in Mason that the mob intended to return and finish what they had started. The following day she added, "Tom Gurley [sic] and Caleb Hall escaped out of jail this afternoon by digging through the partition into next cell."[28]

The mob did not materialize in Mason, but they were nonetheless on the move. A week later they tried to lynch Al Baird, a local cattleman. According to Holmes, "News came in that a party of armed [men] went to Al Beard [sic] ranch after him."[29] Baird escaped, but the situation was quickly proving intolerable to the cattlemen in the area.

Allied with Tom Gamel, thirty-six-year-old Rufus Winn headed the next action. John Ringo may have been with them. Holmes recalled, "Mr. Beard [sic] and Mr. Hey came in and Hal [Henry Holmes] made out a paper for men to sign for the preservation of law and order in the county. Tom Gamel and R. Winn brought in ever so many men with him. They camped out tonight. Nobody knows what they are for."[30] Holmes was mistaken, for one man knew, or at least suspected, their purpose. Sheriff Clark left town the next day and returned on the twenty-second.[31] Lucia Holmes' husband, Mason attorney Henry M. Holmes, wrote, "…the sheriff returned to the town, followed by sixty-two men, mounted and armed, and it was at once remarked that every one of the gentlemen following him were Germans, not one American amongst them.

"The town was held by this party in a kind of semi-military manner for the remainder of the week." Mr. Holmes said both bunches behaved admirably and agreed that there "should be no more mobs or hanging." [32] On the twenty-seventh, the groups left Mason.

Then, reported Lucia Holmes, the "Rangers came in to protect Clark."[33] Clark's actions speak volumes of his guilt, and his choice of allies is revealing. Clark had openly sided with the Germans. He had been, at least in his mind, publicly shamed by the threat to his authority, and the people of Mason knew that a county war had narrowly been avoided.

Lieutenant Dan Roberts and Company D remained in Mason for the rest of the month. On April 1 Roberts reported everything was "quiet in regard to the Mason trouble."[34] Three days later he left Mason, confident that disaster had been avoided. It was a premature decision. On April 8 a notice appeared in the courthouse, ominously warning people not to drive any cattle but their own.[35] The mob was alive and well.

While the ranchers with interests in Mason County eyed each other warily, John Ringo had problems of his own in Burnet. On April 5 the grand jury indicted him for disturbance of the peace. The indictment noted that he had "discharged a pistol across the public square." John W. Calvert and M.B. Thomas posted his $200 bond.[36] Witnesses in the case were Thomas and "N. (or M.) W. Harris"—possibly George Washington Harris, a blacksmith, who had arrived in Burnet in 1858. Ringo was to appear at the next term of court.

April proved deceptively quiet both in Burnet and Mason, and men went about their own business. One of them was John Clark, whose duties as county tax collector included resolving a tax dispute involving Tim Williamson, the foreman of Karl Lehmberg's Llano County ranch.

Timothy P. Williamson was born at Charlotte, North Carolina, on December 23, 1842, to Cyrus and Hannah Alexander Williamson. Cyrus and his sons, Lee, Tim, and Frederick, took ship for Texas during 1855. Cyrus died shortly after their arrival.[37] By 1863 the brothers were living in Burnet County. Tim married Mary Elizabeth Johnson, a cousin of Charley Johnson, and the couple had five children. Sometime after 1870 they moved to Loyal Valley in southern Mason County. At no time during his life in Burnet had Tim been charged with any kind of felony.

The cause of Williamson's tax concern is readily apparent. In 1875 he was assessed for thirty acres of land valued at $30, seven horses at $245, two hundred and twenty cattle at $1,100, miscellaneous property valued at $60, and a single town lot assessed at $1,200.[38] Even though that lot had only a private dwelling, it was assessed $200 higher than John Meusebach's, which had a store.

Clark rode to Loyal Valley to confer with Williamson. Gamel reports that "Williamson was not at home and Clark proceeded to abuse Williamson's wife." When the young rancher learned of the incident he rode to Mason and challenged Clark to fight. Clark refused.[39]

The public humiliation enraged Clark. His next step was to approach Daniel Hoerster, Williamson's bondsman. The *Austin Daily Statesman* reported, "A Mr. Tim Williamson, a stock man living in Mason, was under a heavy bond for his appearance at Mason court. Sometime in May he was met by Mr. Herster [sic], one of his bondsmen, and Wohrlie [sic], deputy sheriff of Mason county, and was surrendered by Herster to Wohrlie."[40]

Wohrle arrested Williamson at Karl Lehmberg's ranch in Llano County on May 13. Lehmberg immediately offered to post bond but was refused. Lehmberg decided to accompany the pair into Mason and post bond there.[41]

The party rode north to Castell before turning west into Mason County. Three miles west of Castell a mob of about a dozen ambushed the men. Williamson reportedly begged Wohrle to let him run for his life. Instead, Wohrle immediately drew his pistol and killed Williamson's horse. The hapless rancher then recognized at least one of his assailants, Peter Bader from Llano County, and asked for his life.

Bader shot him dead.[42]

Tim Williamson's murder sparked great excitement in Mason. Lehmberg had escaped and no doubt spread the story. Henry M. Holmes prepared another petition asking the governor to send help to put down the mob.[43] Like the first petition, it went unanswered. Clark and the mob might have thought they had committed the perfect killing, even though they had left a witness. Evidence suggests that Lehmberg later was intimidated into silence. There was only one small problem.

They had killed the wrong man.

CHAPTER NINE

<hr/>

"Hell has broke loose up here."

If ever a man was born to the feud, it was Scott Cooley. Seemingly from nowhere Cooley suddenly loomed so large on the Mason County scene that other figures shrink in comparison. He was the man of blood, the cold-eyed, ruthless feudist who killed with apparent impunity and turned Mason County into a charnel house. His name became synonymous with terror.

William Scott Cooley was born in Izard County, Arkansas, to Matthias and Martha Cooley in 1855. By 1860 the family had moved to Jack County, Texas.[1] During that time the northern counties of Texas suffered terribly from Indian raids, and the Cooleys grew up hard men. By the early 1870s the raids were a way of life. Though newspapers routinely told of killings and thefts by the raiders, some notable exceptions appeared. The February 10, 1872, *Dallas Herald* reported, "On Saturday the 20th, three young men, Cooley by name, living on Picket's ranche in White prairie, came upon four Indians, and killed two of the four, one of whom they scalped, while the other dead Indian was carried away by his companions."[2] The Cooley brothers again saw action during May 1872. The Galveston, Texas, *Christian Advocate* informed its readers, "We learn from the Texas exchanges that the Indians made a raid on Wise county, but the sheriff and the Cooly [sic] boys got after them and killed them all."[3]

Nor were Indian raiders the only troubles the Cooleys faced. By 1870 Martha Cooley had died, and that year a man named Joseph Horton shot Matthias Cooley to death in a dispute. The next day the Cooleys killed Horton in revenge.[4]

Scott Cooley met Tim Williamson around 1872, hiring on as a drover. James B. Gillett, who served with Cooley in the Texas Rangers, recalled in later years that the pair had made two drives to Kansas.[5] The drives must have been in 1872 and 1873, for on May 2, 1874, Cooley enlisted in Company D of the Rangers.[6] Among the Rangers he acquired a further reputation for courage, and his instincts as a savage feudist first appeared. Reporting on a fight between Comanches and Company D on November 21, 1874, the *Statesman* observed, "The boys brought some fresh scalps with them, and they report that Scott Cooley, who was fired at and run into camp, not only cut a wounded Indian's throat, but stripped a large piece of skin from his back, saying that he would make a quirt out of it."[7]

Cooley received his discharge on December 2, 1874, and rented a farm in Menard County. He would harvest no crops. In contrast to the rapacious leader of freebooting cutthroats portrayed by Burrows and Traywick, Tom Gamel recalled, "It seemed that Cooley's only motive was to find the man or men responsible for Williamson's death—he did not take sides with either element."[8] As early as 1875, the *San Antonio Herald* had similarly reported, "The day news of Williamson's murder came to the Ranger camp, to which force Cooley at one time belonged, he sat down and cried with grief for the loss of one who he said was his best friend in the world, and declared then that he would have revenge."[9]

District court began on July 12, and a number of cases were heard, among them that of Charley Johnson, who had surrendered to Dan Roberts' Rangers. He was freed, a clear indication of the Backus brothers' innocence. No indictments were found in the lynching case or the Bolt murder. Nor was anyone, including John Wohrle, indicted for the Williamson murder. Cooley undoubtedly learned that, as the *Herald* put it, "No effort whatever so far as is known was made by the authorities to endeavor to discover the perpetrators of this outrage further then

[sic] to hold a coroner's inquest over the remains."[10]

On July 20 another man was killed. Henry Doell, a German, had been out on a cow hunt with several other cattlemen. About two o'clock in the morning a rifle shot struck him while he was sleeping in camp. The bullet passed through his stomach and hit August Keller in the leg. Doell died only hours later. The first version of the shooting to reach print blamed it on outlaws disguised as Indians: "These robbers were thought to belong to 'Rance and Co.'s' band of freebooters."[11] Rance was Kimble County rancher Rance Moore.

Doell's killing is often cited as a part of the feud, but he probably was not a member of the mob. In 1944 his son revealed to C.L. Sonnichsen that, shortly after the mob murdered Williamson, Doell had openly questioned the need for that killing. Evidence nonetheless indicates that Doell was, indeed, killed by Indians.[12]

The summer of 1875 saw John Ringo in district court on July 9, when he answered the charge of disturbing the peace. Ringo had posted bond for $200; M.B. Thomas and John W. Calvert were his sureties.[13] The cause was continued at that time.

That Thomas was Ringo's bondsman is hardly surprising. Both men were in the cattle trade, and the Thomas family was considered one of Burnet's finest. It is possible, but not probable, that Ringo might have been involved in the 1874 drive when Thomas and his men were arrested. Certainly he was well thought of by the Thomas family.

Calvert's involvement further indicates that people in Burnet thought well of Ringo. The Calverts had come to Burnet in the 1850s. Hugh Hudson Calvert, John's father, first engaged in stock raising.[14] By 1870 he was running the Calvert House a block south of the courthouse.[15] John Wardlow Calvert was born September 17, 1848. He married Mary Jane Carruth in Burnet on January 17, 1866. The family would pay a high price for supporting John Ringo.

When Ringo's case came to trial on August 5, he failed to appear and the district attorney moved for forfeiture of the bond. The court ordered the sureties "to show cause if any they have or can why this Judgement...should not be made final...."[16] The existing court papers do not reveal the motion's outcome.

Meanwhile Scott Cooley prepared for revenge. In Mason he had a local gunsmith named Miller service his pistol.[17] Then he headed out to track down John Wohrle. He found him on August 10. Wohrle, Charles "Doc" Harcourt, and a third man known only as Doc's little

"Yankee" were digging a well.[18] Sometime between three and four o'clock in the afternoon Cooley rode up to the men and engaged them in conversation. After a time, Harcourt climbed into the bucket and his coworkers began winching him down into the well. Cooley's conversation suddenly changed. "Wohrle, why did you kill Williamson?"

"Because I had to," was Wohrle's startled reply.

Cooley drew and fired. The bullet struck Wohrle in the back of the head, killing him instantly. Doc's little Yankee ran as Wohrle collapsed, releasing his grip on the winch. Harcourt fell to the bottom of the well but survived the experience. Cooley then scalped Wohrle and fled town.

The killing shocked Mason, but apparently had little effect on those members of the mob who believed they were above the law. In a typical press release, obviously printed before Cooley's name was known, the mob again took the opportunity to accuse nonresident cattlemen of the crime:

> Horrible murder at Mason.—From the [Fredericksburg] Freie Presse of the 17th inst., we translate the following:
> "On the 10th of August, during the afternoon, Mr. John Wohrly, a quiet respectable citizen and former Deputy Sheriff, was assisting a man by the name of Harcutt in digging a well, when a young man of about twenty-four years of age, rode up and began conversing with Wohrly in the most friendly manner, stating among other things that he was looking for two horses. He asked Wohrly for a piece of leather with which to fasten his gun to the saddle, which request was complied with. While the villain was apparently fixing the leather to the saddle, Wohrly and another man who was present, began hauling Harcutt up from the bottom of the well. While they were thus engaged the stranger took advantage of the opportunity to shoot Wohrly through in the back of the head, the ball coming out near his nose. Wohrly fell dead, his companion, being without arms, fled, and Harcutt fell to the bottom of the well, a distance of forty feet, where he remained senseless.
> The murderer then fired six shots into the body of Wohrly, stabbed it in four places with his knife, and finally took his scalp; whereupon the fiend mounted his horse and rode off.
> It is probable that the murderer will evade all earthly

punishment, as he is evidently the paid assassin of men who will back him up.[19]

Cooley had picked his first target well. While no one had anticipated an avenging fury, Cooley had deliberately killed the one man who was the most likely target for vengeance. That Wohrle had killed Williamson's horse and denied him the chance to flee was perhaps the worst kept secret of the feud. The mob was not prepared either when Cooley killed Karl Bader on August 19.[20]

Karl "Charley" Bader, a younger brother of Pete Bader, was born on June 4, 1853, to Gottfried and Christina Bader. He had wed Mrs. Katherine Kothmann, the widowed sister of Daniel Hoerster. Cooley possibly intended to kill Peter Bader, misidentifying Karl and shooting him by mistake. Gamel recalls, "John Beard [sic: Baird], Scott Cooley, Charles Johnson and George Glaton [sic: Gladden] made a raid on the Border [sic: Bader] home near Castell, seeking Peter Border to kill him, but they made a mistake." Charley Bader was in a field hauling top-fodder when he was killed.[21] Burrows, citing the *Austin Statesman* of October 17, 1875, and the *San Antonio Herald* of October 6, 1875, asserted that John Ringo was involved.[22] Traywick makes a similar claim without citing the source.[23] The *Statesman's* report of the killing required a single line: "Then came the murder of Charley Bader by some of Cooley's party, supposed by George Gladden and Moses Beard [sic]." The *Herald* did not mention the Bader killing at all. Nor does any contemporary source yet located suggest that Ringo took part in the killing. Evidence shows that only Cooley was involved.[24]

Bader's death, coming on the heels of Wohrle's, changed attitudes among the mob. It was one thing to kill helpless men, and quite another to be killed. The press was fully aroused to the bloody situation. "In Mason county bloodthirsty gangs of murderers ride triumphantly over the rights of law abiding citizens," proclaimed the *Statesman*.[25] They had not seen anything yet.

The swaying allegiance of his followers boded ill for John Clark. Moreover, Clark was himself a fugitive from justice: "His statement that the Sheriff was out of town 10 or 15 miles is true, and generally is, as his usefulness has lately been sadly interfered with by a visit from the Sheriff of Llano County who wants him for over zealously discharging his duty, his friends say, the indictments call it 'Robbery and False Imprisonment.'"[26]

Clark may have been among those who honestly believed Moses

Baird and George Gladden killed Karl Bader, but he never made the charge. Instead, he gathered forces and fortified Hedwig's Hill, a small town along the direct route from Loyal Valley to Mason. Gamel reports, "It is said that Dan Hoerster and Clark paid Chaney [Jim Cheyney] a gambler living in Mason at this time, $50.00 to go to Loyal Valley and get Mose Beard [sic] and George Glaton [sic] to come to Mason."[27] Clark's expectation that Baird and Gladden would come to Mason at his bidding clearly indicates that neither man had any reason not to. The pair simply saddled up and headed north.

At Hedwig's Hill, Baird and Gladden decided to stop at Keller's store. Dan Roberts later recalled, "...when they got pretty close to the store, Sheriff Clark saw that they were Mose Beard [sic] and George Gladden...the Sheriff stepped out on the porch, with his rifle in hand, and the firing commenced...."[28] Gamel confirms Robert's account: "Clark and Hoerster, with about sixty men, who were awaiting them, opened fire on the two."[29]

Baird was hit hardest and could not mount his screaming horse. Rather than abandon his friend, Gladden stopped to help. In a supreme act of courage, he managed to help Baird onto his calmer mount even as bullets slammed into his own body. With Baird safely mounted, Gladden swung up behind him and attempted to flee. Behind them Clark's little army scrambled for their mounts.

At Beaver Creek Gladden fell from the saddle. Baird managed to ride farther along the creek before he, too, fell. The posse was only a minute behind. When they reached Gladden one of the posse drew a bead to finish him off. Charlie Keller, son of the store owner, leveled his pistol on the would-be killer and swore he would kill the first man to shoot Gladden. No one fired.

Gladden would live to fight another day. Moses Baird was less fortunate. Pete Bader overtook the luckless man and unceremoniously killed him. Noting a gold ring on Baird's finger, Bader climbed down and cut off the digit to claim his bloody trophy.

The shootings at Hedwig's Hill were Clark's second mistake, as he would swiftly realize. Documents of the time indicate that Baird, no outlaw, was popular in the Hill Country: "A letter from Fredericksburg, dated Sept. 8th, has been received in this city, and conveys the following startling news: 'H-ll has broke loose up here. Mose Beard [sic] was killed yesterday; Geo. Gladden is badly wounded, but there is some hope of his getting well. He is shot through the arm, and in the face.

All this happened at Keller's store on the Llano.' We fear this is but the beginning of a bloody solution of the difficulties about stock, that have become so serious of late."[30]

In Mason attorney Henry M. Holmes penned yet another letter to Governor Richard Coke:

> Sir
>
> I have the honor to call your attention to the fact that on Sunday the 6th inst. two more men viz. Mose Beard and G.W. Gladden were shot in this county. Beard was killed. Gladden still lives. The stories of the killing are dramatically opposite and I certainly cannot inform you as to whom the cause most attaches. The men shot were alone and were killed by a large number of Germans with Mr. Jn. Clark, Sheriff of the county at their head.
>
> The Germans claim that Beard and Gladden began the fight firing about fifty shots at ten or twelve paces from Mr. Clark. No one was hurt however except the two men Beard and Gladden.
>
> Mr. Beard is a man of large connexions [sic] in Burnet county and if something is not done a civil war will be inaugurated—
>
> The County authorities are completely paralyzed and can do nothing—I write this so that your Excellency may know the state of affairs and if it is found impossible to order troops here some suggestion might be made by your Excellency for our guidance.
>
> Some short time ago a meeting was held and largely attended, which requested the Sheriff and other County officials to resign. The sheriff has not done so but still is leader of a band composed exclusively of Germans. He is a fugitive from justice there being five indictments against him in Llano County for Robbery and false imprison-ment—he cannot be arrested with the force at the disposal of the justices and now holds the County in awe with some fifty men at Kellers, the scene of Mondays killing about eight miles from here. The lives of all those who do not belong to the mob are in danger and quiet can hardly be restored until some steps are taken to bring the perpetrators of the late murders (10) to justice and this cannot be done in this county by any jury grand or petit summoned from the vicinity.

HENRY HOLMES

THE KELLER'S STORE

The authority of the law is apparently gone here, and in my view only a Commissioner with your Excellency's authority backed by a strong force of troops can restore it.

I am

Very Respectfully

Your Obedient Servant Henry M. Holmes[31]

Clark garrisoned Hedwig's Hill with his little army as the news spread. Cooley, sensing natural allies, met with John Baird, Ringo, and others who swore vengeance. In Austin Coke vacillated over a decision. Each man reacted in his own way and time. As Ecclesiastes teaches, there is a time for all things.

The time to kill had arrived.

CHAPTER TEN

"...alias Long John"

In later years, Mason residents recalled that killing Moses Baird was the most foolish thing the mob could have done. "Men came from as far away as San Antonio to avenge him."[1] One of those men was John Ringo.

Word of Baird's killing reached Burnet County quickly. Bill Farris told his grandson, H.V. "Todd" Faris, "They were so upset by the news that they didn't eat before they left. When they arrived they found Mose so ripe that they couldn't eat on the way back. Vultures followed the wagon all the way back to Burnet."[2] Another participant, Sam Tanner, informed his family that he had driven the wagon to Mason County with his rifle across his lap fully expecting to be shot at any moment.[3] Known to have accompanied John Baird were Farris, Tanner, John Olney, and John Ringo. Doubtless more of the family members accompanied them, for the group was reportedly a large one.

Baird's killing marked a turning point in the feud. Scott Cooley, the relentless avenger, seized the moment to rendezvous with the Baird party at Loyal Valley, where Gladden was under a physician's care. The fiery ex-ranger lost no time recruiting allies. Clark, wary of the force gathered within striking distance of Mason, sent word asking Tom

Gamel to meet the Baird party at Loyal Valley.[4] On the tenth Gamel and Deputy Sheriff James Baird (no relation to John and Moses Baird) visited Gladden's home in Loyal Valley. There they found Cooley, Baird, and "a fellow by the name of Ringoe [sic] and Williams at the house."[5] Cooley, having gathered willing allies, was in high spirits and bought a round of drinks at the saloon.

Gamel and Baird returned to Hedwig's Hill, where Clark waited with his forces. Dan Hoerster, still grieved over the death of his brother-in-law, Karl Bader, told Gamel to tell Cooley "the next time we meet one of us is going to die."[6] Anticipating an attack, Clark's forces waited at Hedwig's Hill.

The *San Antonio Daily Herald* reported, "After the killing, Mr. Keller's house was garrisoned for a couple of days, by about 50 men, who were apprehensive that an attack would be made by some parties from Loyal Valley. Mr. John Beard [sic], however, took his brother's body back to Burnet quietly and peaceably."[7] The return of Baird's body to Burnet was the prelude to further tragedy. Laura Olney, pregnant at the time, apparently went into shock at the sight of her brother's decomposing, mutilated body. Nearly a month later, on October 7, she gave birth to a son, Samuel Tanner Olney. The child died the same day.[8]

In Austin Governor Richard Coke moved at last to respond to the pleas from Mason, but it was already too late to avoid violence. Ringo saw clearly that the law had failed, and his childhood aversion to mob rule helped bring him to the Baird camp. Justice, if it was to be had, fell on the hands of Baird's friends and family. In Mason, Clark and his allies waited for some kind of reaction.

They would not wait long.

On September 25, Cooley, Ringo, and a number of other men totaling six or eight brazenly rode into Mason. Ringo and a man named Williams split off from the group and rode to Cheyney's home north of Mason on Comanche Creek. The pair hailed the house, and Cheyney emerged, inviting them in for breakfast. Gamel recalled, "Chaney asked Ringoe and Williams down and they stepped upon the porch and washed their faces. Chaney washed and was drying his face and while he had his face covered with the towel, Ringoe and Williams shot him down and rode back to where their friends were awaiting them."[9] The men ate breakfast at Lace Bridges' with their guns across their laps before departing Mason unmolested.

GEORGE GLADDEN

DANIEL HOERSTER

That brazen raid shocked Mason, and on September 29 the mob learned how truly vulnerable they were. While a confederate named Booker held their mounts, Cooley, Baird, and a recovered Gladden ambushed Dan Hoerster, along with his brother-in-law, Peter Jordan, and Henry Pluenneke, in Mason. A blast from Baird's shotgun killed Hoerster instantly. Jordan and Pluenneke narrowly escaped being killed with him. The killers made good their escape, taking with them a man named Bill Coke. That the gang provided Coke with a rifle casts doubts on reports that he was their hostage.

Ironically the Texas Rangers under John B. Jones had arrived in Mason County the day Hoerster was killed but had been diverted to Loyal Valley. That may account for one writer's unsubstantiated statement that Loyal Valley was "a known hangout for the lower elements of Texas society."[10] No contemporary documentation confirms the allegation, and both the Mason County Historical Commission and the Mason County Historical Society flatly deny it.

The fear which gripped Mason County predominated normal life. Lucia Holmes recorded, "Oh the worry of these dreadful times."[11] The *Austin Statesman*, firing a shot at both Mason and the Sutton-Taylor War, quipped, "The Cuero *Star* should proclaim it, and the people of Mason never forget that few people of the better class care to emigrate to a country where they think it necessary to wear a six-shooter at their side, a bowie knife in their boot, and keep an eye over both shoulders to insure safety."[12]

With Rangers swarming Mason, the Cooley faction retreated to the relative safety of Burnet County. Jeff Ake, an early-day resident and gunfighter of the Reconstruction period, ran across the group hiding out on Table Mountain. He recalled, "When I come to the gap on the way to the mesa—there was a kind of mesa inside the rim—a feller throwed down on me, till he knowed who I was. The Ringo-Gladden crowd was in there, living on beef and roasting ears."[13]

Cooley's crowd could not remain hidden long, and by the end of November they were reported to have had a fight with the Texas Rangers. "For some time past a party of five men have been banded together and encamped in the mountains, fifteen miles southwest of Mason, making a business of not only stealing cattle, but actually killing them for their hides. Warrants for their arrest have been out for some time, but they defied civil authorities. Lieut. Long, of the Rangers, and a squad of his men recently surprised the outlaws in their camp and captured them. The rangers also captured a party under Scott Cooley, wounding that noted leader."[14]

A correspondent signing himself Alazan added details which were translated from the *Freie Presse:* "At last the Rangers appeared to be in earnest, as we hear that on last Saturday they came upon Scott Cooley and John Ringgold. Cooley is reported to be wounded and Ringgold a prisoner."[15] The report of Ringo's capture was erroneous. Ira Long's monthly returns confirm that Company A captured some cattle thieves on November 3. Despite numerous scouts, however, Long failed to encounter any of the Cooley party.[16]

Cooley's strong following in Burnet and the relative security it afforded made him careless. On December 27 he and Ringo were arrested there by Sheriff John Clymer and his deputy, J.J. Strickland. The pair were charged with threatening the lives of Clymer and Strickland. The arrest brought an open show of support:

> WAR IN BURNET.—Ex-Policeman Johnson returned from Burnet Friday, where he had been to conduct a prisoner, and reports a horrible state of affairs in that town. The notorious desperado Cooley and one of his companions had been arrested and placed in the Burnet jail, and when Mr. Johnson arrived there about twenty men were dashing about the town threatening to break open the jail, which was being guarded by fifty or more men, and liberating the prisoners. There was so much excitement in the place in the morning that the sheriff would not receive the prisoner taken up by Mr. Johnson, as he was in constant expectation of an attack. Later in the day, however, the prisoner was received, and Mr. Johnson then started home, meeting many armed men along the road. A feeling of dread and insecurity for life seemed to pervade the entire community, and strangers were anxious to get out of those parts.[17]

Fearing an attempt to liberate the prisoners, Strickland and a dozen guards took them to Austin, arriving on January 2, 1876.

> COOLEY AND RINGGOLD—On Sunday morning the STATESMAN announced that Scott Cooley and John Ringgold, two of the Mason county desperadoes, had been arrested and placed in the Burnet jail, which was under a

heavy guard to prevent the release of the prisoners by an armed body of men that were dashing about the town. On Sunday deputy sheriff Strickland, accompanied by about ten or twelve men, brought the prisoners to this city for safe keeping until the meeting of the Burnet district court on the fourth Monday in this month. Arriving in the city the whole party stopped at Salge's snack house for lunch, and while there a large concourse of people gathered to see the two men who have in the past few months, with others, been "on the rampage" in the counties of Mason and Burnet. The prisoners were apparently cool and reserved, and chatted as freely as any of the guard, and each recognized a person or two in the crowd. Cooley, who is said to have been a very quiet man until about a year ago, is a short solid man, about twenty-eight years old, and looks like he might have some Cherokee blood in him. He is charged with having killed deputy sheriff John A. Whorlie, of Mason county, and it is said that after killing him he also took his scalp off. Ringgold, who is taller and perhaps older than Cooley, is said to have taken an active part in the Mason county war, and he and Cooley are charged with having threatened the lives of Sheriff Clymer, of Mason [sic], and his deputy, Strickland. The prisoners are now in the Travis county jail, and the guard left for home yesterday.[18]

If Cooley and Ringo were safely incarcerated, Baird and Gladden were not. On January 13 they caught up with Peter Bader, whom the *Galveston Daily News* mistakenly identified as one "Bourbon":

The Cooley party in the great vendetta in this county are charged with another murder. Report says that one day last week a foreigner by the name of Bourbon was riding along the public road when he was attacked by a party of men and shot. The party then seeing some men approaching and supposing them to be friends of their victim, told them to take up the man and take care of his valuables, as they (the assassins) did not want money but his life. Bourbon had $400 and a gold watch when shot. It is said that a general warfare is being waged in the county between what is known as the Dutch population and the Americans. At last accounts the murderers had not been captured.[19]

In late January Cooley and Ringo were returned to Burnet:

> DEPUTY SHERIFFS Henry Stokes and Fred Peck arrived yesterday morning from Burnet, where they had been with the posse of ten men that conveyed Scott Cooley to Burnet from the jail in this city. They report that they saw no signs of resistance or of an attempt being made to release the prisoner on the road. They state however, that Deputy Sheriff Johnson, of Burnet, and a man with him were fired upon and pursued several miles while out serving capiases last Tuesday. The speed of their horses saved their lives. A minute company has been organized in the town of Burnet, and recently quite an extensive purchase of firearms has been made in this city by citizens of Burnet, whose lives are said to be endangered because they are determined to enforce law and order.[20]

On February 1 Ringo and Cooley appeared in district court and were indicted in causes 925 and 926 for "Seriously threatening to take the life of a human being."[21] On February 2 Ringo appeared in court again to answer to the disturbing the peace charge. He pleaded guilty, and the jury assessed his fine at seventy-five dollars.[22] Cooley and Ringo then moved for a change of venue to Lampasas County on the other charges. The motion was granted and bail was set at $500 for each count.[23] The district court minutes also indicate that Clymer, Strickland, *Bulletin* editor Swift Ogle, City Marshal J.H. Stapp, and Miss M. McGuire were bonded to appear as witnesses for the case in the amount of two hundred dollars for each count at the next district court term.[24]

While Ringo and Cooley awaited their day in court, mob violence claimed another victim. John Calvert, one of Ringo's bondsmen in Cause 854, was shot to death on February 16. The Burnet *Bulletin* for that period is missing, but family recollections note that he "was shot to death in mysterious circumstances" on the front porch of his home in Burnet. He left a widow and four young children.[25]

Ringo, within the span of little more than a year, had acquired a reputation. The *Galveston Daily News* attested, "Deputy Sheriff J.J. Strickland has acquired some notoriety for his courageous conduct in arresting the celebrated desperadoes, Scott Cooley and one Ringo, alias

'Long John,' both of whom are now in jail at this place."[26]

The pair were transferred to Lampasas and placed in custody of Sheriff Albertus Sweet for safe keeping. Sweet, a veteran lawman, seriously underestimated his new charges' allies. Already the jail's security had been breached by Bud Farris. Farris later told family members that, fearing Cooley and Ringo would be lynched, he had gotten himself arrested on a minor charge to check out the jail's security.[27] Sweet would soon prove unable to hold his charges.

> DISAGREEABLE.—Between midnight and daylight on Sunday last [April 30], four disguised men suddenly sprang upon the jail guard at Lampasas, seized and tied him to a picket fence, his face towards the foe and his back towards the fence. They with pistols presented towards him, commanded him to be silent or die. He didn't die. Two of the four proceeded to the jail, and after handing Scott Cooley a file, they began boring and chiseling to make a hole where by the prisoners (Cooley and John Ringo) might escape. But they were compelled to raise the siege without obtaining their object. The near approach of daylight is supposed to have caused them to abandon their enterprise. The guard was carried about two miles on the San Saba road and turned loose upon the range. He returned to his old feeding place about daylight, and, after calmly surveying the premises and making himself sure that his late companions were all gone, and conscientiously believing that his obligation of silence and secrecy were removed, he dared to speak, and speaking he said he was thankful it was as well with him as it was.—Burnet Buletin. [sic][28]

The jail break attempt prompted Sweet to increase security. The effort proved futile. The night of May 4 a group of men arrived at Sweet's home and forced him to surrender the keys. Bluntly informed that they would kill Sweet and his family and have the keys anyway, Sweet provided them.[29] The party then went to the jail, where they encountered Deputy Sheriff J.T. Walker and a guard. Walker later testified, "I was walking up with one of the guards near Stanifer's store when I saw a party of men coming up some 13 or 15 in no. They told us not to shout that they had the keys & that if we hurt any of them that they would burn up the town with every one in it." Walker prudently concluded not to resist, and the pair were quickly freed. "Their hobbles was laid over a log and cut in two with an old axe which was near the jail door."[30]

Cooley and Ringo immediately headed for Bluffton and the relative safety of Llano County, intending to take Solomon G. Maxwell's ferry across the Colorado River. "Hoss" Maxwell, a huge man with a ready wit, did not know his customers but taking in Cooley's youth and size referred to him as "Sonny." He was preparing to haul a load of hogs across the river when the pair arrived. For obvious reasons, the Ringo and Cooley held their mounts on the opposite end of the ferry from the squealing hogs. Partway across the river, the pigs suddenly became frightened and stampeded to the fugitives' end of the ferry, tipping the craft and plunging men, horses, and hogs into the river. The men swam safely to shore, caught their mounts and rode off. Maxwell considered the incident uproariously funny—right up to the moment a posse arrived and told him who his passengers were.[31]

By May 5 Ringo and Cooley were at Joe Olney's home in Llano when Sheriff William P. Hoskins rode up. The lawman was startled to find himself unexpectedly surrounded by Cooley's allies. Among them was John C. Carson, a brother-in-law of the Baird brothers. Hoskins recalled:

> I saw J.C. Carson on the evening of the 5th of May 1876 with Ringo and Cooley in Llano County. Joe Olney, Andy Murchison, Bud Farris, Jim Mason and Bill Wills & Charley Ferguson and some three or four others were also there in company with Ringo & Cooley. I went to see Joe Olney on official business & got within 25 yards of the house before they saw me. There appeared to be considerable excitement among them when they saw me, some got on their horses and others picked up their guns. I continued to ride up to them and spoke to Joe Olney and he asked me to get down. When I got down Scott Cooley threw a cartridge in his gun & steped [sic] behind his horse.[32]

Hoskins conversed with Olney in his home, then emerged from the house. Ringo approached him. "I was at the back of the house a very short time. Ringo shook hands with me & I asked him what he was doing there & he made some foolish remark."[33]

By May 8 the Cooley faction were back in Mason, hunting Clark no doubt. Clark, however, had fled, and the Mason mob had been broken. Lucia Holmes noted, "Scott Cooley and a crowd here.—No one knows what they are after."[34]

Cooley and Ringo remained through the ninth, brazen as always.[35] The *Galveston News* reported. "A gentleman recently arrived from Loyal Valley, reports that Scott Cooley and Ringgold [sic], who were recently released from the jail at Lampasas by armed men, went to the hotel at Loyal Valley, in broad daylight, armed to the teeth and ate with perfect composure, and rode off unmolested."[36]

The men then returned to Llano County where the Farris family hid them for two weeks or so on Long Mountain.[37] There they separated. Gamel records, "Scott Cooley quit the gang and left Mason en route to Blanco. On his way, he stopped in Fredericksburg and ate dinner at the Mintz [sic: Nimitz] Hotel. When he got ready to leave, he purchased a bottle of whiskey. When he got twelve miles out of Fredericksburg, he rode up to a fellow's house by the name of Moore and got down off his horse and laid down and said, 'Moore, I am an awful sick man,' and in a few minutes he was dead."[38] Cooley died around one o'clock in the morning of June 10 at the home of Dan Maddox in Blanco.[39] Gamel theorizes that Cooley may have been poisoned, and Maddox family tradition concerning his death indicates that this is probably correct.[40]

Meanwhile, Ringo was alive and well, and his reputation as a dangerous man grew significantly as the press spread rumor and innuendo:

> A GENTLEMAN from the frontier says that Scott Cooley, Ringgold and others, who were recently taken out of the Lampasas jail, have gone into camp, and that they defy the law and the authorities, and that there is no protection for life or property in many places up-country. He says that some men who have no viable means of support, and are suspected of being horse thieves, assert that the business don't pay now very well, as horses only command from twenty to thirty dollars in Austin and other places, and that that does not pay for the trouble of getting them and taking them to market. It is currently reported that the whole country is filled with armed men—these snake-hatted, goat skin-leggined chaps—who are the terror to travelers and law-abiding citizens. Perhaps the Governor will yet find it necessary to issue a proclamation authorizing all good citi-

zens to shoot down all notoriously bad characters, and to offer rewards for their scalps. The people are crying aloud for protection, law and order, and they should have it, even if extraordinary measures have to be resorted to. Never has so much lawlessness been experienced in Texas.[41]

With Cooley dead, John Ringo was the premier feudist from Mason County. In the succeeding months his name would appear in print often.

CHAPTER ELEVEN

"State of Texas vs. John Ringo"

While Ringo went into hiding, in California his family appeared to be living comfortably. Mary Ringo was working as a dressmaker, while Fanny had found employment as a milliner.[1] In truth, however, Mary Ringo was ill. Tuberculosis, the disease which had brought the family to California and contributed to her husband's untimely death, the disease which had killed her son Albert, now racked her own body. Mary clearly anticipated her death. On July 5, 1876, she prepared her last will and testament, bequeathing everything to her children: "I do hereby bequeath to my daughters Fanny F. Ringo, Mary E. Ringo & Mattie B. Ringo the homestead, together with the furniture to share & share alike, but with the understanding that the same shall not be sold, until Mattie B. Ringo my younger daughter shall have attained the age of twenty one years. My son John Ringo having been here to fore provided for I bequeath him the sum of one dollar."[2]

That Mary could leave an estate to her daughters speaks well for her finances. Far from the impoverished portrait painted by some authors,

Mary, undoubtedly supplemented by funds from John, was independent of the charity of Colonel Younger. The Ringo sisters, however, would soon be on their own. Less than two weeks later, on July 16, Mary died.[3]

John could not have provided much support for his sisters during that time. While he remained unaware of his mother's death, perhaps for weeks, his problems in Texas mounted. On June 24, 1876, he was indicted for "Aiding a prisoner to escape from the Custody of a lawful Officer."[4] The charge may have stemmed from an attempt by Ringo to liberate John Redding, one of the men implicated in the Lampasas jail break, who had been captured in Llano County. The *Burnet Bulletin* reported:

> Deputy [Joseph] Leverett, of Llano county, who has just returned from carrying Reddin to Austin for safe keeping, reports that thirteen of Reddin's friends were seen ambushed in the cedar brake this side of Austin waiting for them to pass, so as to liberate the prisoners and kill the guard. But, luckily, Leverett and Sheriff Strickland went by Round Rock, and thereby avoiding an attack. It is reported that some one of the waylaying party remarked that they would never get as good an opportunity to kill Strickland and Leverett. The notorious Ringo, who seems to have been the leader, is certainly a very desperate and daring man. All but three of the party finally dispersed, leaving them to waylay Leverett on his return. But the news reached him, and, with the aid of the Sheriff of Travis county and about thirty men, he made a search for but failed to find them. Leverett says that he was assured of the co-operation of the citizens of Williamson and Travis counties in pursuing and hunting down such characters, who are ready to release prisoners and murder county officers while attempting to do their duty.

Adjacent to the article, the *Bulletin* printed a thinly veiled threat. It noted in part, "There are still among us those who fare ever ready to notify these thieves of any move that might be made by the sheriff to arrest them. But the eyes of the people are upon them, and a continuance of harboring and shielding such characters will bring them into trouble."[5]

Ringo made news again in August. On the seventeenth, a telegram from Fredericksburg to the *Galveston News* reported, "Trouble has started again in Mason county. John Ringo and Bill Randall have been driving cattle off from Gooch, Hogan, Neighbors and others. Citizens are after them, and a call has been made on Gillespie county for the Mounted Rifles to help capture them."[6]

Posses swarmed in pursuit. An E.F. Cullen, of Walter Tine & Co. in Austin, reported to the *Burnet Bulletin* that on the August 21 the sheriff of Mason County and "twenty five men, started to Kimble county to capture a party of cattle thieves. It is thought there will be much trouble and probably bloodshed. Ringo is in charge of the stolen cattle."[7] That charge, the only one ever made against Ringo for cattle theft in Texas, proved false. A.T. Taylor, Joe Olney's brother-in-law, knew that Ringo was hiding in Llano County, particularly when he himself was assisting him. Ringo may well have sent Taylor into Burnet to set the record straight. The *Bulletin* noted, "Mr. A.T. Taylor, just from Llano county, informs us that rumors are prevalent that a fight had taken place between the party having charge of the stolen cattle in Kimble county and the pursuers. Several were killed and wounded. R.K. Tucker, who once lived here, was said to have had charge of the cattle and was killed in the fight. Mr. Taylor is certain that it is a mistake about John Ringo being connected with the cattle stealing."[8]

Taylor's opinion was confirmed when the posse overtook Randall and his men. In the ensuing gunfight Randall was killed and the cattle recovered. Ringo was not among the cattle thieves, nor was he ever charged in the incident. On September 5, however, he was in Mason County and Lucia Holmes noted, "Hal started to Bluff Creek and came back on account of Ringold being out there....Heard that Ringold had threatened Hal so Hal got his arms ready if he should come to the house."[9] Why Ringo would have threatened Henry M. Holmes is a mystery, but the mere mention of his name evidently sent fear through the town. Sheriff Jesse W. Leslie of Mason made no attempt to arrest him.

Even with Cooley dead and the Mason mob broken, John Baird's allies lived in fear of the Llano mob that had actively aided their Mason neighbors. In later years, admitted mob member Miles Barler boasted, "We formed a vigilante committee and elected a captain. Well, they were the ones who had to leave the country, and don't forget it; that is, the leaders, and most of the others."[10]

— Abraham Taylor —

In the early morning hours of September 7 two strangers rode up to Joe Olney's house and talked with him before riding on toward a ford that crossed the Colorado on his ranch. Suspicious of the pair, Olney grabbed his rifle and followed them. The men noticed him and rode back, and somehow got the drop on him. Joe threw the rifle down. One of the men then fired. Joe drew his pistol and in the ensuing gunfight shot both men.[11]

Self-defense though the shooting was, it proved catastrophic for Joe Olney. The men were Burnet County Deputy Sheriff Samuel B. Martin, a brother-in-law of Sheriff J.J. Strickland, and Wilson Rountree. Martin died on the eleventh. Rountree recovered, but his older brother, Bob Rountree, a mob leader from Llano, swore vengeance.

The law wasted no time pursuing Olney. Shortly after the shooting, a posse from Llano cornered him in a log cabin in the northeastern part of the county. They rode up to the cabin door and ordered him to come out. "Sure thing boys," yelled Joe. A moment later he stepped through the door laughing and said, "Well, come on and get me."

Clint Breazeale, one of the posse members, recalled his chill of horror as eight or nine rifle muzzles suddenly thrust through the cabin windows. "It was the most stupid thing we ever did. If one cap had been fired we would have all been killed." Olney proceeded to curse the men thoroughly but let them go unharmed. Among those in the cabin were John Ringo, George Gladden, Champ and Bud Farris, and some of the Akes.[12]

Joe Olney had every reason to fear mob action, for on September 11 vigilantes struck unsuccessfully at Ed Cavin. The *Burnet Bulletin* noted:

> Mr. John Haynes, a merchant of Backbone Valley, tells us that he learned that news had reached the Lacy's that Jim Williams, a son-in-law of Mr. Jake Lacy, was killed by a party of men who rode up to his camp about daylight and shot him several times, killing him.
>
> Ed. Cavin who was with Williams, ran as soon as he saw the men approaching. He says, shortly after leaving the camp he heard several shots and heard Williams hollow. It is not known who did the killing, but supposed to be some of the Mason county men who were probably trying to catch Cavin. This occurred Monday morning the 11th, six miles this side of Llano town.[13]

Ed Cavin may have been targeted for death in retribution for his probable role in the killing of Peter Bader. More likely, the attack was simply an attempt to eliminate another one of the witnesses against the Clark posse. Whatever the case, Williams' killing may well have prompted plans for retaliation against the mob. Miles Barler recalled that he was hauling a load of corn from Bluffton to Llano when he was warned that the "Ringo crowd" planned to ambush him. Barler escaped.[14]

John Ringo's luck ran out on October 31, when a combined force of local possemen under Sheriff J.J. Bozarth and a force of Texas Rangers captured him and George Gladden in Llano County.[15] By November 7 the pair was in Austin, where the *Statesman* noted, "John Ringo is the party who was taken from the Lampasas jail last May by about forty armed men. He had been convicted of threatening the life of Sheriff J.J. Strickland, of Burnet, and was regarded as one of the most desperate men in the frontier counties."[16] J.C. Sparks of Company C reported the capture to Adjutant-General William Steele on December 1, 1876:

> Sir—I have the honor to submit to you the following report of the proceedings of Company C, Frontier Battalion:
> On the twelfth day of October I was informed by the sheriff of Llano county that he had been notified to inspect a herd of cattle at the residence of Mr. Neil Cain, ten miles northwest from Llano town, on the following day. Being aware that several parties charged with cattlestealing were in that vicinity, I deemed it advisable to go the point myself, taking a sufficient number of men to make any arrest that I might consider necessary and satisfy myself that no unlawful act was being perpetrated. On my arrival at Mr. Cain's ranche, I found the sheriff, who had already inspected the cattle, and expressed himself satisfied with the title presented by the parties having the herd in charge. On the following Monday, the sixteenth, I detailed Sergeant Robinson to proceed to Loyal Valley in Mason county and ascertain, if possible, the whereabouts of Messrs Gladden, Ringo, Thompson and others, for whom I had warrants, and also to learn the direction taken by a herd of cattle in charge of Eb. Stewart, which I had been informed had passed down the west side of the Colorado river toward Austin.

Sergeant Robinson, on his return, reported that my information was correct, whereupon I detailed nine men, with whom I started in pursuit of the cattle. On the night of Wednesday, the twenty fifth, I arrived in Austin. On the following day I was informed by Deputy Sheriff Carrington, of Travis county, that a small herd of cattle was grazing about thirteen miles northeast of Austin. I immediately started for the point indicated, and found the herd which had been inspected in Llano county on the thirteenth, accompanied by another herd numbering eighty-five head, which latter herd had been stolen from the counties of Mason, Llano, Gillespie and Blanco, in charge of Neil Cain, Eb. Stewart and Frank Enox. I arrested Eb. Stewart and Wm. Thompson [brother of gunfighter Ben Thompson] (who was also with the herds) and brought the prisoners and cattle to Austin, when I lodged the prisoners in jail. I instructed Sergeant Leverett to sell twenty head of the cattle (the owners of which he represented as agent) and to turn the balance over to the inspector of Travis county, which instructions were complied with. The cattle turned over to the inspector of Travis county were advertised ten days, as the law directs, and sold at public auction and the proceeds now remain subject to the order of any person proving ownership of the brands.[17]

Sparks' arrest of Cain and his men effectively ended rustling in the Mason area, at least for the moment. In the same letter he detailed the capture of Gladden and Ringo:

I will now return to the operations of the balance of Company C, at Llano. Soon after my departure information was received that George Gladden and John Ringo, were at Moseley's ranche, in Loyal Valley. Sheriff Bozart [sic: Bozarth] with six men and Sergeant A.W. Robinson with six men proceeded to the aforesaid point, and arrested both Ringo and Gladden and placed them in Llano county jail, where they remained four days, when a courier arrived from Austin ordering all available men to this point by 6 a.m. Monday. The command started for Austin at once, but fearing the release of the prisoners they were taken along and placed in the Travis county jail, where they remain awaiting the action of the courts.[18]

The news that Ringo and Gladden had been taken prompted officials in Burnet to step up their campaign to capture Joe Olney. On November 2, Dan Olney and Alex Erwin, an Olney kinsman, were arrested on a charge of cattle theft.[19] Will Olney was taken in December on a similar charge.[20] The charges, by now all too familiar in the Hill Country, were hastily conceived and may well have been intended to prompt Joe to surrender and relieve the pressure on his family.

For George Gladden the war was over. By the end of November, Sheriff J.J. Bozarth and a strong posse had hauled him back to Llano. On December 4 a correspondent reported to the *Bulletin* that district court was in session and attended by a large crowd. "The case of the State of Texas vs. George Gladden, on indictment for murder, will be taken up this week. Considerable drunkenness and uneasiness the first part of the week but everything is quiet now."[21] On December 7, 1876, Gladden was convicted of murder in the first degree and sentenced to life in the penitentiary.[22]

For John Ringo, too, the fighting was over. His future looked bleak as 1876 closed. In Burnet County he faced two charges of threatening the lives of Clymer and Strickland. In Mason County he faced the charge of murder. From that time forward Ringo was kept under close guard. He would make no more escapes, for even as he faced the prospect of the hangman's noose his allies were fleeing Texas. Jeff Ake would later recall, "Well, both gangs held a compromise meeting with the sheriffs and rangers, and the Beard-Gladden outfit agreed to move out of the country if they was left alone. That was the understanding. They gathered up their cattle, about 1,400 head, and started west. At Brownwood, the sheriff arrested a couple of the boys; but this was breaking the agreement so they forced him to turn 'em loose."[23]

Whatever the facts of the deal, a jail break at Brownwood in May 1877 was very real. At 3:30 in the afternoon four men entered the jail and confronted Sheriff R.B. Wilson with drawn pistols. The raiders liberated four prisoners, including one of the Olneys and Bill Clements, a kinsman of John Wesley Hardin.[24]

Meanwhile, on January 21, 1877, a fire had destroyed the Mason County courthouse, consuming all of the papers and court minutes.[25] Now on May 14, District Attorney F.D. Wilkes "suggested to the Court that the original [indictment] of which the foregoing is a substantial copy has been destroyed by fire together with the entry on the minutes."[26] Those named on the indictment were "John Ringo, Geo. Gladden and others." All of them were charged with shooting James Cheyney in the right side and killing him on September 25, 1875. Hespert Nicholas, S.F. Bridges, and Martin Moran were named as witnesses. The case against Ringo became Cause 21.

On May 31 the firm of Makemson, Posey & Fisher appealed Ringo's March 1876 conviction in Lampasas. Justice E.B. Turner reaffirmed the conviction: "The jury were properly instructed as to the legal presumption of innocence, and the reasonable doubt. Some of the testimony admitted for the prosecution may possibly have been irrelevant, but under charge of the court it is not perceived that any error in this respect can be reasonably supposed to have prejudiced the rights of the accused."[27]

Ringo entered a second appeal which was heard on June 29, 1877, before Justice J. Winkler. Observing that the judge had failed "to charge the alternative punishment," Winkler reversed the decision and remanded the case to Lampasas on July 25, 1877.[28]

In Mason the trial of John Ringo began with a motion to substitute papers for those lost in the courthouse fire. Ringo was indicted in Cause 21.[29] If Ringo harbored hope of a jail break, it was soon crushed. During July J.J. Strickland arrested six men charged in the May 1876 break: Bud and Champ Farris, Andy Murchisson, Ed Brown, Jim Mason, and John C. Carson.[30] In due course others would also be charged including Ed Steadman, George Gamel, John Baird, Bill Redding, and Joe Olney. Only Steadman would serve any time in prison for his role. On September 30, 1878, he entered a plea of guilty, and on October 1 he was sentenced to prison for two years. Writing to his wife, Jane Bowen Hardin, Wes Hardin reported that "ed [sic] Steadman who come here for Breaking John Ringo and Sco Cooley out of the Lampasas Jail is Dead died of Sickness on the 11th."[31]

On November 12 the Mason court issued a capias ordering Ringo's arrest. On November 19, he was returned to Austin under a heavy guard of seven Texas Rangers.[32]

The Travis County jail in Austin held a number of hard men at the time. Among them was Texas gunman Wes Hardin, who had been apprehended in Florida. Hardin recalled in later years, "In that jail I met some noted men. Bill Taylor, George Gladden, John Ringo, Manning Clements, Pipes and Herndon of the Bass gang, John Collins,

Jeff Ake, and Brown Bowen."[33] Burrows offers, without documentation, that Hardin "reputedly and incongruously complained about
being cast into the lock-up with the likes of anyone as mean and
vicious as John Ringo."[34] Considering that Hardin had killed a reported forty men in personal confrontations, that statement would clearly
indicate that Ringo was a mean man. The notorious gunfighter Bill
Longley, however, implied in a letter that Hardin thought highly of
Ringo. Longley angrily wrote from prison:

> Did you see the interview that was given out by John
> Wesley Hardin when he was first brought to Austin? He
> said in that interview that he had never had anything to do
> with Bill Longley, nor any other such characters, and that
> he never had anything to do with anybody except gentle-
> men of honor. Now as a matter of information I would like
> to know where these gentlemen of honor friends of his are
> now? They certainly are not in jail where the Honorable
> John Wesley is himself. I wonder if it is King Fisher, Brown
> Bowen, Bill Taylor, Gladden, Ringo, Scott Cooley,
> Grissom and two or three dozen more whom I might
> name.[35]

In November the trial of John Ringo heated up. Thirty-three men
were ordered to appear as a special venue for the trial on November 12;
on the thirteenth subpoenas for Mrs. Mary Bridges and Ben F. Stewart
were issued; Mrs. James Cheyney was subpoenaed on the fourteenth.[36]

In December Ringo appeared in Mason again. He had been in jail
for more than a year, and in a move to force a speedy trial, his lawyer
filed a writ of habeas corpus. The *Galveston Daily News* reported, "The
rangers, under Corporal Warren, arrived in Mason a few days before
Christmas with John Ringo, who was tried by virtue of a writ of habeas
corpus and the bond fixed at $2,500. The bond was filed and Ringo set
at liberty."[37]

Bond for Ringo was given on January 11, 1878. His bondsmen
included cattlemen William Gamel and Michael Foley, along with
George Anstal, C.W. Wingfield, and Robert H. Moseley. Ringo left
court a temporarily free man, but the threat of prison or the hangman's
noose loomed. If ever there was a time to run, it was now.

CHAPTER TWELVE

"... brave and fearless..."

On Ringo's failure to appear at his August 5, 1875, hearing for "disturbance of the peace" in Burnet County, Traywick comments, "So much for the word of John Ringo which many writers claim was as good as his bond."[1] Ringo's actions after he was released from jail on January 11, 1878, convincingly support those claims, made by men who had actually known him. Now facing charges far more serious than he had in 1875, Ringo had compelling reasons and ample opportunity to flee the hostile environment of Mason County. No one dogged his footsteps, and he was free for more than two weeks, yet he did not run. Moreover, during the last part of January, George Gamel, William Gamel's son, was arrested in Mason County on a charge of assisting Cooley and Ringo's escape from the Lampasas jail.[2] The elder Gamel could hardly have been blamed had he surrendered Ringo's bond. He did not.

On January 19, a flood of subpoenas in the Ringo case were issued to Polk Wynn, Robert Clark, Tom Gamel, J.E. Ranck, W.P. Lockhart, Martin Moran, William Koock, Hespert Nicholas, S.F. Bridges, Mrs. Mary Bridges, Annie King, David Doole, and William Trainer.[3] On February 4, Texas Rangers from N.O. Reynolds' company arrested

Ringo and one Robert McIver in Kimble County for disturbing the peace.[4] He evidently was not held on the charge.

Three months later, on April 18, additional subpoenas for Robert Mosely, Charles Wingfield, William Smith, and O.E. Stewart were issued.[5] The same day Ringo appeared in Mason and filed an affidavit of attachment:

> State of Texas}
> County of Mason}
>   Before one Wilson Hey Clerk of the County Court in and for Said County personally appeared John Ringo who after being duly sworn deposes and says that he can not safely go to trial without the testimony of Bud Farris, Andies Murchison, Wm. Olney who reside in the County of Llano State of Texas and Carl Akard who resides in Bandera Co., Mark Hopkins who resides in Gillespie Co., Westly Johnson, Sam Monroe who resides in Kimble County all of which reside in State of Texas and whose testimony is material for the Defence. He therefore prays that attachments do issue to the sheriffs of the Counties above named Returnable to the District Court of Mason County on the 13th day of May A.D. 1877 that they may then and there testify on behalf of Defendant.
>   Jno. Ringo
>   Sworn and Subscribed before me this the 18th day of April A.D. 1878.
>   Wilson Hey C.D.M. Co.
>   By E.T. Anderson Deputy[6]

What testimony these men would have offered is unknown.

On May 13 another special venue for some forty prospective jurors was issued.[7] Fortune, however, had turned in Ringo's favor. On May 15 the final order in the case was issued at the request of the district attorney: "That testimony cannot now be procured to make out the case. Said case to be dismissed."[8] Ringo walked out of court a free man.

Life returned to a semblance of normality for John Ringo, and evidence suggests that he settled down in Loyal Valley. The charges against him in Lampasas were never seriously pursued. Court records of the case noted a loss of papers on September 12, 1877. Two further entries noted a request for time to substitute papers. Amid unfounded rumors that Ringo had died, the charges were finally dismissed on November 11, 1879, "Upon the death of Deft Ringo being suggested."[9]

With the charges against him for threatening Clymer and Strickland largely being ignored, Ringo resolved to run for constable of Precinct 4 in Mason County. In November 1878 he won election, capturing about two thirds of the votes cast.[10]

On November 22, Ringo registered his brand, a simple V on the left side, in Mason County.[11] Not knowing that it was Ringo's, historian and rancher Janaloo Hill examined a copy of the brand and offered her insight on its owner. "My first thought is that he is either stupid, or a tenderfoot, or both. My second thought is that he might have been playing some sort of double game in which it profited him to look the injured party. A V presents no end of opportunities for brand running or altering."[12] Ringo was neither a fool nor a tenderfoot, and the most likely reason for the brand's simplicity was to prevent his being accused of cattle theft in the harsh environment of Mason County. Indeed, he gave every indication of planning to settle down permanently in Mason. He had selected a brand that precluded him from using a running iron on others' cattle, and he was now a law officer. The Mason County Historical Society's head, Jane Hoerster, pointedly denied writer Frank Tinker's previously cited assertion that Loyal Valley, where John had been elected, had a reputation as a hangout for the dregs of humanity. Quite the contrary, some of Mason County's most respected citizens—John Meusebach, for instance—hailed from Loyal Valley.[13] Furthermore, descendants of Ringo's acquaintances from both sides of the Mason County War dispute Burrows' and Traywick's portrayals of Ringo as a sodden ne'er-do-well. In point of fact, Loyal Valley was a dry community during Ringo's stay there.

Yet John Ringo, for no apparent reason, suddenly threw away all that he had achieved and vanished from Texas. Traditionally writers have ignored the gap in Ringo's life, simply placing him in Arizona during late 1879. Traywick, for example, states, "Conditions being what they were in Texas, Ringo and Joe Hill headed west."[14] But Hill—Joe Olney—had been absent from Texas for more than a year, fleeing the state with his wife and children in 1877.

At least one man encountered Ringo as he headed west. In 1928 N.C. Patterson, a former mail carrier whose family had come to Texas around 1868, recalled that he had encountered a lone horseman while resting during a delivery.

Soon I saw someone coming on horseback. He reined out to the shade tree and said, "If you don't care, I'll share this with you." "Certainly," was my reply, "this is a free shade." I noticed he was pretty well armed. I ventured to ask him if he was afraid of Indians. He said, "I don't know, as I have never met one." He then told me his name was Ringgold. I told him my name, but did not pretend that I had ever heard of him. Some of these old timers around Mason, Fredericksburg and Llano could tell you about Ringgold and Scott Cooley, as I have heard they led some of these folks a cat's life in the early seventies. He told me he was going further West. Some time after this I heard that someone caught him asleep and shot him in the top of the head. I think this happened in New Mexico or Arizona. While under the shade of the tree he called my attention to a buzzard pretty high up circling above us, so I said "Wait till he comes around and I'll stop him," more as a joke than otherwise. So I cut down just to see if I could shoo him off. To my surprise most of his tail feathers came drifting down. He said "That was a good one; try him again." "No, I can't waste any more ammunition on him." The fact was, I knew if I had that buzzard tied to a tree 40 yards away I might use my belt full of cartridges and not get another feather, so I said I was supposed to be in town on schedule, and we parted.[15]

Ringo's undated departure from Texas can be placed logically in December 1878 or early 1879. It remained for Joe Olney's grandson John Olney to explain Ringo's motivation. John was the son of Joe Olney's second son, Joseph Graves Olney, II. In the 1980s John recalled that when he was about fifteen years old, around 1933, his great-uncle Ed Olney had visited the family at Mammoth, Arizona. Ed visited his Arizona kinsmen regularly, staying a month or six weeks for an extended family reunion. One evening Ed recalled how he had left Texas. He and Oscar Olney, the youngest of the Olney brothers, were both arrested in Llano, Texas, on trumped up charges to force Joe's return to Texas. John Ringo went west to tell Joe that Ed and Oscar had been jailed and would "stay in there and rot" until he returned.[16]

After Joe Olney fled Texas in 1877, he moved his family to New

Mexico, then, using the name Joe Hill, bought land in Mexico. Trying to end the Lincoln County War in early 1879, New Mexico Governor Lew Wallace ordered the arrests of thirty-six men, including Joe Olney.[17] The order apparently stemmed from a list of known and suspected outlaws that the notorious Billy the Kid gave Wallace in hopes of getting a pardon. It notes, "Joseph Hill (alias Olney) killing a Deputy Shff. in Burnettown, Texas—sandy complected."[18] On the night of March 23, the Kid, whom Olney knew and disliked, described Mimbres to Wallace, as "situated 30 miles on the road to Cruces from Silver City South. A great many of what are known as the 'Gist Hardin' gang are there. Among them Joe Olney, known in Mimbres as Joe Hill; he has a ranch in old Mexico somewhere near Coralitos. He makes trips up in this country; was at Pinasco not long ago."[19]

When Ringo left Loyal Valley to find Joe Olney, he was fulfilling his obligation from years before when Joe helped liberate him from the Lampasas jail. At the trial of John Carson, Ed Cavin testified, "Mr. Carson said Ringo ought never to forget Joe Olney, that he had ridden day & night to get him out."[20] Ringo did not forget Joe Olney, and it may well have been with this journey in mind that one paper later eulogized, "He was recognized by friends and foes as a recklessly brave man, who would go any distance, or undergo any hardship to serve a friend or punish an enemy."[21]

Ringo and Olney returned to Llano County to free Olney's brothers. Ed recalled that he and Oscar were sitting on their bunks when "suddenly the back of the jail blew out." Then they were in the saddle and riding. The men again headed west for Ysleta, Texas. There, Joe handed his brothers a wad of money and told them to go north because it "might not be healthy for them where he was going."[22] Clearly this was a reference to Joe's fear of Wallace, but he and Ringo would face more immediate problems.

From Ysleta, Ringo and Olney joined a wagon train led by John Parks. Parks, born in Kentucky in 1843, had settled in Acton, Texas, where he married Louise Ann Epley on March 9, 1865. The family resolved to settle in New Mexico in 1879 and arrived at Ysleta during August. Parks' daughter, Jennie, recalled later that the party laid over in Ysleta for some time, fearing Victorio's Apaches, who had left the Mescalero Reservation August 21 and were spreading terror across New Mexico. She added that they intended to leave Ysleta in November, although their departure can be dated to early October.[23]

OSCAR OLNEY

As the wagon train was ready to leave, two men rode up and asked to join them. The pair were heavily armed, each with two pistols, a Winchester, and two belts of cartridges. Parks took their measure quickly as "brave and fearless," hard men who would be good in a fight. One of them was John Ringo. In later years John Parks forgot the name of the second man. Jennie believed it may have been John Baird, who physically resembled Olney. She recalled that her father told her in 1882 that both men "were so courteous and considerate of the other members of the train that they made many friends."[24] Later she would write, "My father thought very highly of John Ringo, and he was a good judge of human character."[25]

The party left for Silver City and reached Mesilla without incident. From there they headed for Slocum's ranch, a popular stop on the road from Mesilla to Fort Cummings. On the way a hard riding, heavily armed party overtook and passed the train. They were hurrying on to Lloyd's ranch, which Apaches had attacked on October 10. Led by Eugene Van Patten, the troop consisted of Dr. William B. Lyon, William T. Jones, J.B. Hinds, Nepomuseno Barragan, Venceslao Lara, Cleto Sanches, Pancho Beltran, Jacinto Armijo, N.L. Hickey, Filoman Barela, and others.

At about one o'clock on the afternoon of October 13, Van Patten's party spotted three horses apparently without owner. The men were suspicious, knowing full well that the Apaches used such diversions for ambushes. After pausing to check their weapons and tighten their saddles, they moved forward. Then the Apaches opened fire from behind some low mounds that the riders had scarcely noticed. They shot Jones through the head almost immediately. His companions fled, and the pursuing Apaches killed Sanches, Barragan, Lara, and Beltran in the rout.

Parks' first inkling of trouble came from M.L. Hickey. Riding ahead of the others, Hickey yelled that the Apaches had ambushed them and exhorted the train to turn back. He was also able to warn a stagecoach following the train.

Parks held a hurried conference with the men. Many of the wagons were drawn by oxen, and they had no chance to reach the safety of Slocum's. The men resolved to circle the wagons and dig a pit in the center from which they could fight. The wives and mothers, however, pleaded with them to make a break for Slocum's for the sake of the children. After some discussion, the men finally agreed and unloaded

ED OLNEY

the horse drawn wagons for the families. The move proved prudent, for the Apaches arrived momentarily but paused to plunder the wagons, giving Park's party time to reach Slocum's safely. When the whites returned later, everything had been destroyed except the wagons, which rain had prevented from burning. It was a cheap price to pay for their lives.[26]

Ringo and Olney left the train at Silver City and headed south to get Joe's family. Joe had his mind set on establishing his family in the San Simon Valley of southeastern Arizona. In later years J.C. Hancock, an early Arizona pioneer, described the area:

> The San Simon Valley lies between the Stein's Peak and Peloncilio mountains on the north and the Chiricahua mountains on the south and empties out into the Gila River at Solomonville. About where the Arizona and New Mexico State line crosses the valley is what is called the San Simon Cienga. This Cienga rises on the New Mexico side and runs toward the Gila on the Arizona side, and on the old maps made by the early Spanish and American explorers was designated as the "San Simon River."...From the head of the Cienga toward the Mexican line the valley was practically unexplored, although it was rumored that some of the old "Rustlers" used to claim there was quite a number of good sized water holes or springs in that section if a man knew just where to look for them.[27]

The San Simon Valley was ideal for ranching. The heavy beef markets of Tombstone and Arizona's other mining camps, not to mention the various army posts, were a relatively short cattle drive away. Equally accessible were the San Carlos reservation and the New Mexico mining camps. To the south were springs that could be utilized for watering cattle being driven north from Joe Olney's ranch. The cattle could be fattened in the San Simon before taking them on to market.

Hancock also recalled the arrival of the first settlers in that area. "In the late 70s some white families settled on the Cienga, among them was J.A. (Gus) Chenowth [sic: Chenoweth], Wm. A. Stark, Al George, Joe Hill and a man by the name of Ware and old Nick Hughes and John McGill, a soldier who had been discharged from the 6th Cavalry at Fort Bowie."[28]

At Chenoweth's William Stark and Al George encountered Ringo for the first time. In later years Stark's sons recalled that he and George had come to Arizona from Colorado, pausing at San Simon because their mules were tired. The men turned the animals loose in a pasture and took a nap, waking later to discover that the mules had strayed. They observed a house on a nearby hill, walked to it, and knocked. Ringo came to the door. Stark explained that the mules had strayed, and Ringo said, "Take my horse and go get them."[29]

With Mason County behind him and no charges pending against him, Ringo could live down his past. Yet it was then that chinks in his armor began to appear. In 1879 the first signs surfaced that Ringo had begun to drink heavily and was developing violent tendencies. The *Epitaph* also reported that "he frequently threatened to commit suicide."[30] Other sources speak of brooding depression. Yet Ringo had never been known as an alcoholic in Texas, and the existing correspondence of Allen Erwin, who was one of the first serious researchers on John Ringo and interviewed John's immediate family, does not even hint of a drinking problem.[31] It was as if a second John Ringo had emerged from the Mason County War.

The evidence suggests that Ringo may have been suffering from post-traumatic stress syndrome, a psychological condition otherwise known as shell shock or battle fatigue and commonly found among combat veterans. In essence, the suppression of trauma can manifest itself over time in various symptoms including drug abuse, alcoholism, depression, violence, and suicide. Evidence of the effects of the Mason County War on the participants is abundant. Peter Jordan in later years suffered vivid nightmares and flashbacks.[32] Ed Olney, a peripheral participant, carried a pocket pistol to the day of his death.[33] Others, such as John Farris, became troublesome. For Farris the symptoms erupted in senseless violence. The *Santa Fe New Mexican* reported, "In a shooting affray at Fort Sumner on the 29th ultimo [December 29, 1879], John Farris was shot and killed by Barney Mason. Farris shot three times at Mason without any provocation, when the latter went off, got a pistol and returning to the store where Farris was shot him twice in the breast."[34]

The first sign of John Ringo's trouble came on December 9, 1879:

More of It.

Last Tuesday night a shooting affair took place at Safford in which Louis Hancock was shot by John Ringo. It appears Ringo wanted Hancock to take a drink of whisky, and he refused saying he would prefer beer. Ringo struck him over the head with his pistol and then fired, the ball taking effect in the lower end of the left ear, and passing through the fleshy part of the neck, half inch more in the neck would have killed him. Ringo is under arrest.[35]

Traywick states, without documentation, that Hancock was unarmed.[36] Armed or not, Hancock, a thirty-one-year-old laborer, had certainly done nothing to provoke the shooting. That Ringo was seriously trying to kill Hancock is less certain. The pistol might well have discharged by accident—a not uncommon occurrence on the frontier—when Ringo struck Hancock with it. Whatever the case, Ringo had announced his entry into Arizona with blood and violence.

He would never live it down.

CHAPTER THIRTEEN

"...disrupting a young economy..."

John Ringo's arrival in Arizona coincides with the establishment of Tombstone in 1879. Tombstone, destined to eclipse those mining camps which came before and after it, was more like Virginia City than the cowtowns of Wichita or Dodge City. James C. Hancock, an early resident of Arizona, related:

> Tombstone was a big rich mining camp filled with mining men from California, Nevada, Colorado and other places in the Pacific slope. The service at the CanCan, Fountain and other first class restaurants were as good in those days as the dining service is today on our railroads. The plug hat was seldom seen on the streets. People were just as rational then as now in the matter of dress. The Can-Can restaurant was named after a very popular dance performed at the Bird Cage by two or more couples in which the ladies were somewhat scantily clad. The Oriental saloon was not considered a very safe place if a man was known to have money on him. The Crystal Palace was the finest saloon in the

camp, and the bar and fixtures were equal to any in San Francisco. The liquors were the finest domestic and foreign that money could buy. The games were all straight and most of the old Faro dealers if they needed money could step into the Bank and borrow on their notes as well as any other business man. Their word and honor was good. The Bird Cage was the principal place of attraction of an evening—I speak from actual knowledge—the girls were all "good sports"—They got a percentage of all the drinks they sold. Nearly all traveling theatrical troops stopped over and put on their shows at the Bird Cage unless it was some high brow outfit and these generally showed at Scheifflein's Hall. Tombstone had the air and personality of the old time mining camps of Nevada in the Comstock days where everybody had money and demanded the best. I have heard old miners say that Tombstone reminded them more of Virginia City than any camp they had been in since leaving Nevada.[1]

Ringo's Arizona arrival also marks his entry into Tombstone folklore, a controversial subject dominated by the conflict between the so-called "Cowboys" and the Earp brothers, of whom Wyatt Earp looms largest. Much of Tombstone literature has concentrated on the theme of the "Cowboy Curse," a term coined by the *Tombstone Epitaph*'s founder, John Clum, an unabashed Earp partisan. While the newspapers of the day took little note of the cowboy troubles until 1881, the problem started far earlier. Historian Larry D. Ball states, "If ever banditti were accused of disrupting a young economy, the highwaymen of Arizona Territory from 1877 to 1882 earned that distinction."[2] Indeed, from the south came the Mexican bandits, men who raided and killed on both sides of the border from California to Texas.

In 1880 the leading outlaw along the Arizona border was Brigido Reyes, who kept himself occupied making life miserable for Mexicans and Americans alike. In a letter to the *Tucson Citizen* dated August 28, 1880, a correspondent signing himself "Occasional" told how Reyes had seized the principal men in the town of Magdalena and held them for a ransom of $10,000. The bandit chieftain, who styled himself "Colonel" Reyes, finally settled for $4,000. Occasional concluded:

> "Coronel" Brigido claims to belong to a party—that of Marquez or Ramirez; he proclaims a plan; but no party

political claims him. People only know him by the plan he acts upon—that of highway robbery; nor does anybody here believe that the proclamation of any plan, promising as it may be, transforms a brigand to a patriot.

Will the people, our neighbors in Arizona, the United States Government, take a different view? If he has made good his escape to Arizona, of which at present we are uncertain yet, will Governor Fremont comply with the treaty and turn him over to the authorities of this State which will surely ask him? For the sake of maintenance of peace and good will we pray let there not be a moment's hesitation.[3]

Reyes led a jack-in-the-box existence, popping back and forth across the border to raid. Nor was he the only Mexican to do so. Acting Governor John J. Gosper would confirm in mid-1881 that Mexicans had perpetrated most "cowboy depredations" up to that time.[4]

Also terrorizing the area were the Apaches, perhaps the best guerrilla fighters of all time. Under the leadership of such men as Victorio, Juh, and Geronimo they struck swiftly, and no accurate figure can be assigned to the people they killed or the livestock they carried off. Much of the problem resulted from the government's forcing the Apaches onto the San Carlos Reservation. Britton Davis, who served in the final campaign against Geronimo, dubbed the San Carlos reservation "Hell's Forty Acres." Nearly fifty years after Davis had served in Arizona, the memory of the reservation remained impressed on his mind: "Rain was so infrequent that it took on the semblance of a phenomenon when it came at all. Almost continuously dry, hot, dust and gravel-laden winds swept the plain, denuding it of every vestige of vegetation. In summer a temperature of 110° in the shade was cool weather. At all other times of the year flies, gnats, unnamable bugs,—and I was about to say 'beasts of the air'—swarmed in millions. Curiously, in the worst heat of the summer most of the flies disappeared; left, evidently, for the mountain resorts."[5] The agency was usually administered by corrupt Indian agents who robbed both the suppliers and the Indians in order to line their own pockets. One of the most despicable chapters in American history, it leaves small wonder that the Apaches were almost constantly on the warpath.

Despite the contemporary newspapers' abundant accounts of the Mexican and Indian depredations, the "Cowboy Curse" holds sway in

Tombstone's history. Writers favorable to the Earps cite the Republican *Epitaph* and a series of documents in the National Archives known as Record Group 60. One author cites as witnesses George W. Parsons, an early Tombstone diarist; John Clum, the editor of the *Epitaph* and the controversial one-time Indian agent at the San Carlos reservation; and Acting Governor John J. Gosper. The same author points to the Clanton family, and others, as the prime movers of the Cowboys.[6] Modern estimates of the gang range from 180 to 300 men.

Historian Ed Bartholomew, often labeled a "debunker" or "Earp basher" by proEarp authors, does not deny the presence of a gang or gangs in Cochise County during the early 1880s. He does point out, however, that Mexican bandits caused many of the problems and that the various newspapers of the time used the term "Cowboy" indisciminantly.[7] Ball concurs, "The most unfortunate aspect of this Cowboy outbreak was that the newspapers failed to distinguish the common, hardworking drovers from the outlaw 'Cowboys.'"[8]

As 1880 dawned John Ringo had other problems. Once again he was in serious trouble, this time facing a charge of assault with intent to commit murder. In March he failed to appear in court, and his bond was ordered forfeited. A March 11 entry in the docket books notes, "On motion of Hugh Farley, Esq., Dist. Atty. it was ordered that as Deft. had failed to appear during this session of the Grand Jury that his Bond be, and this same is hereby declared forfeited, and that a Bench Warrant be issued for the arrest of said Deft."[9]

Ringo, however, had good cause for not appearing. On March 3, 1880, he wrote to "Mr. C. Shib[b]el" from San Simon Valley, New Mexico:

> Dear Sir, being under Bond for my appearance before the Grand jury of Pima Co., I write to let you know why I can not appear—I got shot through the foot and it is impossible for me to travel for awhile[.] [I]f you get any papers for me, and will let me know, I will attend to them at once as I wish to live here. I do not wish to put you to any unnecessary trouble, nor do I wish to bring extra trouble on myself. Please let the Dist-Atty know why I do not appear, for I am very anxious that there is know [sic] forfeiture taken on the Bond. [10]

Traywick says the letter shows that Ringo "had shot himself in the foot."[11] Certainly that is plausible, but Ringo could well have been wounded in any number of other accidents. The disposition of his bond remains unknown.

What is certain is that John Ringo had made a dramatic entrance into Arizona. Contemporary accounts reveal that his reputation, fueled by secondhand stories, confused and garbled accounts, gossip and exaggeration, had swelled beyond reason. One stagecoach driver recalled in 1927, "Never heard of Ringo killing an American in this part of the country but have often heard that there was a fude [sic: feud] in Texas called the 'Ringo War' and that he had killed twenty two men."[12]

Ringo was involved in more mundane matters than killing people on April 2 when he and one M.C. Blakely sold "an undivided two thirds 2/3 in the Blakely Mining Claim situated in the San Simon Mining District" for one thousand dollars. The document was notarized by William R. Brown and witnessed by J.W. Evensen and John R. Phillips at Shakespeare, New Mexico.[13]

On April 7 Ringo again appeared before Brown and appointed James B. Price of Jefferson City, Missouri, to sell "the entire interest in the Sydney Johnson Mine." He authorized Price to sell for no less than $2,000 until October 7, 1880. Anything Price obtained in excess of that amount was his to keep.[14]

In late April or early May, Ringo sold a horse to another possible source of disinformation about his Texas activities, a young transplanted Texan named Billy Grounds. Grounds' letter to his mother dated May 4 communicates his awe for Ringo. "Ma I got 2 horses. I bought one the other day and paid $65.00 for him. I got him from John Ringo the man that was with Scott Cooley that time up at Scold [sic: Cold] Springs."[15]

During the spring of 1880, Joe Olney drove a herd of cattle from his Mexican ranch to San Simon to fatten them for market. That summer he, Ringo, George Turner, and Ike Clanton drove the herd to the San Carlos Indian reservation, where they were to learn firsthand about doing business with corrupt Indian agents.

Indian Agent J.C. Tiffany had arrived at the post in 1879. At first he had organized Sunday schools and Bible classes, but his hand quickly turned to less Christian pursuits such as signing for supplies that were never received and other criminal activities. Tiffany managed to establish a successful ranch at the Apaches' expense, and at one point during

1880, he even wrote to the Tucson firm of Lord and Williams, asking them to send a clerk to the agency in order to make their books agree with his.

The outcome of any dealings with Tiffany or his cronies was predictable. J.B. Collins' July 17, 1880, letter to B.M. Jacobs shows how Hill, Ringo, and Clanton fared:

> I write to ask you to use your influence in getting the parties who tried to wreck your property this week, and who insulted and endangered the lives of your employees at the mill at Safford. I will now fire you a sketch of their doings as I learn them partly from your brother and others. Joe Hill, who they call their King Pin, Dutch Gingo [sic] and Ike Clanton carried about $1,500 or $2,000.00 worth of cattle to the San Carlos. It seems that the contractor found out that these cattle came into San Simon without paying duty, and he caused them much trouble as he would not purchase until he heard from the Gov officer at Silver City who has jurisdiction over that section. I expect N[e]wton made a point on this and got the cattle low of them, which angered them very much. Th[e]y got here about the 12th, and after shooting in Detry's house a few times, they paid me a visit and shot a couple of times. I took Clanton['s] pistol away from him & told him and his Dutch friend if the[y] made any more brakes [sic] I would use my shotgun on them. So they concluded that Safford was a better field for their operations. They reached there in due time and commenced operation by shooting the lamps in John Harrison's Saloon and shooting through Mr. Bill Kirklan's house. Then they opened up in Franklin's store. Shot at everything they fancied, made your brother pour out drinks which they would stir with the muzzle of their pistol. Tried to compel Mr. Wickersham to dance for them by pulling a pistol on him, but it was left for them to have their jolliest time by shooting fifty shots into your mill & make one of your employees furnish the cartridges. They made Katz shut off the water and then compelled him to get up in a corner with a lot of Mexicans and not leave on the pain of being shot, and they wanted to know of Joe Cottrall which one of the party he wished them to kill. Hill the King Pin and Clanton left for Solomon's where they said they were to have another jollification, and they have

Turner under arrest waiting for the return of the J.P.

Now there are but 4 of these fellows all told and it is too bad that they cannot get put through, and I think you have the cause & power to do it. I could not get a single man here to help me arrest them, but I am good for all four of them here. I trust you will see fit after due enquiry to get the Sheriff to send & bring the gang into Tucson and have them put through. It will be a God's blessing for this Vall[e]y to get rid of them. You must excuse this long letter, for I feel like if young Katz was my brother I would not let up on them while the law could reach them.[16]

Since its discovery, writers have offered diverse interpretations of the Collins letter. William A. Duffen suggests the cattle were obtained "without technicality of purchase," even though Collins, who obviously had little love for the men, makes no such implications.[17] Alford E. Turner considers the antics a typical amusement for Ike Clanton and his friends, apparently ignorant of the tradition of hurrahing towns at the end of cattle drives, common throughout the West for so many years.[18] Bartholomew allows the possibility that the cattle were stolen but points out that delaying the drover with various legalities and fine points of the law was a typical pressure tactic which many beef contractors used to get cattle at a lower price.[19]

Had the men been anyone other than John Ringo and his friends, the letter would be nothing more than a curiosity of early Arizona history. Writing of cowboys in general, Philip Ashton Rollins speculates that such events "represented little more than youthful prankishness, and an egotistical desire by passing punchers from distant regions to impress the local inhabitants with the fact of the visitors' presence."[20]

Collins simply repeats what he had heard of the incident, obviously from the contractor. While it may or may not be true that the duty on the cattle had not been paid, neither Collins nor the contractor, Newton, accused them of bringing in stolen beef. Newton had simply made the best of profitable circumstances.

And how did storekeeper A. M. Franklin remember the man who shot up his business during this episode? "I knew John Ringo very well....He saved my life several times."[21]

CHAPTER FOURTEEN

⟨⟩

"... and a stray cat."

The fall of 1880 was an exciting time in Arizona. Word came from Mexico that Victorio and his band had been wiped out. Elections were to be held and, according to one writer, a statement by the Republican County Committee in the *Tombstone Epitaph* contained the first evidence of the Cowboy Curse.[1]

Hugh Farley, the Democratic candidate for District Attorney, is the present incumbent for that office and has held the position since the first of January, 1879. During his term of office there have been more than thirty homicides committed and crimes of all classes have been of frequent occurrence in Pima County....

From the first of October, 1879, to the opening of the present term of court, not less than twenty-five homicides have been committed in this county and fifteen persons have been confined in the Tucson jail awaiting investigation on a charge of murder....

Quite a number of cattle thieves have been bound over to appear before the Grand Jury, and they have not appeared, and the Grand Jury left in ignorance of the evidence against them. There are cases where indictments have been made against cattle thieves and receivers of stolen cattle, and the indicted persons have not even been assigned and the indictments left to slumber in the pigeon holes of the clerk's office until time and dust have hidden them from view....[2]

John Clum, the *Epitaph*'s Republican editor, wrote:

> We understand that the Grand Jury brought in indictments the other day against two Mexicans, and when the cases were called in court the witnesses who had appeared before the jury were nowhere to be found, having probably packed up and started for the Magdalena feast. It appears to us that about enough of this kind of business has been going on in Pima County. Men are shot in the streets and the killers are turned loose because no evidence is brought before the Grand Jury to indict them; men are found dead in various places and a newspaper item is all that is known of the matter; indictments are found and no witnesses are at hand to convict.[3]

Clearly neither Clum nor the Republican Committee were lamenting a Cowboy Curse. Rather, they were attacking Hugh Farley's record in a preelection editorial. The real message is clear—vote Republican!

But if the Cowboy Curse did not exist in 1880, its basis had been established long before John Ringo, the "King of the Cowboys," arrived in Arizona. Governor John C. Frémont reported in January 1879 that one Robert Martin was leading a band of Anglo outlaws that numbered around a hundred.[4] Martin apparently operated out of the San Simon, but that he had so large a gang is questionable. Bob Paul, Republican candidate for sheriff of Pima County in 1880, offered insight into the Cowboy question during January of 1881. At that time the election was being contested, and Paul, with no reason to defend Ringo, Joe Olney, the Clantons, or any other of the oft-named Cowboys, testified under oath:

> Q—Are you familiar with the lower part of the San Simon Valley?
> A—Yes, sir.
> Q—Is it not a fact that it was noted as the headquarters of

the cow-boys?

A—It used to be, but not now.[5]

Paul's testimony is clear evidence that the Cowboys no longer were in the San Simon. At the same time John Ringo and the traditional cowboys had settled in the area. The reference to Martin's gang as "cowboys" again demonstrates the indiscriminate use of the term. E.B. Pomroy, the United States attorney for Arizona Territory, reported to United States Attorney General Wayne MacVeagh, "'Cow-boys' is a generic designation, originally applied to Cow drivers and herders in Western Texas, but the name has been corrupted in the Territories of New Mexico and Arizona and its local significance includes the lawless element that exists upon the border, who subsist by rapine plunder and highway robbery, and whose amusements are drunken orgies, and murder."[6]

Moreover, this designation caught hold quickly, particularly among Easterners and townsmen unfamiliar and, to a large degree, unconcerned with the livestock trade. Eastern tourist C.M. Chase made one such statement in a November 27, 1881, letter from Deming, New Mexico:

> But the Indians are not the worst element in Grant county society. The cow boys, or roughs and thieves, are so numerous that no man ventures any distance from the village without his Winchester rifle, ready to repeat 12 or 16 times without reloading. With this element constantly on the watch for plunder, a man's life goes for naught. A villager told me this morning, in proof that Deming was not a bad town, that the village was eight months old, and only two murders had been committed since it was started. Pretty good evidence of sound morals. Three weeks ago a cow boy rode his horse defiantly over the depot hotel platform, and was about to ride into the dining room, when he dropped off his horse with a charge of buckshot in his back. The first charge struck the dining-room door, and remains there as a reminder of Deming customs. The cow boy was buried without ceremony. He is indebted to Deputy Sheriff Tucker for his change of abode.[7]

The unlucky cowboy was one Charles Hugo. The Silver City, New

Mexico, newspaper reported, "At Deming, on Wednesday evening last [September 28, 1881], Deputy Sheriff Tucker shot and killed one Charley Hugo, who had been deporting himself in a riotous manner, and who resisted arrest."[8] Had Hugo been a gang member or noted outlaw, the newspapers no doubt would have given him more attention. Nor were the Cowboys a preoccupation of diarist George W. Parsons who, on May 22, 1880, noted the Arizonans' primary concern. After looking over a mining property on foot, Parsons recorded, "Don't think I'll tramp it again unarmed. Colonel L [Lewis] says a Mexican might go for a fellow or Indian pop down."[9] Quite obviously Parsons' concern about Cowboys was nonexistent.

During that time in Arizona Territory, crime was prevalent, nonetheless. Ball notes that between 1877 and 1882 at least thirty-six stage holdups took place in Arizona. Many were committed by Mexican citizens who sought refuge in Sonora.[10] The international border also encouraged cattle theft. Texas newspapers reported Mexican raiders striking deep into American territory as early as 1875. Still earlier, in 1871, the *Arizona Citizen* complained bitterly about bandits along the borders.[11] The entire Mexican border from Arizona to Texas suffered raids by Mexican bandits.

During the summer of 1878 Crawley P. Dake was appointed United States marshal for Arizona Territory. Dake began well, and by the fall of 1878 the *Arizona Miner* was praising his attempts to extradite criminals from Mexico. The cooperation was short lived. In December the Mexican government complained about Anglo outlaws who had stolen some Mexican cattle. Governor John C. Frémont denied the charges and accused Mexico of letting bandits use Sonora as a base. Frémont's charge held more than a grain of truth, for the bulk of the raiding on both sides of the border was committed by Mexican bandits.

At times these bandits graced themselves with the title of revolutionaries. The most noted of them was Brigido Reyes, the real terror of the border during the fall of 1880. Governor Luis Torres of Sonora was more than willing to cooperate in removing this thorn from his own flesh, and by August Reyes and his gang were on the run from posses and troops. On August 14 Mexican troops attacked Reyes and his men between Tubutsma and Puente, killing a number of outlaws in the fight. Reyes and his men then fled across the border with Mexican troops in pursuit. The troops overtook them at Doctor Wilbur's ranch near Arivaca. After the stockmen refused to surrender the outlaws, the

Mexican force withdrew. The citizens of Arivaca finally manage to arrest nine of the bandits, but Reyes escaped with five others.

Sheriff Charles Shibell dispatched a Deputy Sheriff Butner to capture Reyes, and on August 18 Butner caught up with the elusive bandit. A gunbattle erupted in which one of Reyes' men was presumably killed. One account concluded, "A posse of men are now on the trail of the remaining fugitives, and although up to the time of going to press no news had been received by Sheriff Shibell, it would seem as though Brigido Reyes and the balance of his murderous gang of cutthroats and horse thieves are about to receive such a check as will deter any future foolhardy and marauding raids into our neighboring state of Sonora."[12]

The pursuit of Reyes was heated. Parsons noted that American troops were in Tombstone hunting the raiders in late August. "Part of a Cavalry Company under Lieutenant Carter in town this a.m. after some Mexican bandits and horse thieves."[13] The *Nugget* provided further details. "A party of soldiers were in town from Camp Huachuca Tuesday hunting for the Mexican bandit, Brigidio Reyes. It is unnecessary to state that they didn't find him.

"Marshal Dake is in Tucson with the avowed intention of capturing the Mexican marauder, Reyes, and putting a stop to all armed incursions on American soil by armed bands of Mexicans."[14]

A Tucson paper, the *Arizona Star*, reported:

> The CITIZEN Monday received a call from United States Marshal C.P. Dake, who arrived on Sunday morning from Prescott. Mr. Dake is here to investigate the circumstances connected with the late raid of Brigido Reyes and his gang into Sonora, and he informs us that it is the intention of the Government to not only prosecute and severely punish, if possible, the participants in the late fiasco, but to take such measures as will make any future demonstrations of the kind very hazardous. The Government is thoroughly aroused to the importance of suppressing these marauding expeditions, and no pains will be spared to prevent them in the future.[15]

The *Star* added, "U.S. Deputy Marshall [sic] Evans has returned from his chase after Reyes. He followed him to the Sonora border first. Reyes then re-entered Arizona and was again pursued till he entered the State of Chihuahua where he is now supposed to be. The soldiery were still near the border when Mr. Evans left and will probably be away another four days."[16]

On September 11 Dake's men captured an important member of the gang named Martinez. The wily Reyes again eluded capture, and for some time the pursuit continued, with local and federal authorities on both sides of the border cooperating fully.

Such was the situation when the 1880 election took place on November 2, an election in which John Ringo played a role. James C. Hancock recalled:

> In this election Charlie Shibell and Bob Paul were both running for the office of Sheriff of Pima County, and the Rustlers that were operating in the county and along the Mexican border at that time, did not want Bob to win the election, so on the morning of election day, John Ringo, Curley Bill, Milt and Billy Hicks, Joe Hill and a few others rode into the little station of San Simon—now quite a thriving city on the Southern Pacific Railroad, and took possession of the voting precinct and all of them preceded [sic] to vote, and to make sure that none had been left out or overlooked, they voted several times over again; then they got all the white people of the little place—men, women, and children, probably eight or ten in all—and voted them in the same manner, then they rounded up the Chinese and Mexican section hands and voted them two or three times over, then they voted all their horses and a dog or two and a stray cat, and finally to make sure no one had been neglected and not given a chance to cast his ballot, they voted every one over again. When the returns began to come into Tucson, Bob took the lead and was quite a few votes ahead of Charlie, but when San Simon was heard from Charlie suddenly shot ahead in the count and Bob was completely "snowed under" by an overwhelming majority...[17]

Other early Arizona residents noted this amusing anecdote, among them John P. Gray and Henry Morgan.[18]

Some writers have accepted this folktale as hard proof that Curly Bill Brocius stuffed the ballot box to make certain Pima County's sheriff was pro-Cowboy. In point of fact the entire story is a bit of humorous fiction. Curly Bill was not even in the San Simon during the election. He was in the Tombstone jail, having been arrested there on October 28 for the killing of City Marshal Fred White. White was responding to some promiscuous shooting when he encountered Brocius. White demanded Brocius' pistol, then seized the weapon by the barrel and jerked it toward himself. The pistol discharged and the bullet hit White in the stomach. Brocius, whom the *Epitaph* identified as "William Rosciotis," was not well known in Tombstone at the time. He was tried and found not guilty in the killing.

Bob Paul contested the election. James K. Johnson, a witness for Paul, testified that "there were not more than fifteen persons present [at the balloting] the whole day." Johnson further testified that the ballots had been left in the hands of Phin Clanton for a time, and added that "the election was first intended to be held at Clanton's, but when Clanton returned from Tucson he said there was a doubt of his house being in Arizona, and the polling place was changed to McGill's house."[19] According to some writers the "Cowboy" Clantons were desperate and lawless men, yet Johnson says they were concerned that the election would be illegal if their home were on Mexican soil—so concerned, in fact, that they asked to have the polling place moved to another home definitely within the territory. Johnson was obviously unaware of the Clantons' "lawlessness," for neither he nor any of the others officiating the election saw anything wrong with Phin Clanton's having custody of the ballots. Nor is there even a hint in the testimony that anyone thought Phin had stuffed the ballot box. Not one witness mentioned the voting of every canine in the San Simon Valley, let alone a stray cat. On the contrary, the Republican representative, testified, "The election was conducted all right so far as I could see."[20]

If the Cowboys did not stuff the ballot box, who did? The testimony in the case indicates that the returns from the San Simon were kept in the Wells, Fargo office in Tombstone with the local agent, Marshall Williams, in charge. Williams testified that the seal he had put on the box had been broken. That, more than any other cause, cast doubt on the election. It is not impossible that Paul's own partisans broke into the ballot box, as they would do in the election of 1884 when Paul's election was again questioned. Paul and some of his friends raided the Wells, Fargo office in Tucson and changed the ballot in his favor.[21]

Finally, contrary to folklore, the San Simon vote was not the only polling place under investigation. Even Tombstone's count was questioned. The San Simon ballots were disregarded for a number of reasons, none of which involved voting livestock. The *Star* published the election's final outcome in April 1881. "The vexed question is settled. The shrievalty contest is ended. Chas. A. Shibell yesterday vacated the office of Pima county, turning over to his successor, R.H. Paul the books, papers, etc., of the office. As long as there was a probability of a final decision in his favor, Mr. Shibell very properly contested the right of his successor to the office; but when it became evident to him that the ultimate success of Paul was assured, he yielded possession immediately."[22]

The folklore aside, John Ringo did play a role in the 1880 election.. The *Tombstone Daily Nugget* listed the Pima County election precincts, naming the officials of Precinct 27, the San Simon, as "J.C. Clanton, Inspector; John Ringo and A.H. Thompson, judges." The polling place was "Joseph Hill's house."[23]

The political controversy intensified animosities that had smoldered between Republicans and Democrats since the end of the Civil War. Tombstone was divided along party lines, and the controversy that has persisted to the present was soon to ignite in a wave of lies, theft, and murder.

CHAPTER FIFTEEN

"John R. Godalmighty"

O n November 1, 1880, John Ringo joined forces with one of the two most controversial families in Tombstone's history. On that day, he and Ike Clanton appeared in Shakespeare to file a ranch claim.

Notice

Know all men by these presence that We the undersigned have this day located for grazing and farming purposes 320 three hundred and twenty acres of land lying in what is called Animas Valley located about five miles West of the Animas Mountains about 28 Miles North of the Gaulupa Canon at the mouth of a cienga running into the Maur Valley from the West, and shall be known as the Alfalfa Ranch or Cienga this the first day of November A.D. 1880.

John Ringo
J.I. Clanton

Witness
W.J. Patrick
Fr.K. Johnson

The document was filed November 26.[1] Ringo's partnership with Ike Clanton places him squarely on the wrong side of the Earps.

Newman Haynes Clanton was born in Davidson County, Tennessee, in 1816 to Henry and Polly Hailey Clanton. He moved to Missouri and on January 5, 1840, married Mariah P. Kelso and began farming. The couple's first three children were born there: John Wesley in 1841, Phineas Fay in 1845, and Joseph Isaac (Ike) in 1847. A daughter, Mary E., was born in Illinois in 1852.

The Clantons moved to Texas in the early 1850s and settled near Dallas. There two more children, Hester and Alonzo, were born in 1854 and 1859 respectively.[2] The family later moved to Hamilton County, where on June 15, 1861, Newman and John enlisted in Captain Wilbur F. Cotton's company of Home Guards.[3] For some reason John also enlisted on August 10, 1861, in the Freestone Boys, Fourth Regiment, Texas Cavalry.[4]

The Clantons' military records indicate that John was arrested for desertion in late 1861 and court-martialed in February 1862. He was found guilty, but due to extenuating circumstances he received a relatively light sentence: pay stoppage from the time of desertion until the end of his enlistment and then a dishonorable discharge. The "extenuating circumstances" were cited as his youth and his ignorance of the Articles of War and the seriousness of his crime.[5] That same year, 1862, the youngest Clanton, William Harrison, was born.

Newman Clanton enlisted again on February 1, 1864, this time in the Company for the Second Frontier District. On June 28, 1864, he was detailed to drive cattle. One record lists him as absent without leave, but the matter cannot have been serious as there is no record of any action being taken against him.[6]

With the close of the war, the Clantons moved west to California. Mariah Clanton died, probably in 1866, although the date is not certain. Young Alonzo Clanton also died during that time.[7] In California, John married Nancy Rose Kelsey and settled in Inyo County. Newman moved to Arizona in 1873 and settled in the Gila Valley.

Many writers point to the Clantons' arrival in Arizona as the beginning of their large scale criminal depredations. Such deeds could hardly have escaped the notice of a watchful press, and the newspapers did, indeed, report the Clantons' activities:

Newman H. Clanton and family settled on the Gila Valley a few miles above old Camp Goodwin August 3 of this year. He at once made claim to water, located a line and now has a ditch two and a half miles in length which carries 1880 cubic feet. There is one body of fully 25,000 acres of very rich land and Mr. Clanton feels sure that with proper management he has water enough to irrigate the whole tract. This year he has cultivated 100 acres and is now preparing and will sow and plant at least 600. He was in Tucson early this week procuring utensils and supplies. He says the settlement now consists of three families—in all fifteen persons, and that more are coming. He is very anxious to have families settle there so that a public school may be opened as soon as possible. Families will be supplied with a water privilege at the actual pro rata cost of the ditch, and accommodated with all information and assistance Mr. Clanton can afford. We have passed over the land and know it to be as rich as can be found anywhere. The water of the river is of first quality and the locality is very healthy so far as known. The settlement is near Camp Grant, not very far from Camps Apache and Bowie, and within reasonable distance of the important mining camp of Clifton. All these places must have much grain, vegetables and all sorts of farm and dairy products.[8]

The paper wrote of Clanton again in 1874:

All who live in the Gila valley, near old Camp Goodwin at Pueblo Viejo, are enthusiastic in their accounts of the richness of the soil and the ease with which a man may make a farm. N.H. Clanton gave us these items last week but after our paper was filled. About twelve months ago he moved to a point near old Camp Goodwin and about 160 miles north of east of Tucson, and within Pima county. The place is now called Clantonville. During the year he has been there, himself and three sons have put a ditch from the Gila river, planted 120 acres with wheat, corn, barley and all kinds of vegetables; and from nothing of consequence to start with, now has a fine farm and plenty about him. All his crops have grown nicely and some of them unusually large. Portions of his corn grew to be twelve to fourteen feet high with two large ears on a stalk. It was so nearly matured two weeks ago that scarcely an ear could be obtained soft enough for table use. He reports grass plentiful and from five to six feet in height. The cattle are fat and everything is in a fine condition. All persons east or west who desire a very fine place to make a good home easily and cheaply cannot do better than to go into the Gila valley. Land is abundant at government price, and the public surveys will be extended there during the present year. Anyone desiring more detailed information can get it by addressing N.H. Clanton, Camp Grant, Arizona.

Last year, we gave Mr. Clanton a quart of white winter rye, which the Commissioner of Agriculture had forwarded to Hon. R. C. McCormick. He sewed it and it grew surprisingly. Fully one half was destroyed by the breaking of a ditch, yet he gathered one and a half bushels of beautiful rye. We lately gave him a few sacks of Winter wheat forwarded as stated in THE CITIZEN last week, from the Department of Agriculture. The best varieties may soon be had in abundance by carefully cultivating the seed received from Washington. The Agricultural Department distributes only the choicest kinds. A few sacks are still at the Territorial Secretary's office.[9]

References to the Clantons' outlawry are conspicuous in their absence. In 1877 the Clantons moved from the Gila Valley and settled along the San Pedro River.[10]

Another of Ringo's friends, George W. Turner, is traditionally identified as a "Cowboy." Turner was, in fact, involved in an incident of stock theft in November, albeit not as his reputation would suggest. Under the title, "Horse and Cattle Thieves," the *Arizona Weekly Star* reported:

> From W.J. Crosby we received the following note:
> SHAKESPEARE, N.M.
> Nov. 25, 1880
> EDITOR STAR:—During the past month a number of horses and mules have been stolen at intervals from various sections of this county, the latest being eight head from Leiterdorf, and several head from San Simon, in Pima county, fourteen head were stolen from the Stage Company at Mason's ranch last week. A posse of San Simon ranchmen, consisting of Messrs. Turner, Marten [sic: Martin], Colt, Raymond and a Mexican named Dominguez, started in pursuit on Monday last following the trail to near

Dowling's ranch, and after a hard fight, lasting from day-light yesterday until three o'clock in the after noon, they succeeded in killing one of the thieves whose name is given as King, and seriously wounding another named Bill Smith. King was a cripple and leader of the gang, which were four in number. The posse captured 22 head of stock and returned with them. They will be well rewarded for this courageous action. They propose capturing the two remaining desperadoes and some 14 head of stock, known to have been stolen by the same gang.

This may be a useful lesson to horse and cattle thieves. Ropes and trees are very convenient in the neighborhood.[11]

Writers on Tombstone's early days have largely ignored that incident, despite its importance. George W. Turner, Ringo's friend and companion at the hurrahing of Maxey and Safford, is clearly described as a rancher by his contemporaries, not a "Cowboy" or outlaw.[12]

Bill Smith, the wounded outlaw, is more commonly known in western history as Six-Shooter Smith. Born in Missouri as John Henry Hankins, he and others had operated around Dodge City as early as 1878. In Dodge, he was arrested for horse theft.[13] Smith migrated to Las Vegas in 1879 with other members of the loosely knit Dodge City Gang and soon proved himself a thorn in the flesh of New Mexican law officers. As the railroad headed southwest, Smith and several of the same ilk "settled" the railroad tank stop of Rio Mimbres. Smith nominated himself for deputy sheriff, a standard tactic of the Dodge City Gang. Fortunately for New Mexico, the Grant County sheriff rebuffed Smith due to his nasty tendency to terrorize the town.[14] Historian Phil Rasch wrote that in late 1880 and early 1881 Smith "was a member of the gang of cowboys who terrorized the San Simon Valley."[15]

Smith was well known in his day, although few authors now mention him. He was certainly well acquainted with Wyatt Earp, if only through his close friend Doc Holliday. In 1882, a Denver newspaper stated in part, "Holliday's history was further given as a partner of the notorious 'Off Wheeler' and 'Six-shooter Smith,' the latter of whom was killed about six weeks ago."[16]

Meanwhile John Ringo, with his court case out of the way, kept a low profile until March of 1881, when his name was again linked to violence in the killing of Dick Lloyd. Aside from one notable paper by Rasch, little has been written of Lloyd. Rasch notes, "Some otherwise undistinguished individuals seem to be picked by fate to participate in a single spectacular incident which results in their names being remembered long after better men have been forgotten."[17] Such is the case with Richard "Dick" Lloyd. Aside from his death, he is virtually unknown. Burns' portrait of a slow-witted waddy, presumably one of the "Cowboys,"[18] is far from true.

One person who remembered Dick Lloyd well before he went to Arizona was Lily Klasner. In her memoirs, Klasner recalled that Lloyd's real name was Kelly, but that he usually went by the last name of his stepfather, Will Lloyd. Dick was a good friend of Lily's brother, Will. She recalled, "He was a good-hearted, hard-working boy about whom it was told that he would drink too much mean whiskey. He liked to go to Lincoln, get good and drunk, then race up and down the street firing his six-shooter. He always shot into the air, and never tried to hurt anyone. So far as I know, Dick Lloyd never killed anyone or stole anything." [19]

Klasner remembered Lloyd as a high spirited man who once traded five horses for a racehorse belonging to Manuel Romero Kline. It was a good trade, but Lloyd's fondness for whiskey made him squander his assets. On one spree in Lincoln, he rode into a herd of milk cows and oxen that were being driven up the street. Lloyd struck a steer and his mount suffered a severely stoved shoulder, which ended its racing days.[20] Lloyd was an active member of the "Murphy-Dolan" faction during the Lincoln County War.

Lloyd went to Arizona as a drover with a herd that was delivered to the San Carlos Indian Reservation around November 1878. Others on the drive included George and Bill Graham, the latter sometimes being identified as Curly Bill Brocius.[21] He then took a job with Jerome B. Collins at the Bear Springs ranch. Lloyd next surfaced in Tombstone, where he broke a horse before an admiring crowd in 1880.[22]

The admiration was short lived, for on the very day that Lloyd's bronco-busting exploit hit the papers he was among the cowboys arrested after the October 28 shooting of City Marshal Fred White. Evidently following Stuart N. Lake's lead, writers on the Earp brothers traditionally have contended that Wyatt arrested such men as Ike and Billy Clanton, Pony Diehl, the McLaury brothers, and others for their roles in the disturbance. Under the heading of "Police Court," however, *Epitaph* editor John Clum noted, "Edward Collins, A. Ames, R. L[l]oyd, Frank Patterson and James Johnson were brought before Judge

Gray yesterday morning on charge of violating city ordinances. A. Ames plead [sic] guilty to carrying concealed weapons and discharging the same on the public streets. He was fined $40, which he paid. Edward Collins, R. L[l]oyd and James Johnson plead guilty to carrying concealed weapons, and were fined $10 each, which was paid. Frank Patterson was discharged, it being made apparent to his Honor that he had used every effort to prevent the disturbance by his companions."23

In March 1881 Lloyd ran head on into John Ringo. Breakenridge recounts that Ringo, Joe Hill (Olney), Tom Norris, Curly Bill, Jim and Nick Hughes, and others brought a herd of cattle up from Mexico, probably from Hill's ranch, and held them in the San Simon Valley to fatten before final delivery to the San Carlos Reservation. Considering their experience the year before, they may also have been waiting for a customs agent to pass the herd.

After finally delivering the cattle at San Carlos the men adjourned to Jack O'Neil's saloon to blow off some steam in a card game. Lloyd was present, but drunk, and the men refused to let him play cards with them. Angered, Lloyd left the saloon and met Ed Mann, a former justice of the peace. Words passed between the pair, and Lloyd shot Mann. The drunken Lloyd then proceeded to steal Joe Hill's horse. Still angry that the card players had slighted him, he drew his pistol and rode into the saloon, firing as he went. The men at the table promptly shot him from the saddle. The horse bolted through the door with an irate Joe Hill in pursuit.24

Breakenridge, who was not present, heard of Lloyd's death secondhand. Eyewitness Melvin W. Jones, another early Arizona resident, also described the shooting:

> Dick Loid was killed in Jack O'Neal's [sic] at Camp Thomas two years after the drive there with them. I happened to be at the killing and was on the cor[o]ner's jury.
>
> At the time of the killing there were in the saloon Jack O'Neil, proprietor, Barney Clark and Pete Brewer, bartenders, Curley Bill Graham and his brother George, John Ringo, Joe Hill, Tom Norris, Jimmie Hughes, old man Hughes, Charley Dook [Doak?] and two others that I can't remember. Jack O'Neil claimed he acted in self defense, so did the shooting. Anyway, I am sure that while Curley Bill looked on he did not fire a shot at Dick Loid. They were good friends.25

Contemporary news accounts confirm Jones' version. The *Arizona Weekly Citizen* titled its story "Triangular Shooting Affray": "This evening a desperado named Dick Lloyd shot and dangerously wounded E. Mann, ex-Justice of the Peace of this place. Lloyd afterwards threatened to kill others, and in attempting to ride into O'Neill's [sic] saloon, was instantly killed. The jury in this case exonerated O'Neil, who acknowledged to have done the killing, by a verdict of justifiable homicide. It is expected that Mann will recover; the attack on him was unprovoked."[26]

In an account entitled "Justice at Last" and dated March 9, *Epitaph* editor John Clum, who had lauded Lloyd only months before, now did not even spell his name correctly: "A Star special from Maxey of the 8th says: Dick Floyd, a notorious cowboy, shot E. Mann, Justice of the peace, this evening. After the shooting he rode into O'Neil & Franklin's saloon. O'Neil shot him dead, and then gave himself up. Mann, it is thought, will survive. Floyd has taken the town several times, riding into saloons, stores and private houses. He was a desperate character."[27]

By then Ringo's notoriety was well established in Arizona. Contrary to more modern accounts, he was rarely called "Johnny Ringo" in Texas or Arizona. Rather, he was referred to as John R. The designation appealed to his vanity, but vanity has a way of being pricked. Bartholomew recorded the recollection of a man who purchased some mules from Ringo. The latter signed the bill-of-sale simply as "John R."

"John R. what?" questioned the buyer.

"John R. Godalmighty," retorted an exasperated Ringo, who signed the paper accordingly.[28]

For John Ringo 1881 would be filled with trouble. His vastly inflated reputation had awed all but his oldest friends, and evidence suggests that men such as Ike Clanton would look to him as their defender. Psychologically he was deteriorating. Already his drinking was becoming heavier, perhaps to ward off flashbacks of the Mason County War. And when he was drunk, all sources agree, he was a hard, mean man. Violence and charges of murder were soon to be laid at his doorstep once more.

CHAPTER SIXTEEN

"...a killer and professional cutthroat..."

A botched stage robbery on the evening of March 15, 1881, would prove pivotal in drawing John Ringo into the Earp-Clanton feud. The Kinnear and Company stage left Drew's Station on its way to Contention with Eli "Budd" Philpott holding the reins. Shotgun guard Bob Paul, his contest for sheriff still in dispute, also rode in the box. As they reached a small incline some two hundred yards from Drew's, an armed man stepped onto the road from the east side and shouted "Hold!"

The *Epitaph* picks up the story:

> At the same moment a number of men—believed to have been eight—made their appearance and a shot was fired from the same side of the road instantly followed by another. One of those shots struck "Budd" Philpott, the driver, who fell heavily forward between the wheelers carrying the reins with him. The horses immediately sprang into a dead run....[1]

As the horses bolted Paul opened up with his shotgun and the highwaymen returned the fire. Peter Roerig, a miner riding on top of the coach, was hit in the back and tumbled to the ground.

The alarm reached Tombstone around eleven o'clock. Marshall Williams gathered the Earp brothers and some other men and started for the scene. In the meantime, A.C. Cowan, the Wells, Fargo agent at Contention, had dispatched thirty men after the killers. Paul, who had driven on to Benson, also assembled a posse and gave pursuit. Parsons recorded:

> A most terrible affair of last evening. First intimation I had of it was when Doctor Goodfellow burst into room and asked for rifle. Abbott finally—let him have his upon Doc's assurance he didn't want to kill any one. I stopped our chess—got revolver and followed him up—not wishing him to get hurt if I could help it. Men and horses were flying about in different directions, and I soon ascertained the cause. A large posse started in pursuit—$26,000 specie reported on stage. Bob Paul went as shot gun messenger and emptied both barrels of his gun at the robbers probably wounding one. "I hold for no one" he said and let drive. Some 20 shots fired—close call for Paul. Captain Colby wished me to form one of another posse, to head the robbers off at San Simon if we could get necessary information upon arrival of stage, and we worked the thing up. Probably six in all. Information didn't come as we expected, so delayed, and several of us shadowed several desperate characters in town, one known as an ex stage robber. Couldn't fix anything. Budd Philpott—the driver was shot through the heart and the passenger—a miner—through the back. Doc showed me the bullet that killed him—an ugly 45 caliber. Some more tracking tonight. Our birds have flown....[2]

One bird had not flown fast or far enough. On March 19 Sheriff John Behan and a posse that included Virgil, Wyatt, and Morgan Earp, Billy Breakenridge, and others apprehended Luther King at the ranch of Len Redfield. The story of the arrest varies according to which side tells it. They generally agree, however, that King told the posse they were trailing Bill Leonard, Harry Head, and Jim Crane. Parsons learned of Leonard's involvement the next day: "Marshall Williams in from hunting stage robbers. Told me at ball that they would have them and who they were. Know one of them Leonard—very well by sight and have had business with him. Know him to be a hard case. Hard chase of 200 miles to present time."[3]

King's information has proven controversial, some writers claiming that only the four men he named were involved in the aborted robbery. Fred Dodge, an acknowledged friend of Wyatt Earp, wrote to Stuart N. Lake:

> Yes, 'Doc [Holliday] was a tough citizen and a bad egg,' and I was fully aware of the situation between Doc and Wyatt. Doc never played square with any one in that country. Bill Leonard was as hard as nails and was a stage robber and everything else in the line of crime. Marshall Williams did do some tipping off [of Wells, Fargo treasure shipments], but *Doc was a full fledged member of the gang that Leonard was in with* [emphasis added]. I know who was present at the holdup at the time Bud Philpot [sic] was killed and I know who killed him.[4]

Dodge elsewhere named the robbers as King, Leonard, Head, Crane, Holliday, and Johnny Barnes.[5] He did not name Philpott's killer but strongly implied that it was Holliday. Indeed, Holliday was seen riding a badly lathered mount from the scene of the robbery at about the time it took place. Among the witnesses to his headlong flight were Billy Clanton, John H. Slaughter, and an unidentified Indian. Some authors have speculated that the latter might have been Florentino Cruz, a woodcutter, but the evidence for this theory is only circumstantial.

John Henry Holliday was born August 14, 1851, at Griffin, Georgia. Before his arrival in Tombstone, Holliday led a checkered career throughout the West and was closely associated with Wyatt Earp. He had killed at least one man at Las Vegas, New Mexico, where he ran with the Hoodoo Brown gang of con men, pimps, thugs, and killers. Las Vegans recalled him well. The *Optic* said, in part, "Doc was always considered a shiftless, bagged-legged character—a killer and professional cut-throat and not a whit too refined to rob stages or even steal sheep."[6] Among his close friends at Las Vegas were Bill Leonard and Harry Head.

Dodge was not the only man who linked Earp, however indirectly, with the attempted stage robbery. Although Wyatt obviously had not taken part in the robbery, Jim Crane later told John Gray that he had planned it.[7] Nor was the March 15 debacle near Drew's the only Arizona holdup to which friends of Earp were linked. Bob Paul wanted both Sherman MacMasters and Pony Diehl in 1881 for another stage robbery.

Marshall Williams was another acknowledged friend of Earp, and Dodge was not the only one to name him as the inside man on the holdups that plagued Cochise County. Sol Israel told Joe Chisholm that Williams rousted him out of bed one night in a panic to liquidate his holdings. Israel refused to do business under such mysterious circumstances, but another man was less scrupulous. Shortly after Williams' departure, a Wells, Fargo agent arrived to investigate the holdups.[8]

One of the most interesting points concerning King's arrest is that Earp recalled telling Behan and Breakenridge he did not want anyone talking to the prisoner, and he was highly disturbed when he caught Redfield doing so. Since Wyatt held only limited, if any, legal authority at the time, this is most curious. Earp supporters insist Behan was in league with the outlaws, but Wyatt more likely was concerned that King would finger Holliday and, perhaps, himself.[9]

King did not remain in jail long. He escaped from the custody of Deputy Sheriff Harry Woods, who also happened to be the editor of the *Nugget*. Woods put the best possible face on the incident:

> Luther King, the man arrested at Redfeld's ranch charged with being implicated in the Bud Philpot [sic] murder, escaped from the sheriff's office by quietly stepping out the back door while Harry Jones, Esq., was drawing up a bill of sale for a horse the prisoner was selling to John Dunbar. Under-sheriff Harry Woods and Dunbar were present. He had been absent but a few seconds before he was missed. A confederate on the outside had a horse in readiness for him. It was a well-planned job by outsiders to get him away. He was an important witness against Holliday. He it was that gave the names of the three that were being followed at the time he was arrested. Their names were Bill Leonard, Jim Crane and Harry Head.[10]

Woods justifiably came under severe criticism for his incompetence in allowing King's escape. George W. Parsons noted, "King the stage robber escaped tonight early from H. Woods *who had been previously notified* [emphasis added] of an attempt at release to be made. Some of our officials should be hanged. They're a bad lot."[11] In June 1881 Woods was fined for dereliction of duty. Earp supporters have charged Jones, Woods, and Dunbar with aiding King's escape. It is hard to believe, however, that the trio could not have created a better story than the *Nugget*'s to avert suspicion. The entire incident appears to have been a true case of carelessness.

What is obvious from the article is that King's escape kept Holliday—whom he had named as a would-be robber—out of jail as well. Doc had every reason to hamper King's recapture. On April 1, 1881, the *Epitaph* reported:

> False Alarm.

> A report was current on the streets that King, the missing cow-boy, had been killed by some of his companions near the Huachucas, in revenge for what information covering their crimes he is alleged to have given the officers. One of the rumors was to the effect that Crane, one of the Contention murderers, was in Charleston yesterday boasting of King's death. A telegram to Charleston, however, elicited the fact that the rumor of it was false, and it is thought the stories about King's death were started to throw the officers off the scent.[12]

Despite being dismissed, the report of King's death was probably true. At this point he vanishes from history. His most likely killers, of course, were the men he had implicated. Wyatt Earp himself indirectly confirmed King's death. In June 1881 Earp approached Ike Clanton with a plan to trap Leonard, Crane, and Head—to be captured according to Earp, killed according to Clanton. Significantly, Earp and Clanton both omit King from Earp's wanted list. The logical reason is that Earp already knew King's fate.[13]

Another factor in Ringo's alliance with the Clantons may well have been his knowledge of Earp and Holliday from the Kansas cowtowns. Holliday is said to have hated Ringo. The feeling was reciprocal.

Other events occurring in Arizona at the same time would inflame the border country and further strengthen Ringo's links with the

Cowboys. Outlaws, both Anglo and Mexican, raided Cochise County increasingly during 1881. One of the victims, T. W. Ayles, wrote an angry letter to the editor of the *Epitaph*:

> I am not a growler or chronic grumbler, but I own stock, am a butcher and supply my immediate neighborhood beef, and to do so must keep cattle on hand, and try to and could do so always if I had not to divide with unknown and irresponsible partners, viz: 'Cow Boys,' or some other cattle thieves. Since my advent into the territory and more particularly on the San Pedro River, I have lost 50 head of cattle by cattle thieves. I am not the only sufferer from these marauders and cattle robbers on the San Pedro, within the last six months. Aside from 50 head of good beef cattle that I have been robbed of, Judge Blair has lost his entire herd. P. McMinnimen has lost all of his finest fat steers. Dunbar at Tres Alamos, has lost a number of head. Burton of Huachuca, lost almost his entire herd, and others—and in fact all engaged in the stock business—have lost heavily from cattle thieves. And not always do these thieves confine themselves to cattle; horses and mules are gobbled up by these robbers, as well as cattle. Is there no way to stop this wholesale stealing of stock in this vicinity or in the county?
>
> T.W. Ayles, Cattle Dealer
> March 18, 1881[14]

Ayles' concerns were well founded, and neither the law nor the ranchers managed to curb the stealing significantly. While Ayles mentions the "Cow Boys"— a clear reference to the old Martin gang—he entirely omits the Mexican raiders, not because there were none but because Arizonans already knew who was behind the bulk of the thefts. The newspapers, Governor John C. Frémont, and Acting Governor John J. Gosper all made this abundantly clear. The Clantons, the McLaurys, Ringo, and the Hills (Olneys) were raided as often as anyone. Moreover, not one of the Cowboys named by Earp had been charged with cattle theft. In fact, other than Curly Bill and Ringo, none of them had been charged with any crime whatsoever.

The situation in Arizona could not, and had not, gone unheeded. The outlaw activity there prompted the military to report to Robert

Todd Lincoln, United States secretary of war. Lincoln naturally brought the reports to the attention of United States Attorney General Wayne MacVeagh on April 12, 1881, noting "...certain facts concerning 'Cowboys' and their outrages in Arizona and Sonora, and suggesting as a remedy that they be arrested by the U.S. Marshal upon the direction of the Honorable Attorney General."[15]

Why had neither Arizona Territory's United States Marshal C.P. Dake nor United States Attorney E.B. Pomroy reported the powerful outlaw gang known as the "Cowboys" to their superior? MacVeagh was understandably upset that the secretary of war had to inform him of the band, while his own law enforcement people in Arizona seemed oblivious to the situation. He acted quickly, writing Pomroy a letter which barely concealed his anger. "You will forthwith upon the receipt of this letter make diligent inquiry and report to this office the facts as you find them concerning the outrages committed, as is alleged, in Arizona and Sonora by a gang of desperadoes called cowboys who make their escape across boundary lines."[16]

The reason Pomroy failed to report the "Cowboy Curse" may well be that he was unaware of it. Samuel Mulliken, chief clerk, sent some papers regarding "Cowboy depredations" to Pomroy on the fifteenth. Mulliken's letter reached Pomroy ahead of MacVeagh's. Unaware of the elusive Cowboy horde lead by John Ringo, Curly Bill, and the Clantons, Pomroy wrote to Mulliken on the twenty-first to find out what the department wanted of him.[17] And well he might wonder, for not one word of the "Curse of the Cowboys" had yet appeared in print, despite the fact that the accused leaders of the band had been in Arizona for some time. Indeed, men such as Ringo, Brocius, and the McLaurys were so unknown that the papers often spelled their names incorrectly.

By late April the "King of the Cowboys" himself, John Ringo, had left Arizona, headed back to Missouri. The trip, no doubt, combined business and pleasure. At Austin, Texas, Ringo stopped to dawdle with the ladies of the evening:

> Mr. John Ringo was in town early Sunday morning and was passing his time down in a house in the jungles. Along about 4 o'clock he missed his purse, and stepping out in the hall where some three or four of Austin's nice young men were seated, he came down upon them with his little pistol and commanded them to 'up hand,' he quietly searched the

whole tea party. Not finding his purse he smiled beamingly upon the young men, and retired to his room while they quietly slid out and reported the facts to the police. Marshal [Ben] Thompson in person went down to the house, but was refused admission to the room, whereupon he cheerfully kicked open the door, and to the infinite disgust of Mr. Ringo, scooped him in. He was disarmed, and Officer Chenneville, who had arrived, marched him to the station, and yesterday he was fined $5 and costs for disturbing the peace, and $25 and costs for carrying a pistol. He settled with the city and left a wiser if not sadder man.[18]

The arrest occurred about 6:00 A.M. Ben Thompson, a tough gunfighter, cared little for John Ringo's reputation or that he had shared jail time with his brother, Billy. The Record of Arrests gives Ringo's name as "John Ringold" and lists his occupation as "stockman."[19]

During Ringo's extended absence from Arizona his friend, George Turner, was killed. The *Nugget* reported:

> THE FRONTERAS MASSACRE.
> The Names of the Parties Killed.
> From a very intelligent Mexican, who arrived yesterday from Sonora, we learn that the first account of the Fronteras killing, as reported in the NUGGET, was substantially correct. The parties killed at that time—May 13—by Jose Juan Vasquez's party, were McAllister, a butcher from Galeyville; Oliver, a Mexican named Garcia, and a white man, supposed to be Turner. These four men had rounded up a band of cattle and were camped for the night, when they were surrounded by the Mexicans and their surrender demanded. Their answer was a volley from their pistols and rifles, which was returned with such deadly effect that three of the party fell dead, the other lived long enough to kill Vasquez, the best friend the Americans ever had in that section. If the matter is ever investigated it will be found that
> WE ARE CORRECT IN THE NAMES
> of the parties killed. Our informant says that letters and papers found upon the dead bodies places the truthfulness of this beyond a doubt.
> A reporter of the NUGGET was detailed to interview Con. S. Cutler, from that section, and is well acquainted

with the people, but he was reticent, merely saying he had nothing to report regarding the matter; that he was engaged in mining in Sonora, and all he knew of the case was what he had read in the papers. The evidence we have before us, however, convinces us that we are correct in our statement.

It is rumored that in case certain parties are convinced McAllister has been killed, a company will be raised to go to Fronteras and 'clean out' the town. We trust no such measures will be taken, as it would result in loss of life on both sides, and no benefit be derived.[20]

Writing to Acting Governor Gosper later that year, Joseph Bowyer noted Turner's death and added what he had heard of the matter:

Last spring George Turner and M. McCalister [sic], two well known cow-boys, obtained the contract at Fort Bowie for furnishing beef to the command; they and two assistants went to Sonora to either buy or steal beef-cattle; they succeeded in driving a large herd as far as Fronteras, when they were attacked by the Mexican citizens. They (the cow-boys) were all killed, and one Mexican citizen was killed. Upon the bodies of Turner and McCallister [sic] was found the money which they ostensibly took to purchase cattle, which amount, compared with what they were known to have started here with, proved that the cattle they were driving had not been paid for.[21]

Bowyer's account is hearsay at best. The only people who could have carefully counted the dead men's money and reported the amount to the authorities were the Mexicans. Moreover, who would have known how much money Turner was carrying when he left for Sonora?

Cutler's reluctance to discuss the case in order to protect his own mining interests from Mexican retaliation speaks volumes, but it remained for Deputy United States Marshal Joe Evans to determine the truth of the affair through his contacts in Mexico. "The cowboys number about 380. They are constantly raiding in Sonora bringing out stock and killing Mexicans when they interfere. A great many Mexicans have been killed by the cowboys. In one instance the Mexicans retaliated by killing law abiding American citizens."[22] Evans overestimated the number of men involved in the raids, unless he was including Mexicans. He was, however, confident of the men's innocence.

After Turner's death the mood along the border turned ugly. On June 9 General Orlando B. Willcox reported that Lieutenant Craig had returned from a scout and learned of "threats made that people at Fronteras, Sonora should have to pay for so called murder of Turner's party." Craig's belief that "forty or fifty Cow-boys of bad character are ready for action between Los Animas and Galeyville" added fuel to the volatile border situation.[23]

The United States government could not and would not tolerate an invasion of Mexico by American citizens. Leander H. McNelly had led his company of Texas Rangers into Mexico on November 18, 1875, in pursuit of stolen cattle. In the gunplay that followed a number of Mexicans were killed. McNelly withdrew only after the Mexicans promised to return the stolen cattle. The incident sparked an international furor,[24] a furor which officials had no wish to repeat in 1881.

They would not get their wish.

CHAPTER
SEVENTEEN

"...armed with a Henry side..."

The violence that swept the Arizona border country in 1881 began with George Turner's death in Sonora, a direct parallel to the killing of Tim Williamson in Mason County, Texas, six years earlier. The similarities would not have escaped John Ringo. Once again a "mob of foreigners" was killing ranchers over cattle, and if justice was to be done it would be up to the victim's friends. That the "foreigners" were citizens of another country made no difference to Turner's avengers, and they cared little about international incidents. The June 16, 1881, *Arizona Star* heralded the beginning of the "policy of retaliation":

PROBABLY A RAID.

From reliable sources we learned yesterday that a party of seventy cow-boys left Willcox for the purpose of making a raid on Fronteras, Sonora, near the border and about sixty miles from Willcox, their purpose being to avenge the death of the four parties who were killed three weeks ago in that neighborhood by the Mexicans. It has been known for some days that they were recruiting their force for the purpose of making this trip, and they openly avowed they would wipe out the town of Fronteras in revenge of the Americans killed. This intelligence was sent to the commanding general of the department, who at once notified Mr. Morales, the Mexican Consul at this place. He at once sent word to Fronteras, and to the troops' station on the San Bernardino ranch, so that, ere the festive gang reaches the desired point, they will most probably have to measure bullet range with the Mexican Federal troops. Should they meet, there will be a warm fight. The cow-boys are reckless, daring fighters, good shots, ride good stock, and don't place much value on life. The Mexicans will stand their ground, unless the quarters grow too close. We have no doubt, however, that ere this, the whole business has been determined, and should any damage be done to our Mexican neighbors, the United States cannot escape censure. This whole affair has been organized on American soil, and with an open and avowed purpose of murder, robbery and outlawry. We will await development of events.[1]

The *Star*'s report stunned the Southwest, and the story grew in the telling. On June 21, the Las Vegas, New Mexico, *Optic* reported:

Dispatches from Tucson of last Thursday, announced that about 70 cowboys, well armed and equined were marauding the country, raiding the small towns and scattering consternation in their path, with the avowed purpose of avenging the death of four of their comrades. The dispatch expressed the general fear that there would be bloody work, as they are the most reckless gang of outlaws ever banded together. What these 70 cutthroats have done is not yet known, but they and their gang will soon, without a doubt meet their just deserts. Arizona is being settled, and the U.S. troops will give the honest settlers assistance necessary to put down these lawless vagabonds, who are more of a disgrace to this country than the worst Bandits were in Spain or Italy.[2]

Even Joe Evans was taken in by the rumors. In a June 18 letter to

Dake, he wrote, in part:

> There is much excitement here and in Sonora relative to depredations being committed by the cowboys. It is reported that a few days since that they went into Fronteras Sonora and killed about forty Mexicans in retaliation for the killing of four of their companions by the Mexicans some weeks since. The state of affairs existing on the border has been communicated to our Govt at Washington by the Mexican minister resident....The Mexican Consul here keeps me posted.[3]

Did the Cowboys, in fact, raid Fronteras? Not according to Governor Luis Torres, who had been alerted by the Mexican consul. On June 24, Torres wrote his old friend, Joe Evans, in Tucson, asking for help. "The time has come when your aid will be of great importance to me as it was in the time of Brigidio Reyes and his crowd. I mean the invasion intended by the 'Cow Boys' to our territory near Fronteras."[4] Torres clearly indicates that no raid had yet taken place. These lines further suggest that Torres had had no significant trouble with cowboys, or anyone else, since Brigidio Reyes. Torres' decision to work with Evans in Tucson rather than Virgil Earp in nearby Tombstone is intriguing. Indeed, none of the early documents in Record Group 60 mention any of the Earps.

The raiders proved elusive. T.S. Williams, of Willcox, challenged the *Star*'s initial report:

> You say, in your edition of the 16th instant, that you are reliably informed that a party of seventy cow boys left Willcox for the purpose of making a raid on Fronteras. I can only say that you were wrongly informed; and I think you did us a great injustice to publish the report. Who would wish to settle in a town which could produce seventy cow boys in so short a time? If there are any cow-boys here they are gentlemanly fellows, and behave themselves like all other good citizens. This is a quiet place—almost too quiet. My opinion of the matter is that it is all a hoax. I think the cow-boys here have too much sense to engage in anything of that sort, at least on so large a scale.

The *Star* hedged its response:

> We have made diligent enquiry since publishing the facts above referred to, and find that our informants were mistaken as to the band leaving Willcox; that it left San Simon instead. But as to the whole matter being a hoax, we only wish it was. The evidence appears to be all the other way up to the present writing. The band has been seen by several parties and it is a notorious fact that they have been recruiting their forces for this raid in the vicinity of San Simon and Galeyville for the last three weeks. We fully endorse the writer when he says that the cow-boys of Willcox are gentlemanly fellows and frown upon all kinds of lawlessness. We did not intend to convey the impression that the cow boys were citizens of Willcox, or even recruited there, but that they left the vicinity of Willcox. The STAR has too much respect for that thriving town and its citizens to do an intentional injury.[5]

General Orlando B. Willcox responded quickly to the rumors and had already dispatched troops to scout the area on June 8, eight days before the *Star*'s initial prediction of the raid. Willcox reported to the adjutant general:

> Captain McLellan, who left Bowie Seventh [sic: June 8], on scout down Eastern side of Chiricahua mountains, reports his return by way of the Tanks and Camp Rucker to Bowie on fifteenth. His orders were to protect persons and property and prevent raids into Sonora threatened by cow-boys. He discovered no evidence of raiding parties either to or from Mexico. He says that if any such parties were organizing, Lieutenant Craig's Scout, previously reported, broke them up. I think this true so far as members within the borders of Arizona are concerned, but from Craig's report and all other accounts these outlaws still invest Southwestern New Mexico.[6]

McClellan's scout is of great importance in understanding what was and, more importantly, what was not happening in Cochise County. During the time that the great cowboy raid was supposedly being organized, McClellan found no evidence of the raiders and concluded that Craig's expedition had broken them up. Yet Craig had returned from his scout two weeks before the *Star* printed its story. The raiders were always someplace else, and no one found a trace of them anywhere they were reported to be. The entire episode, reminiscent of the raid by Roberts and his men, appears to have been generated by rumor and sensational dispatches originating at Tombstone.

But if Ringo was not involved in the fictitious cowboy raid on Fronteras, folklore has linked him to two real outlaws who made news in early June. On June 10 Ike and Bill Haslett ambushed and shot Bill Leonard and a man identified as Harry the "Kid." Leonard died on the twelfth, but the Kid was still alive when the *Star* printed the story on June 23.[7] Days later Jim Crane and a group of men avenged the killing.[8] Several writers have theorized that Ringo might have been involved.[9] That was impossible, however, for he was still absent on his trip to Missouri until mid-July. Then he returned to Tombstone, registering at the Grand Hotel as "John Ringo, Liberty, Mo."[10]

The furor in southern Arizona greeted Ringo. In his absence E.B. Pomroy had completed his investigation of the Cowboys and filed his report on June 23. After defining "Cowboy" as a generic designation, he stated that the crimes involved were territorial responsibilities, "but owing to its magnitude the Territorial officers are unable to cope with the difficulty." Pomroy recommended federal intervention and, specifically, the appointment by of deputy United States marshals "to act in concert with the sheriff."[11]

C.P. Dake himself had written Washington earlier concerning the border troubles: "I have the honor to report that I am constantly in receipt of communications complaining of the depredation of 'Cow Boys,' and other organized bands of Outlaws, who are operating in the Southern part of this Territory and raiding into Mexico."[12]

Washington officials must have wondered why, if Dake received constant reports of these depredations, they had to be advised by the War Department rather than an officer in their own department.

This seeming proof of cowboy outrages is tempered, however, by the letter's overall tone—how much money could he spend? Dake's request for funding information was in order, as his authority extended only to federal matters. Yet as 1881 progressed, his cry for funds would become a familiar refrain. Was he really in need of more money? More particularly, was he really in need of more money to combat depredations of which he apparently knew nothing until his superiors took him to task? Leigh Chalmers, a federal investigator, was asked the same question in 1885. Chalmers reported that Dake himself admitted to having received in excess of $50,000 during his term of office—around five million dollars in today's currency. Yavapai County Recorder William Wilkinson testified that Dake had purchased $22,907 worth of property during the same period. Still others testified that Dake had deposited all of the funds to his personal bank account.[13] Dake later blamed Wyatt Earp for some of the unaccounted for funds; Earp naturally accused Dake.

More trouble struck the border in late July. Hancock reported that John McGill, Alex Arnett, and Milt Hicks stole a herd of cattle in Mexico and drove it north across the border. The men split up near the Double Adobe ranch. Hicks started his part of the herd toward Galeyville; McGill and Arnett headed for Lordsburg. Forewarned by the sensational news accounts from Arizona, a party of Mexican ranchers rode in hot pursuit. Hancock wrote:

> The Mexicans overtook the two outfits before they were out of sight of each other. They first took in after McGill's outfit and McGill and those with him abandoned the cattle and lit out over to where Milt was. They sized up the situation and concluded they were not strong enough to stand off the Mexicans so they all pulled out for the Lang ranch where they found John Ringo, Curly Bill, Joe Hill and some of the other boys. They saddled up and took after the Mexicans. They overtook them in the San Luis Pass and 14 Mexicans were supposed to have been killed and the cattle and some of the horses recaptured. I never heard that any of the boys were wounded.[14]

Hancock was not an eyewitness, but John Gray was. In 1940, sixty years after the fact, Gray recorded:

> In a frontier land where there is no law in reach and where it is one hundred miles to the County seat, taking two days of time at the best to reach by any kind of travel, a quick decision as to the right thing to do is often necessary. And it might lead to embarrassing consequences, no matter what the decision. Such a crisis for both brother Dick and

myself happened one bright morning at the old Animas Valley Ranch. Long before sunup a stranger rode up and appealed to us for help.

His story was that a well-armed bunch of Mexicans had appeared in the night at his camp at the old Double Dobies and had seized about one hundred head of cattle he was holding there while his partner had gone to Lordsburg for grub. The Mexicans, he said, were now rushing these cattle back to Mexico, and he asked us to help to recover them. We did not know the man, but the fact that he was white and a fellow American seemed in his favor—and a quick decision *was* necessary. We did not hesitate but agreed to go at once. We of course knew that these cattle might have been stolen from the Mexicans and that they might be only taking judgment into their own hands. But there was the other side to look at—a man of our own kind had appealed to us for aid, and we feared too that our horses might have been picked up on the way.

If on overtaking the herd, we found the Mexicans were only regaining their own stock which had been stolen, and had done no harm, we could turn back.

So we started and rode to overtake the Mexicans if possible before they reached the Mexican border. We picked up four more cowboys at the Lang Ranch who willingly joined us on hearing the story, and, seven strong, we dashed ahead.

We knew they must be heading for Deer Creek, the only possible pass that cattle could be driven through into Mexico, and true enough, we soon saw the dust raised by the herd. As a precaution against an ambush we took to the high ground on each side of the pass, and scattering out, we each fired a shot in the air to suggest to the Mexicans we might be a bigger force than we were. This evidently worked, for despite our waving of hats when we came in sight of the herders to show our 'friendly interest,' they fired a few shots which came close enough to alarm us. We dismounted and hid behind our mounts, and then saw the Mexicans had abandoned the herd and were speeding up their mounts in an evident attempt to get away. We had won the fight with our bluff and the poor bunch of panting cattle were ours by conquest.

No loose horses were in the herd, and we suddenly realized the rustler (which he then admitted to be) had worked us to a finish. But we took our medicine with good grace, feeling we could not have done otherwise from our point of view—and if again we were called upon to make a choice between a white man and a Mexican, and there were no known extenuating circumstances in favor of the Mexican, we would have to step to the side of our countryman. Such was the universal law on the border involving relations of the 'gringo' and the 'greaser.'[15]

Burns claimed on unknown authority that the Gray party was made up of Curly Bill, John Ringo, Joe Hill, Jim Hughes, John and Charlie Green, Charlie Thomas, Tall Bell, and one or two others—undoubtedly the Gray brothers. In addition he identified the original cattle thieves with the herd as Milt Hicks, Alex Arnett, Jack MacKenzie, John McGill, Bud Snow, and Jake Gauze. [16]

Both Gray and Hancock stated that the cattle were stolen, but a contemporary account in the *Nugget* differs:

Cattle Thieves Routed.

From Bob Clark, who recently returned from New Mexico, the NUGGET learns that about the 26th of last month, a party of Mexicans from Sonora made a raid into the Animas and adjoining valleys, and rounding up several hundred animals, started with them through the Guadaloupe Pass for Mexico. The Mexicans numbered about thirty all told. The cattlemen organized about twenty in number, and pursuing the marauders, overtook them on the plains near the Pass. A running fight ensued, which resulted in the flight of the Mexicans, and the recovery of the cattle. He also states that in Skull Canyon he struck a pack train of about thirty mules which had evidently been stampeded, as their packs were turned upside down, and there was no one in charge of them. He expressed the opinion that the train was a smuggling one from Sonora, and that the owners had been attacked by the Rustlers and killed, and the train had stampeded during the melee. It is reported that a smuggling trail leads through this neighborhood, and that very often trains are taken in by the marauders who infest that country. The Mexicans can make no complaint to the authorities, being engaged in an unlawful business themselves. [17]

JIM HUGHES

JOE OLNEY ALIAS JOE HILL

Clark's knowledge of New Mexico cattlemen, including John Ringo, is valuable, and clearly he regarded Ringo and the others in the cattle raid fight as ranchers—not outlaws.

Clark's views on the smuggling train are equally valuable. That incident provided the basis for what Burns enlarged as the Skeleton Canyon Massacre, in which Ringo was allegedly involved. The simple story was expanded further by later writers, but it is important that Clark was offering an opinion. He found no dead Mexicans, and quite obviously the mules in question could have stampeded for any number of causes, natural or otherwise. But if the Skeleton Canyon Massacre was largely inflated, the next incident was not. The *Nugget* reported:

Another Outrage.

Report comes to us of a fresh outrage perpetrated by the cowboys in Sonora. Early last Monday morning [probably July 25] a party of sixteen Mexicans from the interior of Sonora, on the way to this Territory to purchase goods and carrying $4,000 for that purpose, stopped at a curve in the road at Los Animas near Fronteras, to prepare their frugal breakfast. While busily engaged preparing their tortillas they were saluted with the music of twenty rifles fired by cowboys who lay in ambush awaiting them. The Mexicans took this as an invitation to leave and did not stand on the order of going but left all their mules and pack saddles in which they carried their money for the purchase of goods. When they stopped running they were at Fronteras and their party was four shot. The missing men are supposed to have been killed. The citizens of Babispe and troops are after the cowboys and are disposed to take summary vengeance if they overtake them.—Citizen.[18]

The Mexican government quickly notified Evans in Tucson, and he promptly reported the affair to Dake on August 4: "The Mexican Consul here has just received dispatches confirming the reported raid of the cowboys into Sonora near Fronteras, killing four Mexicans and robbing others of $4,000 and other property. The Mexicans express great dissatisfaction at the seeming neglect of our Gov't and threaten to take revenge on all Americans in Sonora."[19]

The unveiled threat against American citizens, innocent and guilty alike, got action from Dake—but not too quickly. Never one to miss a chance to cry for more money, Dake telegraphed MacVeagh in Washington. In this his duplicity is transparent, for he doubtless received the letter during business hours yet waited until 2:31 A.M. to send his wire so that it took on an added sense of urgency.

> Follow dispatch just rec'd from Tucson. 'Cowboys have just maid [sic] another raid into Sonora killing four Mexicans and robbing others of four thousand dollars. The Mexican government are very much incensed and threaten to take matter into their own hands if they are not protected by our government. (signed) J. W. Evans Deputy marshal.' Have sent deputy and posse after cowboys. Expense will be five to ten thousand dollars if pursued until successful. What amount allowed on my estimate for witnesses and marshal. Shall be governed in regard to my efforts in this matter by amount allowed on estimate over expense of courts about to convene. Owing to washouts on railroad no eastern mail rec'd here for past ten days. Answer.[20]

Unaware that Dake had sent him after the Cowboys, Evans wrote Dake again from his office in Tucson, in part, "Gov. Torres informs me that there are three hundred soldiers on the border of Sonora who will render us every assistance possible. The Mexican Consul does not think it possible for them to obtain the names of the cowboys who made the late raid into Sonora."[21] Evans agreed with the consul, but believed that sufficient evidence would be found in time in Arizona.

Factual evidence not withstanding, tradition has linked John Ringo, Newman Clanton, Jim Hughes, and others, depending on which author tells the story, to the brutal attack. Most, if not all, of these folktales are apocryphal, usually aimed at tarnishing the names of the "participants" to make up for the lack of indictments against the individuals. A case in point is Newman Clanton. Considering Clanton's role as an outlaw chieftain in Tombstone folklore, it is mind-boggling that he was not charged in a single indictment. Nevertheless, court records indicate that this was the case. According to J.C. Hancock, Milt Hicks confided that he, Jim Hughes, and Hughes' brother-in-law Jack MacKenzie had attacked the Mexicans at Fronteras.[22]

By now all of the depredations were being credited to the Cowboys. When outlaws ambushed three of General Pesqueira's Mexican soldiers, killing one, the *Epitaph*'s headline screamed, "The Murdering Cowboys."[23] When some mules and a horse were stolen from a freighter named Leopold Graff, the paper called for lynch law.[24]

By August 1881 Ringo was drinking more, trying to forget the Mason County War while living in a new war zone. He was more erratic, with a growing tendency toward flawed judgment. Such was the case in Galeyville, where he was playing poker and losing heavily. When Ringo asked for credit, one of the players refused to take his word for it. An angry Ringo rounded up a friend, Dave Estes, and the pair returned to the game. The *Nugget* reported:

A Social Game

Galeyville is noted as the rendezvous of the festive 'cowboy.' It is there he most congregates and joins in the amusement peculiar to his clan. On last Friday one of them known as Ringold entered into a game of poker and not being as expert with the 'keards' as he is with his 'gun' he soon went 'broke.' But, the Star adds, he returned with a companion named David Estes, one being armed with a Henry side and the other with a Six Shooter. The players were promptly ordered to hold up their hands and the cowboys proceeded to go through the party securing in the neighborhood of $500.00. Some of the party were so frightened that they broke for the woods where they remained concealed until daylight. A well known saloon keeper who was in the room had $500.00 on his person. He dodged the Henry rifle and the Six shooter and escaped into the darkness returning shortly with a shotgun, but the bold desperados had vamosed. When the robbers left the town they took with them a horse belonging to one of the citizens.[25]

Ringo had simply intended to teach the man a lesson. At Ringo's request, Joe Olney later returned the money to the poker players.[26] Ringo thought he deserved an apology. Instead, he and Estes found themselves charged with larceny for their ill-conceived object lesson.

CHAPTER EIGHTEEN

"...the sympathy of the border people seem to be with them."

Once again John Ringo found himself facing serious charges in Arizona. As late as the fall of 1881, however, he was not well known to the people of Tombstone, a town he rarely visited. That was evident in his arraignment for robbery in the Territory of Arizona Plaintiff v. John Ringgold Defendant when "the defendant was asked if John Ringgold was his true name to which he replied that it was not."[1] Ringo was actually better known among the cattlemen of southwestern New Mexico and southeastern Arizona.

Even while Ringo faced robbery charges and imprisonment if convicted, events unfolding along the border would profoundly affect not only his life but all of Tombstone's history. As day broke on August 13, a party of Anglos trailing a herd of cattle to Tombstone was ambushed; five were killed, among them Newman Clanton.

The situation along the border is central to the events leading up to Newman Clanton's death. The violence perpetrated on both sides of the border by American and Mexican alike continued to strain relations between Mexico and the United States. In addition, the Apaches were restless up in "Hell's Forty Acres." In June an Apache mystic and healer named Noch-ay-del-klinne had become the center of revival type meetings. The medicine man reportedly promised to resurrect two Apache chieftains from the dead, and agent J.C. Tiffany determined to put a halt to the business. On August 29 General Eugene A. Carr started out to arrest the Prophet with a force of 117 men.[2] The Apache restlessness alone was enough to put the settlers on the alert, even without the border skirmishes.

In New Mexico Territory Jim Crane was having second thoughts about being on the run. Once, gunman Buckskin Frank Leslie had sought him out, intent on killing him. Leslie had learned that Crane was in the habit of taking his noon meal at the Gray ranch. John Pleasant Gray recalled the confrontation between the men vividly, "Jim Crane rode up at his usual time on a fine saddle mule, unmistakably a refugee from some army post. And as dinner was ready I asked both [Crane and Leslie] in to the meal. It happened we three were alone, except for our old cook, Moody. Jim Crane packed his carbine—a short, Sharp's rifle—into the cook tent and sat down on Leslie's right with the gun across his lap and the muzzle in Frank's direction.

"I don't think any one of us relished that meal much."[3]

Leslie departed peacefully, but Crane realized he was marked for death and became nervous. In consulting with Gray and others in the area he became convinced that his best option was to surrender to the authorities, "thinking that he had a good chance for a light sentence."[4] That would be better than being constantly on the *qui vive* with the likes of Frank Leslie gunning for him. Crane had also begged for trouble by telling Gray that the Earps had planned the March 15 stage robbery that cost Budd Philpott his life.[5] Although the Earps' involvement is impossible to prove today, Crane's confession provides additional evidence that they were at least in part responsible for the robbery.[6] Fred Dodge admitted to Stuart N. Lake that Doc Holliday was among the highwaymen. If Holliday was, indeed, involved, the Earps certainly would have been aware of it.

On the evening of August 12, Crane rode into the camp of Billy Lang. Lang was driving a herd of cattle to Tombstone, and Crane was hunting a meal.[7] Perhaps he was also seeking protection. Gray's brother, Dixie Lee Gray, had joined Lang for the same reason. With typical western hospitality Crane was permitted to stay the night. In Lang's party were Newman Clanton, Billy Byers, Charley Snow, and Harry Ernshaw.

The next morning a hail of gunfire ripped into the camp. Byers lived to tell the tale:

> We pitched our camp in a small swag between three low hills, which formed a sort of triangle around the camp, and at daybreak the cattle appeared uneasy and showed signs of stampeding, when Will Lang said to Charley Snow, who was guarding the cattle, 'Charley, get your gun; I think there's a bear up there, and, if so, kill it.' Charley then rode up one of the hills when the Mexicans opened fire, shooting him and pouring a volley into the camp. At the time they fired Dick Gray, Jim Crane and myself had not got up, but Will Lang, old man Clanton and Harry Ernshaw were up or dressing. Gray, Crane and Clanton were shot at the first fire, and almost instantly killed. When they first fired and killed Charley Snow I thought the boys were firing at a bear, jumped up out of my blankets, and as I got up the boys around me were shot. As soon as I saw what was up I looked for my rifle, and not seeing it I grabbed my revolver, and seeing them shooting at us from all sides, started to run, but had not gone forty feet when I was shot across my body, but I didn't fall, and in a few more steps was hit in my arm, knocked the pistol out of my hand and I fell down. When I was down Harry and Will passed me both running for the canyon. Soon Will fell, shot through the legs, and he then turned his revolver loose, and I think killed one Mexican and wounded another, as one man was killed and another badly wounded, and he was the only one that did much fighting. You must remember that the reason we had no chance to fight was that the Mexicans had crawled up behind the low hills mentioned, and being almost over us fired right down among us. We could see nothing but little whiffs of smoke.[8]

In 1982 author Glenn G. Boyer wrote that the assailants were the Earps.[9] More recently Boyer stated the Earps were rumored to be "suspected" of killing Crane and the others.[10] Byers' eyewitness account contradicts those assertions, as it does Ten Eyck's explanation that the

Earps were mistaken for Mexican militia because two of their party wore Mexican hats.[11]

> I saw some Mexicans coming from the direction Will and Harry had run, wearing their hats, and I then thought they had been killed or had lost their hats in getting away. When I saw the Mexicans begin stripping the bodies, I took off what clothes I had, even my finger ring, and lay stretched out with my face down, and as I was all bloody from my wounds, I thought they would pass me by, thinking I was dead, and already had been stripped. I was not mistaken, for they never touched me, but as one fellow passed me on horseback he fired several shots at me, one grazing my head, and the others striking at my side, throwing the dirt over me. But I kept perfectly still and he rode on. They stripped the bodies, cut open the valises, took all the horses and saddles, and in fact everything they could, possibly getting altogether, including money, $2,000. The only way I can account for Harry's escape is that when Will began shooting at them they turned most of their guns on him and that gave Harry a chance to get away.[12]

A indignant howl swept the border as newspapers picked up the story:

A MEXICAN OUTRAGE

> The Journal has the following special from Tombstone: This town is excited over the killing of five Americans by Mexicans. Dick Gray, Billy Lang, ——- Clanton, Chas. Snow and Billy Byers were those killed, and a man named Harris wounded. John Gray and Mr. Ames arrived from New Mexico this afternoon and gave the following particulars of the killing: Five days ago Billy Lang, son of Mr. Lang, butcher, left here for his cattle ranch, accompanied by Billy Byers and Chas. Snow, to bring in cattle. Old man Clanton, formerly living in San Pedro, and Dick Gray, of Tombstone, who owns two ranches in the vicinity of Lang's ranch, were helping to get up the cattle. The camp was surprised while all were asleep by a party of Mexicans. Three Americans killed by the first fire, two others were killed, outright and the sixth, Harris [sic: Byers], was shot through

the abdomen and left for dead, but is still living. James Crane, one of the noted single robbers, came to Lang's camp the night before the assault to get something to eat and remained there during the night, and is among the killed. He is the last of the gang of robbers who participated in the stage robbery when Bud Philpot was killed. There is great indignation and excitement here. The Mexicans made good their escape across the line.[13]

The *Star* reported:

BORDER WARFARE
The Recent Massacre in New Mexico

The Tombstone Nugget of the 16th inst., contains full details of the recent massacre of Americans in Guadalupe canyon, New Mexico. Parties who were on the ground within a few hours after the murders were committed are now in Tombstone. The following is the story of one of them, John Gray, brother of one of the victims of the horrible tragedy.

A party of seven started on the morning of the 12th from Lang's ranch with a band of cattle for the Tombstone market. They camped that night at Guadalupe canyon, and in the morning, the 13th, at about sunrise, while all but two of the party were asleep, they were surprised by a party of twenty-five or thirty Mexicans, who opened fire upon them, and killed my brother, Dixie Lee Gray, Billy Lang, old man Clanton, Charley Snow, and Jim Crane. Billy Byers was shot through the right arm, and, I think, through the stomach, and he will probably die, if not already dead. The seventh man was known as 'Harry.' I don't remember his other name. He says after the firing commenced, he concealed himself behind a large brush and emptied two revolvers at the assailants. At this time he was joined by Billy Lang, and they concluded to try and escape and started to run, when the Mexicans opened a full volley at them and Billy fell. The bullets whistled all around him, one grazing the bridge of his nose, but he succeeding in getting away without any further injury and made his way back to Lang's ranch. Immediately upon his arrival there the boys at the place hurried to the scene of the killing and found the bodies of the five men. They then commenced to search for

Billy Rogers [sic: Byers] and found that he had been taken in by a rancher near by, but had in a fit of delirium again wandered off. In a short time they found him in an exhausted condition, and took him to Lang's ranch.

The D. L. Gray mentioned as among the killed was a son of Col. Mike Gray, well known in Tucson and also throughout California. The prevailing impression in Tombstone now, is that the murders were committed by Mexican Troops. It is known that a company of soldiers, under command of Capt. Carrillo, were scouring the country in the vicinity of the massacre in search of a party of cowboys who had been depredating on Mexican soil. It is not unlikely that this affair may lead to serious complications between the two governments. At any rate it will result in bloody border feuds between representatives of both nationalities, as the victims of the outrage were well known and have many friends, and their deaths will not be allowed to pass unavenged.[14]

And in New Mexico:

Another Killing.

The following letter was received last Wednesday evening and fully explains itself.

SHAKESPEARE, N. M.)
Aug. 17, 1881.)

I have just heard the particulars of the massacre in the Animas Valley, which are as follows: On Saturday morning, the 13th inst. a party of seven men were camped about five miles below Lang's ranch, and near to Skeleton Valley. About daylight they were attacked by a large party of Mexicans, five out of the seven were killed outright, one mortally wounded and one missing. The names of the killed were Mr. Clanton, father of I. & P. Clanton, Richard Gray, son of Judge Gray of Arizona, James Crane and William Lang. The name of the fifth is unknown. The wounded man lived long enough to tell the particulars. His name was William Byers. The missing man's name is Charles Snow. There were one or two more men missing at the time my informant left Gillespie.

If I hear any further particulars I will let you know.
GREAVES.

The outrage of the murders shocked the border, and men converged on the area from Arizona and New Mexico, among them some of the best citizens from both territories. John Ringo was one of many men who examined the scene. Mayor John Clum then threw the military into a panic by irresponsibly reporting that the men sought revenge. From the Presidio in San Francisco, Assistant Adjutant General Kelton reported to the adjutant general in Washington, DC:

> Following telegram received from Commanding General Department of Arizona:
> 'Clum the Mayor of Tombstone reported seventeenth killing of party of Americans by Mexicans in Guadalupe Canyon and starting of large parties from Tombstone and vicinity for Mexico in retaliation.'
> These reports confirmed from Camp Huachuca and Fort Bowie. The Mayor of Tombstone asks what steps the Military have taken. I have not been called upon by civil authorities to make arrests as in the case contemplated by Attorney General, but have ordered troops to be sent to the border to intercept all armed parties raiding into Mexico with hostile intent and disarm them, or if found returning, to aid the civil authorities to arrest them. The troops seem powerless to act under the posse commitatus law, and, local Commanders have done nothing beyond asking information and reporting. The last parties killed are said to be Cowboys, but the sympathy of the border people seem to be with them and I doubt whether any local civil authorities can, or will do anything to prevent retaliation.[16]

The troops were unnecessary, for the large parties were simply men who wanted to recover the bodies and were taking no chance of a Mexican troop ambush.

Yet the government, swayed by the irresponsible yellow journalism of an elected official, further fueled the cowboy curse. Parsons also noted the incident, and in a callous journal entry, revealed much about both him and his misunderstanding of the West:

> Bad trouble on the border and this time looks more serious

than anything yet. Dick Gray—the lame one—was killed by some Mexicans along with several others among them the notorious Crane and revenge seems the order of the day, a gang having started out to make trouble. This killing business by the Mexicans, in my mind, was perfectly justifiable as it was in retaliation for killing of several of them and their robbery by cow-boys recently this same Crane being one of the number. Am glad they killed him, as for the others—if not guilty of cattle stealing—they had no business to be found in such bad company. I hope no trouble will be had as our mill and mines being near to the line might suffer and some of us be taken in.[17]

Despite Parsons' self-righteous and heartless attitude toward the murder of innocent men, all of these documents are of interest. Notably, neither the newspapers of the day nor any of the correspondents involved knew Newman Clanton's first name. Historian Chuck Parsons has pointed out, "Today we think of Old Man Clanton as if he is as well known as Satan himself...but at the time of the events the press couldn't or didn't want to bother even to give him a name."[18]

Cattlemen along the border were furious. Among the men who swarmed to the area to recover the bodies was John Ringo. Unlike the Germans back in Mason County, who had names and distinct identities, the Mexican troops who committed these brutal and cowardly murders were relatively anonymous.

Ringo had no intention of taking on the Mexican army, but he might have contemplated an opportunity for revenge later. A.M. Franklin, Ringo's friend from Maxey, encountered him sometime after the ambush. In 1925 Franklin recalled that L.M. Jacobs & Co., of Tucson, sent him to the San Simon to take charge of a herd of cattle being driven north from Durango and Chihuahua. Franklin had arranged for the customs agent at Silver City, New Mexico, to meet him and clear the herd, which was in charge of a man named Jim Sprague.

The herd reached the San Simon around 4:30 P.M. Sprague, Franklin, and four of the Mexican herders were detailed to take the first watch. Everything was calm until shortly after midnight. Franklin recalled:

About five minutes after the shift had changed there was

considerable noise and commotion that frightened the cattle. They were up and on their feet—the whole bunch of them. The greater portion of them were moving to where I was camping. I had not as yet unsaddled my horse, so I jumped on him thinking I would be able to get out of the way, not appreciating in the least what was really happening.

It seemed to me the faster I rode away from those cattle down the valley the greater was the desire of the cattle to overtake me and as split minutes passed by more and more was this desire made manifest. Riding on the extreme edge was Joe Browning, one of our Cowboys and a very trustworthy fellow. He was on a very fleet horse, waving his red handkerchief as if to attract my attention. The cattle were all the time gaining on me and I expected if I swerved from my course that they would run me down and that would be the last of yours truly. There were 998 steers in the bunch, all weighing from 700 to 1000 pounds and their hoofs would have made human hamburger out of me—bones, machinery and all.

Browning seeing how I stood rode towards me; he caught up and said without introduction: 'You damn fool, haven't you got sense enough to circle around so as to get the cattle milling and stop this damn stampede? You've been the ringleader of it for the last four miles, leading the cattle.'

This was the first information that I had that the cattle were stampeding; it was certainly the first information I had that I was leading the stampede.[19]

The drovers settled the cattle and again bedded them for the night.

In the morning Sprague, along with two hundred of the cattle, were missing. Sprague apparently had reported the herd's arrival to Ringo, who, along with six or eight other men, had stampeded the herd, cut out some cattle and driven them toward Galeyville. Franklin saddled his mount and headed toward the town. As he rode on he "saw other bunches from 3 to 10—not a man or horse in sight. I arrived at Galeyville, went to headquarters—the saloon without a name—and there John Ringo was the first man I met."[20]

Ringo was surprised by Franklin's appearance. After a few rounds of drinks the conversation turned to why Franklin had come. Franklin told Ringo that the herd had stampeded during the night and that th herd was about 175 head short.

He looked at me with his baby blue eyes, which actually danced with excitement and first said: 'Did you see anything as you were coming up the trail?' I answered: 'I thought I did but I'm not sure.'

He then said 'Why in the hell didn't you send your Mexicans up to get your cattle?'

I answered: 'They've got as much as they can attend to and if you and your fellows will round up the cattle I've lost and deliver them to me at the San Carlos Apache Indian Reservation it will be worth $10 a head to me, or it will be worth $5 a head to me if you can deliver them to me at San Jose, which was a little settlement—the first settlement on the Gila river after the river leaves the mountains and the first place to water the cattle.

He joshed with me a little while and said again: 'I'm sorry you didn't send your Mexicans.'[21]

Ringo finally agreed to round up the cattle in return for $100—an obvious indication that he had more interest in ambushing the Mexicans than in stealing cattle. As Franklin turned to leave, Ringo asked again, "Why in hell didn't you send your Mexicans up to get them anyhow? They're the fellows we wanted to have some fun with."[22]

Franklin clearly believed the beeves had been stolen. Equally clear is that they had been scattered, something no cattle thief would have done. Two possibilities exist. Either Ringo was indulging in some good-natured leg pulling of his friend, or he had attempted to lure the Mexican wranglers into an ambush—most probably the latter. If so, he was simply following the law of the feud.

Franklin's account also provides a good description of Ringo at this time.

John was over six feet tall, rangy, bony and strong as a horse. He had light blue, baby eyes, that would cause you to love him when he was looking at you, but you wanted to travel from him like lightning when he was under the influence of liquor. He was admittedly the best pistol shot in the country. His best trick was to hold a .45 caliber Colt on the index finger of each hand, barrels down, and at the word would give the pistols a three-quarter turn, simultaneously shooting both at beer bottles and always knocking the neck off one or two. I recall that John made a bet that he would send the bullets into the open necks of the bottle twice out of five, at fifty feet. He won many a bet of this kind.[23]

Ringo's reputation had grown, and with it the tendency to drink heavily as his depression spiraled out of control. This time there would be no respite. The cold-eyed feudist had again emerged.

CHAPTER
NINETEEN

"...desperate and dangerous..."

According to Wyatt Earp, his family's feud with Ringo originated in a September 1881 stage robbery. On September 8, the Bisbee stage left Tombstone carrying a Wells, Fargo box containing $2,500. Five miles from Bisbee, two masked men halted and robbed the coach. The *Nugget* reported:

> Upon receiving the news, Marshal [sic] Williams, Wells, Fargo and Company's agent here, informed Under Sheriff Woods of the case, and Deputy Sheriff Woods was soon in the saddle en route for the scene of the robbery.
>
> Later a party consisting of Marshal Williams, Wyatt and Morgan Earp, and Frederick Dodge also started to hunt the trail of the highwaymen. Nothing positive is known as to who the road agents were, but circumstantial evidence points to several parties well known in Tombstone. Though having a long start, if their trail is struck, we have no doubt of their capture. The Sonora line has heretofore been no bar to pursuit of other criminals, by some of the pursuing party, and in all probability will not this time.[1]

A few days later two suspects were apprehended.

Important Capture.

> Wyatt and Morgan Earp, Marshal [sic] Williams and
> Deputy Sheriff Breakenridge, who went to Bisbee to arrest
> the stage robbers on Sunday evening, brought in Depty
> Sheriff T.C. Stilwell and P. Spencer, whom the evidence
> strongly points out as the robbers. They were examined
> before Wells Spicer, Esq., yesterday and were admitted to
> bail in the sum of $7,000 each—$5,000 for robbing the
> mail and $2,000 for robbing D.B. Rea. The evidence
> against Deputy Sheriff Stilwell is circumstantial, and rests
> principally upon the tracks made by his bootheels in the
> mud, which corresponded with those he had removed by a
> shoemaker upon his return to Bisbee. The Epitaph has no
> desire to prejudge the case, but if it turns out as now antici-
> pated, that the officers of the law are implicated in this
> nefarious business, it would seem to be in order for Sheriff
> Behan to appoint another deputy.[2]

The arrest of John Behan's deputy, Frank Stilwell, was a political
embarrassment which the Republican *Epitaph* used to full advantage.
Stilwell and Spence were bound over for trial. By coincidence, Pony
Diehl and Sherman MacMasters also come into the picture at this time.
In mid-September Diehl was arrested at Harshaw, a mining camp some
thirty-five miles from the robbery site, on the old charge involving the
February stage robbery. Sheriff Bob Paul soon learned that MacMasters
was in Tombstone and wired that city.

Somehow MacMasters learned of Paul's telegram and planned to flee
Tombstone. In the process Virgil Earp spotted him and ordered him to
halt. MacMasters ran and Earp ineffectively emptied his pistol after the
fleeing man. Since Earp's authority did not cross the city line, he asked
Behan, just back from Yuma, to pursue the fugitive. In the meantime,
the cunning MacMasters stole two horses from E. B. Gage and headed
for Harshaw. Bartholomew theorizes that Diehl and MacMasters may
have committed the September 8 holdup. Spence was later cleared of
the charges. Stilwell was still under investigation at the time of his
death.[3]

Wyatt Earp would later testify under oath that John Ringo had threatened his life because of his involvement in the arrests of Stilwell and Spencer.

> Morgan Earp and myself assisted to arrest Stilwell and Spencer on the charge of robbing the Bisbee stage; the McLowrys and Clantons have always been friends of Stilwell and Spencer, and they laid the whole blame of their arrest on us, though, the fact is we only went as a Sheriff's posse; after we got in town with Spencer and Stilwell Ike Clanton and Frank McLowry came in; Frank McLowry took Morgan Earp into the street in front of the Alhambra, when John Ringgold, Ike Clanton, and the two Hicks boys were also standing by, when Frank McLowry commenced to abuse Morgan Earp for going after Spencer and Stilwell; Frank McLowry said he would never speak to Spencer again for being arrested by us; he said to Morgan "If you ever come after me you will never take me"; Morgan replied if he ever had occasion to go after him he would arrest him; Frank McLowry then said to Morgan: "I have threatened you boys' lives, and a few days ago had taken it back, but since this arrest it now goes;" Morgan made no reply and walked off; before this and after this Marshall Williams, Farmer Daly, Ed Byrnes, Old Man Winter, Charley Smith and three or four others had told us at different times of threats to kill us made by Ike Clanton, Frank McLowry, Tom McLowry, Joe Hill and John Ringgold; I know all these men were desperate and dangerous men; that they were connected with outlaws, cattle thieves, robbers and murderers; I knew of the McLowrys stealing six government mules and also cattle, and when the owners went after them—finding his stock on the McLowry boys' ranch— that he was driven off, and told that if he ever said anything about it they would kill him, and he has kept his mouth shut until several days ago
> FOR FEAR OF BEING KILLED.
> I heard of Ringold shooting a man down in cold blood near Camp Thomas....[4]

In Prescott Dake found time to advise MacVeagh that he was "solicited to take active measures for the protection of mail-stages and routes of communication from the depredations now being perpetrated by Indians and other outlaws." Dake detailed a number of attacks on stages and the death of his deputy, George L. Turner should not be confused with the George Turner killed earlier that year. On September 6, 1881, Deputy Turner and Henry Moody had ridden from Globe, Arizona, to the Middleton ranch with the news that Apaches were raiding in the vicinity. A group of Apaches arrived about the same time as Turner and Moody. After speaking peacefully with the ranchers for a short time, the Apaches suddenly opened fire, killing Turner and Moody instantly. The Middletons barricaded themselves in their home and fought off the attackers.

Dake told MacVeagh, "I have no doubt that at the present time many of the depredations reported by the Indians are committed by outlaws, both Mexicans and whites." Dake's point was the familiar refrain, how much money could he spend?[5] He added an interesting twist in blaming the Indian raids on outlaws, however. Usually it was the other way around. Moreover, it clearly shows that after six months Dake had done nothing to suppress the "Cowboy Curse" other than write letters asking Washington for money.

While Dake was soliciting funds, Acting Governor John Gosper was responding to an August 29 letter from Secretary of State James G. Blaine on two matters concerning Anglo-Mexican relations: the lynching of a Mexican rustler and the Cowboy situation: "While it is true Americans on our side of the line dividing the U.S. from Mexico are often guilty of murder and theft upon the citizens of Mexico, it is equally true that Mexicans on their side of said line are equally guilty with Americans of murder and theft, and until recently—until the cow-boy combination along the border for common plunder—the crimes committed against citizens of both the governments of the U.S. and Mexico along the border were in most part committed by citizens of Mexico."[6]

Adding to the chaos, Apaches swept down from the north to strike the outlying ranches. Parsons noted on October 5, "Late last night Bulford informed that Indians and soldiers were fighting in Dragoon Pass north of town and having a regular battle. The Indian scare spread through town."[7]

Parsons was among those who joined John Behan's posse to run down the hostiles. "We then called off by fours every fourth man to hold horses in engagement and quickly went for the trail which we followed sometime and then thinking to cut it, struck across Sulphur

Spring Valley. Hay ranches deserted. At one place, food left as parties were eating, they not having stopped for anything not certainly on the order of their going, but went at once."[8] One of the ranches hit was the McLaury brothers'. Frank McLaury was reported to have lost twenty-seven horses to the hostiles, and he and brother Tom, with the aid of the Clantons, had begun gathering their stock with the intention of selling out and leaving Arizona. On October 25 Tom McLaury and Ike Clanton arrived in Tombstone from the McLaury ranch.[9] The men stabled their mounts at the West End Corral on Fremont Street, then separated.

According to Ike Clanton trouble began with Doc Holliday and the Earps early on the morning of October 26, when he was at the Occidental's lunch room. Clanton said that Holliday came into the room and began cursing him, called him a "son-of-a-bitch of a cowboy" and told him to go for his gun. Ike was unarmed and attempted to reason with Holliday, who yelled that he had threatened the Earps. "All the time I was talking, he had his hand in his bosom and I supposed on his pistol. I looked behind me and saw Morgan Earp with his feet over the lunch counter. He had his hand in his bosom also, looking at me." Clanton wisely decided that discretion was called for and left the room, the enraged Holliday and Morgan Earp on his heels. Outside both men challenged Clanton to fight. Wyatt and Virgil Earp watched nearby. "Morgan Earp told me if I was not heeled, when I came back on the street to be heeled. I walked off and asked them not to shoot me in the back."[10] Wyatt Earp's testimony confirmed Ike's, in part.[11]

Ike Clanton then got into a poker game with John Behan, Tom McLaury, and Virgil Earp. Why the men would play cards together is curious indeed, but they did, until eight o'clock in the morning. Ike later testified that Virgil Earp kept his pistol in his lap during the game. When they were done, Ike retrieved his weapons, a clear violation of city ordinance if he was not then on his way out of town. Between 8:30 and 9:00 he met E.F. Boyle, a night-shift bartender who was coming off duty. Boyle testified that Clanton told him he intended to fight the Earps and Holliday.[12] Saloon owner Julius Kelley concurred, "I asked Clanton what trouble he had been having. He stated that the Earp crowd and Doc Holliday had insulted him the night before when he was not heeled; that he had now heeled himself, and that they had to fight on sight."[13]

Clanton then began hunting the Earps. At R.F. Hafford's saloon he again complained that Holliday and the Earps insulted him.[14] Ike next made his way to the Capitol Saloon. Between 1:00 and 1:30 in the afternoon he emerged and headed for the Pima County Bank. As he did, Virgil and Morgan Earp approached from his rear, and Virgil struck him on the head from behind with his pistol. The men disarmed Clanton and took him to Judge Wallace, who fined him twenty-five dollars. While Ike was in the courtroom, Wyatt Earp arrived and, according to Clanton, "He called me a thief and a son-of-a-bitch, and told me I could have all the shooting I wanted." Wyatt then offered Ike his rifle, muzzle first.[15] Wyatt confirmed some of Ike's testimony, but said that Morgan had offered Ike a pistol and that Ike had started the bickering.[16] Clanton wisely refused the rifle, and Virgil and Morgan deposited his weapons at the Grand Hotel Bar.

Wyatt then stepped out onto the street, where he met Tom McLaury. Wyatt testified later that McLaury "had a pistol in plain sight" and offered to fight him anywhere. Earp stated that he slapped McLaury, then struck him over the head with his pistol. Curiously Wyatt made no attempt to arrest Tom for carrying weapons, the most logical reason being that in reality Tom was not armed. A number of reliable witnesses contradicted Earp's statement. A. Bauer, a local butcher, saw Earp hit McLaury in the face while Tom's hands were in his pockets. Earp had asked if McLaury were "heeled," then struck him "two or three or maybe four blows with his pistol." As the rancher lay bleeding on the ground, Earp shouted, "I could kill the son-of-a-bitch."[17]

J. H. Batcher, a bookkeeper, confirmed Bauer's testimony, adding that he heard Tom say that he did not know what Earp had against him, that he had never done anything against him, and that they were friends. According to Batcher, Tom also said that "whenever [Wyatt] wanted to fight, [Tom] was with him [on his side]." Earp then drew his pistol and struck him.[18] A third witness, Thomas Keefe, a carpenter, also saw the beating.[19]

At two o'clock Billy Clanton and Frank McLaury arrived in Tombstone from Antelope Springs. Billy Allen recalled later that Doc Holliday greeted both men cordially.[20] Soon thereafter, Billy and Frank met their brothers and, learning of the day's events, immediately made plans to leave town. It was already too late.

The events of the next few moments—the notorious "Gunfight at the O.K. Corral"—are embroiled in controversy. Confronted by conflicting testimony, writers have charged that witnesses such as Sheriff John Behan, Billy Claiborne, Billy Allen, and Wes Fuller all lied under oath. For example, Turner states that Allen was a "cowboy partisan" and was "believed" to have fired a number of shots at the Earps.[21] Turner's foundation for this claim is unknown; no one ever testified of any gunfire from any unseen shooter. R. F. Coleman, a witness standing beside Allen during the fight, completely failed to notice Allen's alleged gunplay, and Turner neither offers a source for the allegation nor attempts to impeach Coleman's testimony. Not surprisingly, historians favorable to the Clantons counter that statements such as Turner's were created from whole cloth, simply to discredit witnesses whose testimony was damaging to the Earps.

One common story holds that Ike Clanton and Frank McLaury planned to kill the Earps to prove to their "gang" that they had not lured Leonard, Crane, and Head into an ambush. That theory fails to account for Joe "Hill" Olney, who would have had as much or more reason to fear reprisal if Earp's statements were true. Olney would certainly have joined the Clantons and the McLaurys, also bringing his brothers Dan and George, both veterans of the Mason County War, into the fight. With them would have come John Ringo, whose loyalty to Joe was undiminished. None of these men were in Tombstone that day.

The Earp supporters' most common claim is that Virgil Earp, the town marshal, deputized his brothers and Doc Holliday to disarm and arrest the four "cow-boys." As the Earps approached, Billy Clanton and Frank McLaury went for their guns. Others argue that the Earps fully intended to kill their victims, who raised their hands (or in Tom McLaury's case, threw open his coat) and were unceremoniously shot down. The inquest testimony of those witnesses with no interest in the fight sheds light on what really happened in Tombstone on October 26, 1881.

Did the Earps plan to kill the Clanton and McLaury brothers? As they passed Bauer's butcher shop, Mrs. Martha J. King saw and heard them plainly:

> I stepped to the door and looked up the sidewalk and I saw four men coming down the sidewalk. I only knew one of the party and that was Mr. Holliday....Mr. Holliday was next to the buildings, on the inside. He had a gun under his

coat. The way I noticed the gun was that his coat would blow open, and he tried to keep it covered. I stood in the door until these gentlemen passed and until they got to the second door. And what frightened me and made me run back, I heard him say, 'Let them have it!' And Doc Holliday said, 'All right.'[22]

Did Tom McLaury throw open his coat as some witnesses stated? Coroner H.M. Matthews stated that Tom had been hit by twelve buckshot in the right side.[23] There were no wounds on Tom's arm, plainly indicating that his arms were away from his body, undoubtedly holding his coat open as witnesses stated.

Did Frank McLaury start the fight by drawing on the Earps before they fired? James Kehoe saw it clearly: "In less than a minute, I heard two shots in quick succession. I saw Frank McLaury running out on the street, *drawing his pistol* [emphasis added]."[24]

Was Billy Clanton shot with his hands in the air? Thomas Keefe, who examined Billy immediately after the shooting, stated that he had been shot about two inches above the wrist, and the wound "went from the inside to the outside."[25] Keefe also said that the wound on the outside of Clanton's wrist was the larger, clearly the exit wound made when his hands were in the air.

Was Tom McLaury armed? Both Andrew Mehan and J.H. Allman stated that Tom's weapons were checked at the time of the shooting.[26] Keefe testified that no weapons were found on his body. No one—except the Earps—saw Tom McLaury fire a gun.

Were the men noted troublemakers and outlaws? Bartender E.F. Boyle testified:

> A. Knew Tom McLaury about 18 months, never knew him to be in a difficulty with anybody.
>
> …
>
> A. Knew Billy Clanton about the same length of time. Never was on intimate terms with him. Never knew him to be in any difficulty.
> Q. Did you ever of your knowledge know of Frank McLaury to be in any difficulty?
> A. No sir.[27]

Billy Clanton and the McLaury brothers were dead. Their bodies lay on display in a store window until their funeral on October 27. John

Clum's *Epitaph* summed up the feelings of the community.

The Funeral.

> The funeral of the McLowry brothers and Clanton yesterday was numerically one of the largest ever witnessed in Tombstone. It took place at 3:30 from the undertaking rooms of Messrs. Ritter and Eyan. The procession headed by the Tombstone brass band, moved down Allen Street and thence to the cemetery. The sidewalks were densely packed for three or four blocks. The body of Clanton was in the first hearse and those of the two McLowry brothers in the second, side by side, and were interred in the same grave. It was a most impressive and saddening sight and such a one as it is to be hoped may never occur again in this community.[28]

Nearly 2,000 people attended the funeral, one of the largest in Tombstone's history.

John Ringo did not arrive in Tombstone in time for the funeral, but the *Nugget* of November 8 noted that "John Ringo, New Mexico" had arrived at the Grand Hotel. Ringo, following in the footsteps of Scott Cooley, had come to observe the Earp-Holliday hearing before Justice Wells Spicer and to learn his own status regarding the August robbery. His partner in that escapade, Dave Estes, had already been cleared in the affair.[29] In Tombstone, Ringo heard the version of the gunfight that he believed—Ike Clanton's. Ike looked to John Ringo for support and for leadership, and Ringo naturally rode to the San Simon to meet with his old friend, Joe Olney. In late November, "Joe Hill, San Simon" registered in the Grand Hotel, along with W.H. Miller of Camp Thomas, a close friend of the Olneys.[30] Three days later, "J. Ringgold, San Simon" registered at the Grand.[31] The next day Joe's brother, George, checked in from the San Simon.[32]

Ringo arrived in Tombstone to surrender. On November 30 Deputy Sheriff Dave Neagle arrested him. The next day he appeared in district court, charged with a felony for the August poker game robbery. After he pleaded not guilty, his trial was set for the next day.[33] The same day of Ringo's arraignment, Wells Spicer, who was also a business partner of Marshall Williams, ruled the evidence did not warrant holding the Earps for trial and ordered them freed.

In Arizona both Republican and Democratic newspapers castigated the Earps, the exception being Clum's *Epitaph*. The Prescott *Democrat* noted of the Earps, "Those distinguished swashbucklers honored Prescott with their presence some two years ago," and "the odor of their unsavory reputation still taints the nostrils of our citizens." The Republican *Miner* stated that the Earps had acted "without provocation."[34]

The farce of the Spicer decision was not lost on the citizens of Tombstone and Cochise County. They had mourned the murdered ranchers in one of the largest funerals Tombstone ever saw. They had seen Judge Spicer twist the law to permit irrelevant testimony without cross examination. And they had seen the court free men whom most believed to be cold blooded murderers. Talk turned to lynching.

The time to kill had returned.

CHAPTER TWENTY

"Ringo...the cowboy leader..."

John Ringo, now facing charges for robbing the poker game in Galeyville, was in a position to observe the troubles in Tombstone develop. Rumors that the Earps would be lynched abounded, and John Clum panicked. Using his office as mayor, Clum wired Acting Governor John J. Gosper for weapons. It was easy to gain Gosper's support by blaming the "Cowboys" for the threats. Gosper immediately wired President Chester A. Arthur on December 12, 1881:

> Following telegram just received from Mayor of Tombstone—'Tombstone Eleventh Dec.—Gov. J. J. Gosper, Prescott. Please send those fifty stands of arms care P.M. Smith soon as possible. John P. Clum.'
>
> Arms will be furnished, and are for use. The committee of safety discharge of the Earps enrages Cow Boys. New dangers apprehended. Give us use of military and we will give you peace on the borders. Public peace in this Territory imperatively demands repeal posse commitatus

act so far as our southern Border is concerned. Our people much pleased with your notice of our troubles.[1]

Clum, however, was in no frame of mind to wait for weapons. As talk of lynching increased, he decided a quick trip to Tucson was in order.

On December 14, Clum boarded the Kinnear stage with Jimmy Harrington at the reins. Behind the stage rumbled a bullion wagon driven by Whistling Dick Wright. Trouble struck some four miles from Tombstone, shortly after the wagons left Malcolm's water station on the way to Contention. Highwaymen attempted to rob both the stage and bullion wagon. From the roadside came the cry, "Halt!" followed by "a volley of shots evidently aimed at the horses for the purpose of disabling them and thus stopping the coach."[2] One of the lead horses was killed, and Wright took a bullet in the leg.

In the early hours of December 15, Sheriff Behan led a posse to the site of the bungled holdup attempt. At Contention he learned the full story of the attempted robbery:

> The six-horse coach driven by Jimmy Harrington and the bullion wagon driven by 'Whistling Dick' had just left Malcolm's water station, which is the last house on the road to Contention, and only about four miles from Tombstone and were bowling along at a rapid gait when the order to 'Halt' was given from the roadside and almost simultaneously a volley was fired into them. The off leader of the coach was struck in the neck and all the horses became unmanageable. Dick was hit in the calf of the leg and received a painful flesh wound but kept his seat and his wagon right side up. The horses ran for about half a mile when the wounded one weakened and fell.[3]

Clum helped cut the dead horse from its harness, but apparently terrified that the robbers were trying to kill him, fled to the Grand Central mill where he obtained a horse and rode on to Benson. From Benson the badly shaken Clum penned an editorial and forwarded it to the *Epitaph* office:

> It is a well known fact that the night stages do not carry either treasure or the mails; therefore the ordinary excuse

for plunder cannot be alleged as an incentive to the deed. Since the late unfortunate affair rumors have been rife of the intended assassination of not only the Earp brothers and Holliday, but of Marshal [sic] Williams, Mayor Clum, Judge Spicer and Thomas Fitch. Why the feeling of deadly hatred should exist in relation to the Earps and Holliday everyone here can understand; but as against the others it is one of those inscrutable mysteries that none but the most depraved can possibly assign a reason for. That the affair of Wednesday night was intended for the murder of John P. Clum, we are fully satisfied.[4]

Subsequent writers have stated without reservation that the incident was an attempt to kill Clum. Traywick writes, without documentation, "Three of the men who attempted to murder Clum, were Frank Stilwell, John Ringo, and Ike Clanton."[5] Not one shred of contemporary evidence supports that assertion. Actually, the attempted robbery of both the stage and bullion wagon has marked similarities to the bungled holdup attempt on the Kinnear stage the previous March when Philpott and Roerig were killed. Once again, trigger-happy outlaws had botched the attempt with a promiscuous burst of gunfire. Aside from Clum's ramblings in the *Epitaph*, not a hint of evidence exists that the men ever planned to do anything but rob the stage and bullion wagon. That none of the shots struck the coach obviously indicates they were aimed at the horses.

Nonetheless, threats had been made. One of the people who heard them was Parsons. "Threatening letters have been sent to certain parties with orders to leave town among them Sheriff and others well known."[6] Parsons' statement that Behan was threatened has apparently been missed by modern writers. Certainly it was missed, or ignored, by Clum who may have been using the threats for political purposes. Two days after Clum's blistering editorial, Wells Spicer added fuel to the fire in his response to a threatening letter dated December 13, signed by "A. Miner," and published in the *Epitaph*.

There is a rabble in our city who would like to be thugs, if they had courage; would be proud to be called cow-boys, if people would give them that distinction; but as they can be neither, they do the best they can to show how vile they are, and slander, abuse and threaten everyone they dare to. Of all such I say, that whenever they are denouncing me they are lying from a low, wicked and villainous heart; and that when they threaten me they are low-bred, arrant cowards, and know that 'fight is not my racket'—if it was they would not dare to do it.[7]

Crawley P. Dake, meanwhile, made good use of this period to forward another request for more money. "Yours at the instance of the President received my deputies at Tombstone have struck one effective blow to that element killing three of five. They had threatened the lives of my deputies on sight. Not braver men in Arizona than I have employed with a strong posse I have confidence will drive them from our border. A special allowance for this particular purpose should be made and the paying of actual expenses of posse authorized. Wrote you December third on this subject. I have acting Governor Gosper's cordial support."[8] It was all a matter of money of course, and Dake took the opportunity to employ Gosper's weight behind his request for funds. Gosper also wrote to Phillips, "Marshall Dake has consulted me reference to yours at instance of President. He informs me he must be authorized to employ posse before making expense. I have confidence he can secure proper men if authorized."[9]

Tombstone lapsed into a disturbing calm as the Christmas season passed. Then, on December 28, vengeance fell on Virgil Earp. Earp was walking from the Oriental Saloon to his room in the Cosmopolitan Hotel. As he passed the Eagle Brewery Saloon, shotgun fire blazed from the darkness. The blast shattered his left arm, inflicting a wound that permanently crippled him. The *Epitaph* reported that five shots were fired in quick succession and speculated that three men were involved. Parsons noted, "It is surmised that Ike Clanton, 'Curly Bill' and McLowry [sic: Will McLaury] did the shooting."[10]

No one was ever convicted for the attack. Among historians, DeMattos writes simply, "Ringo has often been listed as one of the assailants who ambushed and crippled Virgil Earp on December 28, 1881."[11] Traywick lists the assailants as Ike Clanton, Frank Stilwell, John Ringo, Hank Swilling, Pete Spencer, and Johnny Barnes, again without any contemporary evidence for his assertion.[12] Ike Clanton was provably out of town at the time of the shooting. Ringo's whereabouts are uncertain, but he may well have been at Joe Hill's ranch, where Joe's children fondly recalled him as "Uncle John." Both men may have known who the shooters were, but neither ever talked of it.

Wyatt Earp sent a telegram about the shooting to Dake in Prescott.

Dake in turn appointed Wyatt as a deputy United States marshal. Virgil's days as city marshal were over, however, and Tombstone voters made clear their regard for Republicans as represented by the Earps. On January 3, Parsons mourned the Republican ticket's defeat. Shorn of most of their legal power, the Earps faced the beginning of their end in Arizona.

Eighteen eighty-two began with more stage robberies. On January 6, three, possibly five, men held up the W.W. Hubbard and Co.'s Tombstone-to-Bisbee stage and engaged shotgun messenger Charles A. Bartholomew in a rifle duel eight miles from Bisbee. Finally the robbers "met a Mexican wood-hauler, whom they compelled to carry a message" to the stage. Believing resistance was futile, the passengers persuaded Bartholomew to cease resistance. The robbers, one of whom was not masked, netted $6,500 and stole one of the coach's horses.[13] DeMattos states that Ringo was a prime suspect, along with Curly Bill Brocius, Stilwell, and Spence.[14] If so, their involvement was only rumor, for none of them was ever charged in connection with the holdup.

On January 7, two robbers hit the Sandy Bob stage. The *Epitaph* commented that the pair apparently were not novices. Among the passengers was James B. Hume of Wells, Fargo. The robbery occurred about 1:00 A.M. between Contention and Tombstone.[15]

For John Ringo the Earps represented justice thwarted and power abused once again. He understood clearly that the cycle of revenge had begun. Area ranchers looked to Ringo for leadership, at the very time that he was deteriorating mentally. Perhaps the flashbacks of the Mason County War were growing more intense. Certainly he was drinking more, seeking oblivion in a bottle, a situation which could only exacerbate his condition. Friends would later recall that his mental state made him "subject to frequent fits of melancholy" and that he was "certain of being killed."[16] He was being drawn into a situation over which he had no control.

On January 17 Ringo spotted "the Earps" (probably Wyatt, Morgan, and younger brother Warren), Doc Holliday, and others of their clique. He resolved to give Wyatt a chance to prove his courage. Walking up to the group he cordially invited Wyatt to step out onto the street and draw. Earp refused, but Holliday was game. Only the intervention of Policeman James Flynn averted shooting. Parsons wrote, "Ringo and Doc Holliday came nearly having it with pistols....Bad time expected with the cowboy leader and D.H. I passed both not knowing blood was up. One with hand in breast pocket and the other probably ready. Earps just beyond. Crowded street and looked like another battle. Police vigilant for once and both disarmed."[17]

Earp's defenders have postulated that Wyatt refused the fight because he intended to run for sheriff in the fall—an unconvincing theory, since the Republican party had just gone down to defeat in the city elections. Whatever the case, the locals' thoughts on the incident are clear. Hancock would write, "Ringo gave those fellows every opportunity to fight it out but when he found them to be only a bunch of cowards he ignored them."[18]

Hancock claimed that was not the only time Ringo offered to fight Earp and his cronies. "It was no swashbuckling on John's part. He told them what he thought of them and what they were and they took it....Ringo gave those fellows every opportunity to fight it out..."[19] Hancock's assertion is supported by Ben Olney's recollection that his grandfather, Joe Hill, saw Ringo offer to fight it out with knives. "Wyatt went pale and backed out of the saloon."[20]

Officer Flynn arrested Ringo and hauled him to jail. He would not long remain incarcerated. On the mistaken belief that Ringo's bond had been approved, Breakenridge permitted him to take his guns and leave town on January 23.[21] That same day, James Earp, the oldest of Wyatt's full brothers, swore out an affidavit against Ringo. Earp claimed that on January 23 he had seen Ringo escape from the sheriff without any approved bond. The purpose of Ringo's "escape," he said, was to intercept "Wyatt S. Earp a marshal intrusted with the execution of warrants for the arrest of diverse persons charged with violations of the laws of the territory."[22] A posse started in pursuit, and Parsons would comment, "Was routed out of bed night before last to help get a horse for posse which left about 4:00 a.m. for Charleston to rearrest Ringo. Jack [J. Jackson] headed them and they had quite an experience but no shooting. The Earps are out too on U.S. business and lively times are anticipated."[23]

Lively times indeed. The *Epitaph* reported:

The Official Scandal.

Up to the time of going to press nothing has been heard from the posse that went out with Marshal Earp. After the escape of Ringo it was decided to send out another posse to bring him in as the marshal of course had no warrant for his arrest. Accordingly, yesterday morning [January 24] about 4 o'clock a posse of eight, led by Mr. J. Jackson, left town with a warrant for his arrest. Arriving at Charleston at daybreak they put their horses in a corral to grain and after leaving their arms at a convenient place proceeded to the Occidental hotel to get their breakfast. Upon passing the threshold they were intercepted by Isaac Clanton and another man with drawn weapons, while the barrels of other Winchesters suddenly gleamed over the adobe wall. Mr. Jackson stated his errand. After a few words by some of the party that nobody would be arrested unless they wanted to be, Clanton stated that Johnny had always acted the gentleman toward him and he would see what could be done, the result of his efforts being that it was arranged that Ringo would return with the posse to Tombstone. A little while afterward Mr. [Briggs] Goodrich rode up and took Ringo [to] one side for conversation. A few moments afterward Clanton informed Mr. Jackson that Ringo had left but would [be] in Tombstone within an hour or an hour be [sic] and twenty minutes at most, and in just about the allotted time he appeared, gave himself up and was placed in the county jail. The posse returned to town about four o'clock, the intent of their mission having been achieved by the voluntary act of Ringo. They report about twenty-five cow-boys congregated at Charleston and from a gentleman who came in late from the southern country we learn that he was passed by a quartet about four miles above Charleston, who were making excellent time in the direction of Hereford.[24]

The *Epitaph* also explained Ringo's "escape": "The bond by which John Ringo had heretofore been admitted to bail was decided to be insufficient by Judge [W. H.] Stilwell in court yesterday, and Ringo was ordered to be confined in the county jail until further orders."[25]

James Earp's personal appearance fully illustrates his concern for his brother and, conversely, his fear of Ringo. Wyatt was with a posse of some forty or fifty men. Having been appointed a deputy United States marshal to succeed Virgil, Wyatt headed to Charleston to arrest both Ike Clanton and his brother, Phin. Although the men refused to be arrested by Earp, they did surrender peacefully to Jackson. The *Nugget* reported, "It was represented that the parties for whom warrants were issued had a well grounded fear that it was not for the purpose of getting them to answer the charges but for the purpose of committing a grave offense upon the accused."[26]

If the Earps failed to arrest the Clantons, they did succeed in alienating Charleston. With from forty to fifty possemen "patrolling" their town, Charleston's angry citizenry telegraphed Tombstone, "Doc Holliday, the Earps, and about 40 or 50 more of the filth of Tombstone, are here, armed with Winchester rifles and revolvers, and patrolling our streets, as we believe, for no good purpose. Last night and today they have been stopping good, peaceable citizens on all roads leading to our town, nearly paralyzing the business of our place. Some of them, we believe, are thieves, robbers, and murderers. Please come here and take them where they belong."[27]

Such events could not go unnoticed. In New Mexico, the *Optic* reported:

> Holliday's High Handed Hoodoo.

> Doc Holliday and the Earp boys are at it again in Arizona, and are acting a great deal worse than they ever dared to carry on in Las Vegas. The other day these frontier terrors got acquainted with Uncle Sam and gained his affections sufficiently to secure the appointment to positions called United States Marshals. Under this coat of authority, they swooped down on a little camp called Charleston and raised the awfullest din the poor people had ever listened to. There were forty men in the party and they felt that they could stand off a regiment of cavalry. They found no cowboys, but had lots of fun.[28]

The Charleston siege telegram has been denounced as a fake to discredit Earp; however, Parsons, an acknowledged Earp supporter, confirms the raid's impact on Charleston. "Met the Earp posse on outskirts Charleston returning to town, their parties having surrendered at Tombstone. Charleston looked almost like a deserted village and as though having undergone a siege."[29] Although writers often portray Parsons as an impartial observer, his hatred of the Democratic party colored his view of the Earps. By his own admission, he was willing to and did believe only the worst of Democrats, particularly those from the South: "Garfield...represents the best interest of the country. The Republican party saved it 17 years ago. I have some fears of a solid south from the action of that south....The old issues are not forgotten. I can now see the hollowness of southern chivalry....What other government under heaven would have granted Amnesty to its traitors....The South broke the law but didn't suffer the penalty it should have....Perhaps the Republican party the party of law and peace will be called upon again in an emergency."[30]

John Ringo was arraigned on robbery charges on January 27. On January 31 he was freed on bail once more.[31] Tensions would continue high throughout February. On the fourteenth Sheriff Behan took the Earps to Contention for another hearing. Surrounded by their heavily armed cohorts, the justice was intimidated and refused to bind them over for trial. They, too, emerged free men.

The battle lines were drawn.

CHAPTER TWENTY-ONE

"Blood will surely come."

Weather rainy and very disagreeable. Bad time on street today. Policeman just prevented Ben Maynard and [Dan] Tipton from shooting one another. Yesterday Earps were taken to Contention to be tried for killing of Clanton. Quite a posse went out. Many of Earp's [sic] friends accompanied armed to the teeth, they came back later in day, the good people below beseeching them to leave and try case here. A bad time is expected again in town at any time. Earps on one side of street with their friends and Ike Clanton and Ringo with theirs on the other side—watching each other. Blood will surely come.[1]

Parsons' February 15, 1882, journal entry proved prophetic. Only one side could remain in Tombstone, and by March the citizens had had enough. Living in fear of the Earps, seeing the courts cowed by armed men, convinced that legal justice was impossible, they resorted once more to the gun.

Many old-timers in Tombstone told local writer Grace McCool that the vigilantes drew lots from a hat to decide who would kill the Earps.

One of them had a black cross on it.[2] That assertion, if true, is of great importance. On March 18 Ringo sent his attorney, Briggs Goodrich, with a message to Wyatt Earp, stating that he had no grudge against him and only wanted to be left alone. Coming from John Ringo, an avowed enemy, the message might have raised suspicions, but if it did the Earps took no precautions. That same night, violence again struck their family. Under the headline, "THE DEADLY BULLET," the *Epitaph* reported:

> At 10:50 Saturday night while engaged in playing a game of billiards in Campbell & Hatch's billiard parlor, on Allen street between Fourth and Fifth, Morgan Earp was shot through the body by an unknown assassin. At the time the shot was fired he was playing a game of billiards with Bob Hatch, one of the proprietors of the house and was standing with his back to the glass door in the rear of the room that opens out upon the alley that leads straight through the block along the west side of A.D. Otis & Co's store to Fremont street. This door is the ordinary glass door with four panes in the top in place of panels. The two lower panes are painted, the upper ones being clear. Anyone standing outside can look over the painted glass and see anything going on in the room just as though standing in the open door. At the time the shot was fired the deceased must have been standing within ten feet of the door, and the assassin standing near enough to see his position, took aim for about the middle of his person, shooting through the upper portion of the whitened glass. The bullet entered the right side of the abdomen, passing through the spinal column, completely shattering it, emerging on the left side, passing the length of the room and lodging in the thigh of Geo. A. B. Berry, who was standing by the stove, inflicting a painful flesh wound. Instantly after the first shot a second was fired through the top of the upper glass which passed across the room and lodged in the wall near the ceiling over the head of Wyatt Earp, who was sitting a spectator of the game. Morgan fell instantly upon the first fire and lived only about one hour.[3]

Ringo's message to Earp hints that he knew some kind of action was planned against the family, an action which he obviously wanted no part of. It could have been intended as a veiled warning. Certainly it was too obvious to have been intended as an alibi. Whatever the case, it could only have heightened suspicion that he had, indeed, played a role in Morgan Earp's death.

Somewhat surprisingly the inquest named not one, but five men as Morgan Earp's killers: Pete Spence, Frank Stilwell, John Doe Freis, an Indian named Charlie, and another Indian, name unknown. Disregarding the spectacle this quintet must have made in the alley, the coroner's jury named them largely on the testimony of Marietta Spence, Pete's wife, who said they had all been at her home the night of the killing. Marietta also testified that her husband beat her. Traywick adds the unsubstantiated details that Ringo held the assassins' horses and that Stilwell claimed to have been the triggerman.[4]

Was Stilwell the gunman as charged? His movements at the time are well documented. On Sunday, March 19, he arrived at Tucson to appear before the grand jury on the stage robbery charges.[5] Bob Paul, who had no reason to lie for Stilwell, later testified that he had seen him in Tucson about three o'clock in the morning, a mere four hours after Earp's shooting. Yet Marietta Spence placed him in Tombstone at midnight. That would allow him only three hours at night to ride the seventy-five miles to Tucson. Upon reaching Tucson he would almost immediately have had to find someone who knew him. Why would he make such a ride when he could create an alibi far more easily by having some of his so-called cronies lie for him?

In any event, Stilwell was never allowed to prove his innocence. On the morning of March 21, his body was found in the railroad yard. The *Epitaph* reported that on the evening of March 20, Morgan Earp's body had arrived in Tucson, accompanied by Wyatt, Virgil, and Warren Earp, Doc Holliday, Sherman MacMasters, and "Turkey Creek Jack" Johnson. The party was reported to be "heavily armed with shotguns and revolvers." The *Epitaph* continued, "A few minutes before the train started Stilwell and Ike Clanton (brother of Wm. Clanton who was killed in Tombstone by the Earps) went to the depot to meet a man by the name of McDowell who was to have come in as a witness before the grand jury. On their arrival at the depot they saw the Earp party walking on the platform. Stilwell advised Clanton to leave at once saying they wanted to kill him."[6]

Writers dealing with Earp have repeated a story created by Lake that Wyatt confronted and killed Stilwell. "Wyatt surprised Stilwell, chased him down the railroad track and loaded him with buckshot. Doc Holliday put a few rounds into him for good measure...."[7] The pro-Earp *Epitaph*, however, makes it clear that the killing was more like a gangland hit than a one-on-one confrontation: "Four of the armed men who were on the platform soon followed. One was described as a slender, light complexioned man wearing a white hat. Just as the train was leaving six shots were heard in the locality of the assassination, but attracted no particular attention and nothing was known of the tragedy until this morning when the body was discovered." Stilwell had been shot six times—four rifle balls and two loads of buckshot. One charge of buckshot fired through his breast "must have been delivered close, as the coat was powder burnt, and six buckshot holes within a radius of three inches. Stilwell had a pistol on his person which was not discharged. He evidently was taken unaware...."[8] In time, murder indictments were handed down for Wyatt and Warren Earp, Holliday, Sherman MacMasters, and John Johnston.

Having robbed and murdered Stilwell, the Earps made their way back to Tombstone, only to flee when Behan attempted to arrest them.[9] The following day Behan took a posse in pursuit. Parsons, influenced by the Republican *Epitaph*, angrily noted, "Excitement again this morning. Sheriff went out with a posse supposedly to arrest the Earp party, but they will never do it. The Cow-boy element is backing him strongly. John Ringo being one of the party. There is a prospect of a bad time and there are about three men who deserve to get it in the back of the neck. Terrible thing, this, for our town, but the sooner it is all over with the better."[10]

The Earps were on the run, but they found time to pause at Pete Spence's wood camp the morning of March 22. The *Epitaph* reported:

STILL ANOTHER KILLING.
A Mexican Found Dead This Morning
The Act Supposed to be the work of the Earps

This afternoon Theodore D. Judah came in from Pete Spence's wood camp in the South Pass of the Dragoons and gave an Epitaph reporter the following information: Yesterday morning, about 11 o'clock, Wyatt and Warren Earp, Doc Holliday, McMasters, Texas Jack and Johnson, came into camp and inquired for Pete Spence and Indian Charley; also as to the number of men there and their whereabouts. Judah informed them that Spence was in Tombstone and that a Mexican named Florentine was looking for some stock which had strayed away. Judah indicated the direction taken by the Mexican and the party immediately left as directed, passing over a hill which hid them from view.

A few minutes later ten or twelve shots were heard. Florentine not returning, this morning Judah proceeded in search of him and found the body not far from camp, riddled with bullets. Judah immediately came to town with the news. He states that had the sheriff's posse come a mile further they would have had all the information they wanted.[11]

The coroner stated that Florentine Cruz was probably laying on the ground when he was shot. Possibly he was sleeping. He had been shot ten or twelve times, and all of the wounds were in the back.

It was big news. Assuming that Cruz and Indian Charley were one and the same, all of Arizona was surprised that the Earps had killed him. The most surprised Arizonan of all, however, might have been Indian Charley. The day after the Earps murdered Florentine Cruz, the *Epitaph* reported, "Deputy Sheriff Bell arrived from Charleston today in charge of Indian Charlie [sic], charged with the murder of Morgan Earp."[12] If Florentine Cruz was not Indian Charley, who was he? Why was he killed? Was it simply a case of mistaken identity, or is it possible that, as some have asserted, Cruz had witnessed the Philpott killing and could place Holliday at the scene? Nothing appears certain except that the Earps had killed the wrong man.

Parsons felt that it was capital work, however, no matter who had been killed. He confided to his diary, "More killing by the Earp party. Hope they'll keep it up...."[13]

The *Epitaph,* desperate to somehow justify the brutal murders hit upon a unique concept. The opportunity arose on March 25 when a report that the Earps had killed Curly Bill arrived in Tombstone. The "Battle of Burleigh," as it was called, described how Curly Bill and eight "cowboys" had ambushed the Earp party as they rode down on Burleigh Spring. Citing an anonymous informant, the *Epitaph* alleged that Wyatt had killed Brocius.[14] The *Nugget* disputed the account, and in time the *Epitaph* itself reported the true story:

On Friday last, Dick Wright, better known in Tombstone as 'Whistling Dick' and Tony Kraker were out on the mesa west of Drew's ranch below Contention, in search of strayed mules, and just at evening they rode down to the spring when they were suddenly confronted by four men with leveled guns pointed directly at them. Tony sung out, 'what are you doing there you lop-eared Missourian?' This original salutation disarmed the cowboys, who lowered their guns and invited Tony and Dick to get down and make themselves at home, which they did. Sitting around the campfire the four cowboys told them their version of the story which was as follows: They said they were camped at the spring when they saw the Earp party ride down, and not knowing how they stood with them they thought that they would

Give Them a Shot

just for luck so they blazed away and shot off the pommel of Wyatt Earp's saddle and killed the horse that Texas Jack was riding. They said that not one of the Earp party charged upon them but Wyatt, the balance all running away. Wyatt dismounted and fired his gun at them but without effect. Texas Jack is said to have jumped up behind one of the other boys a la Mexicana, and off they went as rapidly as they could. These are about as near the two sides of the fight as can be got at this time.[15]

Breakenridge confirmed this version, identifying two of the men as Alex Arnold and Pink Truly.[16]

Pursuit of the fleeing Earps proved futile. The *Nugget* published a full report of the chase:

THE POSSE'S PURSUIT.
Return of Sheriff Behan and Depu-
ties—A Fruitless Search for the
Absconding Earps.

The Sheriff's posse returned from the pursuit of the Earp party yesterday evening at 5 o'clock. The bronzed and weather-beaten appearance of the posse—more especially of Sheriff Behan and Under-Sheriff Woods—was ample proof of the arduous and exhausting nature of the trip which had just been brought to an unsuccessful termination. The posse left Tombstone Monday morning [March 27] at 5 o'clock, numbering 15 men all told, including the Sheriff and Under-Sheriff. The trail of the fugitives was struck by the pursuers four miles from town, and led in the direction of Summit Station, in Dragoon Pass, to which point the posse proceeded with all possible speed, fearing that the Earp party had boarded a passing train at the station and left the country. Arriving there, however, it was ascertained that the fugitives had crossed the railroad and proceeded north toward Hooker's ranch. The pursuers immediately pushed forward, and camped near Winchester District Monday night. They started early Tuesday morning, and

ARRIVED AT HOOKER'S

at 7 a. m., where it was learned that the party they were in quest of had been the day previous and had left on Monday evening. The proprietor of the ranch utterly refused to impart any information concerning the direction taken by his whilom guests of the day before; said he didn't know and wouldn't tell if he did know, and concluded by saying, 'D—n the officers and d—n the law.' He furnished the posse with food for themselves and animals—for which he received liberal compensation—but positively refused to supply them with fresh horses. It was also learned by Sheriff Behan that Tipton had here joined the Earps, and that Hooker had outfitted the entire party with provisions, fresh horses, etc. After breakfast at the ranch, and being unable to discover the trail of the fugitives, Behan and Woods started for Fort Grant, 25 miles distant, with the intention of securing the services of Government scouts as trailers, the remainder of the posse mean while continuing their efforts to discover the trail in the mountains west and north of Hooker's. On arrival at Grant, Colonel Biddle who was in command, received our county officials with great cordiality, but informed them that the Indian scouts had been ordered discharged only a few days previous. Sheriff Behan offered $500 reward, but the much coveted assistance of the

SLEUTH-LIKE APACHES

could not be obtained. The discomfited officials then retraced their way to Hooker's, when, no trace of the lost trail having been discovered in their absence, the entire posse took horse and departed for Eureka Springs at the head of Aravaipa Canyon. They remained there until Wednesday morning, and becoming satisfied that the fugitives had not effected their escape in that direction, again returned to Hooker's. The Graham county cattleman was not quite so reticent as on the former visit of the posse. He now informed the Sheriff that the Earp party was much the better armed, and in case of an encounter would undoubtedly 'get away' with the Sheriff and his posse. The mountains to the south of the ranch were thoroughly scouted for traces of the fugitives, and none being found, they

PROCEEDED TO WINCHESTER DISTRICT,

where camp was made for the night and three fresh horses obtained, and from there the return trip was made yesterday.

Under-Sheriff Woods speaks in the highest terms of the treatment of the posse by the citizens of both Cochise and Graham counties, with the single exception already noted, Mr. H. C. Hooker, of the Sierra Bonita ranch, a man whom, from the large property interests he had in the country, would naturally be supposed to be in favor of upholding the constituted authorities and the preservation of law and order.[17]

Some writers cite Hooker's support for the Earps as evidence of their good work in putting down the Cowboys. Yet Hooker's contemporaries did not care for him. Commenting on Burns' *Tombstone*, Hancock wrote, "Ask some of the old timer cow-men what they think of 'Col' Hooker. I have seen Hooker's cows and unbranded calves left in the roundup when it was trimmed up and every one ready to pull out. If Hooker had stood well with his neighbors they would have cut his cows and calves with their own and brought them back as near as possible to his ranch." Nor, according to Hancock, was Hooker above buying stock whose title was shaky. "A story is told on him that he once made a deal with some of the boys for a bunch of cattle. Title was all right as long [as] they were from far enough away so as no one would claim them....There were very few of the ranchers but what would traffic with the Rustlers if they seen a bargain. It made no difference whether the stuff was stolen or not."[18]

Whatever Hooker's reason to cover for the fugitives, the result was the same. None of the Earps were ever brought to trial. They fled to Colorado, where Bob Paul attempted to extradite Holliday. While languishing in jail, Holliday told some tall tales: "...[John Behan] has five Rustlers under him as deputies. One of these men is John Ringo, who jumped on the stage of the variety theater in Tombstone one night about three weeks ago, and took all the jewels from the proprietor's wife in full view of the audience."[19] No such incident occurred.

As the Earps fled Arizona justice, further violence, perhaps linked to the Earp-Clanton feud, struck Cochise County. On the evening of March 25, M.R. Peel, George W. Cheyney, William Austin, and F.F. Hunt were seated in the office of the Tombstone Mill and Mining Company at Millville, across the San Pedro River from Charleston. At twenty minutes past eight someone fumbled at the door, then struck it a blow. Austin shouted for the men to come in. The door burst open and two men armed with rifles barged in. The leader fired point blank into Peel's chest. The second man fired at Austin, who escaped death by dropping to the floor. The killers turned and ran to their horses, which a third man was holding.[20]

The intruders made no attempt to rob their victims.[21] Indeed, the crime has overtones of premeditated murder. Peel's father, Judge B.L. Peel, placed at least part of the blame on Holliday's old friend, Six Shooter Smith; as the Tombstone Mill and Mining Company had taken an anti-Earp position, the claim may have merit.[22]

Suspicion also fell on Billy Grounds and Zwing Hunt, two minor cattle thieves who had been indicted the previous fall for stealing stock from Robert Woolf and James Pursley. When word reached Tombstone that Grounds and Hunt were holed up at J.J. Chandler's milk ranch, Billy Breakenridge gathered a posse made up of jailer Hugh Allen and two miners, Jack Young and John Gillespie. At Chandler's, Breakenridge detailed Young to watch the farther of two cabins while the others surrounded the nearer. On reaching their positions, the posse hailed the cabin, and all hell broke loose.

"Bull" Lewis, John Elliot, and a third man named Caldwell emerged quickly from the house. Zwing Hunt followed and immediately turned loose his gun, firing three bullets into Gillespie. Hunt dodged around to the south side of the cabin where he shot Allen, the bullet creasing his neck. Allen returned Hunt's fire, knocking him to the ground with a bullet in the chest. Young, rushing to help his friends, caught a bullet in the thigh and went down. While Hunt was busy decimating the posse, Grounds leaped out of the cabin and began shooting at Breakenridge with his Winchester. Billy fired one barrel of his shotgun into the crouching outlaw's head and chest, and the fight was over.

Gillespie was dead, and Grounds died the next morning. Hunt survived his wounds and escaped custody from the Cochise County Hospital, only to be killed by Apaches on May 31. Smith had already escaped to New Mexico. He died June 23, mortally wounded by a posse the day before in LaSalle County, Texas.

Of the Earp party, Holliday appears to have died first. He coughed out his dissipated life at Glenwood Springs, Colorado, on November 8, 1887. Warren Earp went on to a criminal career spotted by violence. Johnny Boyette, a cowboy he had bullied, finally killed him on July 6, 1900, at Willcox, Arizona. Virgil Earp, a lifelong cripple, died of pneumonia on October 19, 1905, at Goldfield, Nevada. Others of the group, notably MacMasters, Johnson, and Tipton, are said by various writers to have come to violent ends, but that has not been confirmed.

As for Wyatt Earp, the end came many years later from a lingering cancer of the prostate. His entire career was dotted by petty crime. In the 1920s the aging Earp convinced at least two writers, both concerned more with sales than truth, of his importance in "cleaning up Arizona." Despite much of that fiction's having been disproved, the myth persists. Earp died January 13, 1929.

With the departure of the Earps and John Clum's yellow journalism, the "Curse of the Cowboys" abruptly ended. Tradition attributes the calm to the Earps' having killed Curly Bill and, thus, eliminating that threat to the border. Indeed, the troubles had drawn the attention of President Chester A. Arthur. John Ringo, however, remained. His next court appearance was scheduled for May, and it is likely that he visited his sisters in San Jose during April. He could well have stayed in California and, as the Earps did, avoided the possibility of prison. Ringo returned to face his accusers.

CHAPTER
TWENTY-TWO

======➤●✦=======

"Many friends will mourn him…"

On May 8, 1882, the *Epitaph* noted, "Jack Ringo is in Town." He had returned for his trial, evidently from an April 1882 trip to see his family in San Jose, California. His sister, Fanny, had married Frank Moses Jackson on November 16, 1880, and John wanted to visit them. Several notices in the *Epitaph* of letters to Ringo confirm his absence from Tombstone. An April 15 notice of a letter for "Ringe, [sic] Jno" was followed by one on April 30 for "Ringold, [sic] Jno." Another notice for Jno. Ringold on May 6, may have been a repeat of the April 30 listing.

The same day that the *Epitaph* announced Ringo's presence in Tombstone, his attorney, Briggs Goodrich, motioned for J.S. Robinson to be added as associate counsel for the defense.[1] On May 16, Cochise County's Great Register entered Ringo as number 2649. The entry listed him as a speculator, born in the United States. It incorrectly gave his residence as Tombstone and his age as thirty-nine.[2] He had barely turned thirty-two.

Both charges against Ringo were scheduled for trial on May 12.[3]

They were continued and finally tried May 18. Both cases were ordered "dismissed and the defendants bail exonerated."[4]

A free man, Ringo decided to go back to New Mexico. One of those happy to see him there was Mary Hughes, a younger sister of Jim Hughes.

> John Ringo...was an especially welcome guest at the Hughes home. He was the hero of 11-year-old Mary Hughes....Whenever Mary, scanning the country from the watchtower, saw him coming, she put on her prettiest dress and combed her glossy, black hair. John Ringo, when he spoke to her, made her feel like a great lady. He had read many books, and he told her of what he read, and thus made Mary want to learn how to read. So he taught her English from the family Bible, and Spanish from a book he had picked up in Tombstone. He taught her how to write, and she took enormous pride in copying his beautiful Spencerian chirography.[5]

Ringo had now reached the peak of his fame. His reputation remained intact, and he was well thought of by most of his contemporaries. At the same time he was still suffering from post-traumatic stress syndrome, and his efforts to blot out the flashbacks and dreams had led him to heavier drinking. That could only serve to aggravate his condition, which in turn led to growing depression and more drinking.

By late June, Ringo's bouts of depression had increased, intensified by the recent events in Cochise County. In late June or early July he returned to Tombstone, where he was reportedly on an "extended jamboree."[6] On July 2 he confided in an *Epitaph* reporter that "he was as certain of being killed, as he was of being living then. He said he might run along for a couple of years more, and may not last two days."[7]

Ringo left Tombstone on July 8, arriving at "Dial's in the South Pass of the Dragoons." From Dial's he rode on to Galeyville, where he continued drinking. Billy Breakenridge ran into him on the road.

> ...I met John Ringo in the South Pass of the Dragoon Mountains. It was shortly after noon. Ringo was very drunk, reeling in the saddle, and said he was going to Galeyville. It was in the summer and a very hot day. He offered me a drink out of a bottle half-full of whiskey, and he had another full bottle. I tasted it and it was too hot to

drink. It burned my lips. Knowing that he would have to ride nearly all night before he could reach Galeyville, I tried to get him to go back with me to the Goodrich Ranch and wait until after sundown, but he was stubborn and went on his way.[8]

The following day Ringo was found dead in Morse's Canyon. The *Epitaph's* long obituary demonstrates the public's regard for him.

DEATH OF JOHN RINGO.
His Body Found In Morse's Canyon—
Probable Suicide.

Sunday evening intelligence reached this city of the finding of the dead body of John Ringo near the mouth of Morse's Canyon in the Chiricahua mountains on Friday afternoon. There was few men in Cochise county, or southeastern Arizona better known. He was recognized by friends and foes as a recklessly brave man, who would go any distance, or undergo any hardship to serve a friend or punish an enemy. While undoubtedly reckless, he was far from being a desperado, and we know of no murder being laid to his charge. Friends and foes are unanimous in the opinion that he was a strictly honorable man in all his dealings, and that his word was as good as his bond. Many people who were intimately acquainted with him in life, have serious doubts that he took his own life, while an equally large number say that he frequently threatened to commit suicide, and that event was expected at any time. The circumstances of the case hardly leave any room for doubt as to his self destruction. He was about 200 feet from water, and was acquainted with every inch of the country, so that it was almost impossible for him to lose himself. He was found in the midst of a clump of oaks, springing from the same stem, but diverging outward so as to leave an open space in the center. On top of the main stem and between the spreading boughs, was a large stone, and on this pedestal he was found sitting, with his body leaning backward and resting against a tree. He was found by a man named John Yost [sic] who was acquainted with him for years both in this Territory and Texas. Yost is working for Sorgum Smith, and was employed hauling wood. He was driving a team along the road, and noticed a man in the midst of the clump of trees, apparently asleep. He passed on without further investigation, but on looking back, saw his dog smelling of the man's face and snorting. This excited curiosity and he stopped the team, alighted and proceeded to investigate. He found the lifeless body of John Ringo, with a hole large enough to admit two fingers about half way between the right eye and ear, and a hole correspondingly large on top of his head, doubtless the outlet of the fatal bullet. The revolver was firmly clenched in his hand, which is almost conclusive evidence that death was instantaneous. His rifle rested against a tree and one of his cartridge belts was turned upside down. Yost immediately gave the alarm and in about 15 minutes eleven men were on the spot. The Subjoined Statement was made by eye witnesses to Coroner Matthews:

TURKEY OR MORSE'S MILL CREEK

Statement for the information of the Coroner and Sheriff of Cochise County, Arizona: there was found by the undersigned, John Yost, the body of a man in a clump of oak trees, about 20 yds. north from the road leading to Morse's mill, and about a quarter of a mile west of the house of B. F. Smith. The undersigned viewed the body and found it in a sitting posture, facing west, the head inclined to the right. There was a bullet hole on the top of the head on the left side. There is, apparently, a part of the scalp gone, including a small portion of the forehead and part of the hair. This looks as if cut out by a knife. These are the only marks of violence visible on the body. Several of the undersigned identify the body as that of John Ringo, well known in Tombstone. He was dressed in light hat, blue shirt, vest, pants and drawers. On his feet were a pair of hose and an undershirt torn up so as to protect his feet. He had evidently traveled but a short distance in this foot gear. His revolver he grasped in his right hand, his rifle resting against the tree close to him. He had on two cartridge belts, the belt for revolver cartridges being buckled on upside down. The undernoted property was found with him and on his person; one Colt's revolver, calibre 45, No. 222, containing five cartridges; one Winchester rifle octagon barrel, calibre 45, model 1876, No. 21,986, containing a cartridge in the breech and ten in the magazine; 1 cartridge belt, containing 9 rifle cartridges; 1 cartridge belt, containing 2 revolver cartridges; 1 silver watch of American Watch company, No. 9339, with silver chain attached; two dollars and sixty cents ($2.60) in money; 6 pistol cartridges in pocket; 5 shirt studs; 1 small pocket knife; 1 tobacco pipe; 1 comb; 1 block matches; 1 small piece tobacco. There is also a portion of a letter from Messrs. Hereford & Zabriskie, attorneys at law, Tucson, to the deceased, John Ringo. The above property is left in the possession of Frederick Ward, teamster between Morse's mill and Tombstone.

The body of the deceased was buried close to where it was found.

When found deceased had been dead about twenty-four hours. Thomas White, John Blake, John W. Bradfield, B.F. Smith, A.E. Lewis, A.S. Neighbors, James Morgan, Robert Boller, Frank McKenney, W.J. Dowell, J.C. McGray, John Yoast, Fred Ward.

From Fred Ward, who arrived in the city on Sunday evening, an EPITAPH reporter learned that the general impression prevailing among people in the Chiricahuas is that his horse wandered off somewhere, and he started off on foot to search for him; that his boots began to hurt him, and he pulled them off and made moccasins of his under-shirt. he could not have been suffering for water, as he was within 200 feet of it and not more than 700 feet from Smith's house. Mrs. Morse and Mrs. Young passed by where he was lying Thursday afternoon, but supposed it was some man asleep, and took no further notice of him. The inmates of Smith's house heard a shot about 3 o'clock Thursday evening, and it is more than likely that that is the time the rash deed was done. He was on an extended jam-boree the last time he was in this city, and only left here ten days ago [July 8]. He had dinner at Dial's in the South Pass of the Dragoons one week ago last Sunday, and went from there to Galeyville, where he kept on drinking heavily. We have not heard of his whereabouts after leaving Galeyville, but it is more than likely that he went to Morse's canon. He was subject to frequent fits of melan-choly and had an abnormal fear of being killed. Two weeks ago last Sunday in conversing with the writer, he said he was as certain of being killed, as he was of living then. He said he might run along for a couple of years more, and may not last two days. He was born in Texas and is very respectably connected. He removed to San Jose, California, when about sixteen years old, and Col. Coleman Younger, one of the leading citizens of that town is his grandfather.

Ringo was a second cousin to the famous Younger brothers now in the Minnesota penitentiary, for their partnership with the James boys. He has three sisters in San Jose, of whom he was passionately fond. He was about thirty-eight years old, though looking much younger, and was a fine specimen of physical manhood. Many friends will mourn him, and many others will take secret delight in learning of his death.[9]

John Ringo's death, like so much of his life, has proven controversial. Since his demise in 1882, theorists have named a number of men as his killer. The most popular theory in recent years is that Wyatt Earp, still seeking vengeance for his brother Morgan, returned to Arizona to kill Ringo. Among the various others blamed for murdering Ringo have been Doc Holliday, Buckskin Frank Leslie, and a young gambler nick-named Johnny-Behind-The-Deuce.[10]

Burrows opts for suicide.[11] He quotes a letter from Charles Ringo to William K. Hall which states in part, "I have another story from a Mrs. Travis whose husband was of that family, that the sisters would not let him in the house. You will notice that the body was left in Arizona and not brought back."[12] Based upon that and other correspondence from Charles Ringo, Burrows concludes that John Ringo attempted to return to his family but met a grim reception and despondently went back to Arizona, where he killed himself.[13] Traywick is silent on this incident.

Burrows further refers several times to letters Ringo received from his family and quotes John's nephew as stating that he never wrote back. That in itself poses an interesting question, for if John did not write to his family, how did they know where to find him once he left Missouri in the early 1870s? Moreover, if his family had disowned him, why was he found with a letter from Fanny Jackson in his pocket? The *Citizen* clearly noted, "In one of the pockets [of his coat] were three photographs and a card bearing the name Mrs. Jackson."[14]

The statement made for the coroner has also provoked controversy, both for what it did and did not say. The points of contention may be summarized as the report's failure to mention that a bullet had been fired from the pistol, its failure to mention powder burns, and its description of "...a bullet hole in the right temple, the bullet coming out of the top of the head on the left side. There is apparently a part of the scalp gone including a small portion of the forehead and part of the hair. This looks as if cut out by a knife." If John Ringo's gun had not been fired, he did not commit suicide; and if he did not commit suicide, who killed him?

The weaknesses in the statement for the coroner can be explained at least in part by the backgrounds of the fifteen witnesses. None of them were physicians. They were describing what they saw as completely as they could for the coroner. Concerning their failure to mention the discharged weapon, Ringo's obituary in the Tucson papers provided some additional information: "The pistol *with one chamber emptied* [emphasis added] was found in his clenched fist."[15] Such papers as the *Phoenix Gazette* and the *Citizen* picked up that news release. The *Phoenix Gazette* noted:

> John Ringgold, one of the best known men in southwestern [sic] Arizona, was found dead in Morse's canyon, in the Chiricahua mountains last Friday. He evidently committed suicide. He was known in this section as 'King of the Cowboys' and was fearless in the extreme. He had many staunch friends and bitter enemies. The pistol, with one chamber emptied, was found in his clenched fist. He shot himself in the head, the bullet entering on the right side, between the eye and ear, and coming out on top of the head. Some members of his family reside at San Jose California.—*Citizen* [16]

Witness Robert M. Boller also confirmed that Ringo's pistol had been fired. "His pistol with one empty shell was caught in his watch chain...."[17] Clearly the failure to mention the discharged shell was simply that, a failure, which was corrected when the weapon was examined later.

The report's failure to mention powder burns could have resulted from either of two possible causes. First, as with the cartridge, the untrained observers might simply have overlooked any powder burns. Second, by the time Yost found Ringo, the body was beginning to decay in Arizona's summer heat. It was swollen and blackened. Boller recalled the "body was in such condition, that we buried it right there...."[18]

Finally, despite the strange exit wound, the men who found Ringo never doubted that he had killed himself. Hancock recorded, "[A.E.] 'Bull' Lewis who was in the coroner's jury told me there was absolutely no question but what Ringo committed suicide."[19] Boller recalled, "There is no question in the minds of any of the five [sic] who found him but what [he] committed suicide."[20]

Ringo's horse wandered until July 25. "A son of Mr. B.F. Smith, says the Tombstone Independent, found John Ringo's horse, on Tuesday last, about two miles from where deceased was found. His saddle was still upon him with Ringo's coat upon the back of it. In one of the pockets were three photographs and a card bearing the name of 'Mrs. Jackson.' It seems strange that the horse should have wandered about all this time without having been discovered before. Mr. Smith brought the horse into town with him. It is a bay, weighing about 1,000 pounds."[21]

Misfortune hounded Ringo's friends. William Claiborne somehow took the notion that Frank Leslie had killed Ringo. On November 18, 1882, Claiborne rode into Tombstone, intent on killing Leslie. Leslie's aim was more accurate, however, and he killed Claiborne for his trouble.

On December 13, 1884, the *Arizona Silver Belt* reported, "From the Willcox Stockman we learn that Joe Hill, a well-known cattle man, met with a fatal accident at Bowie, on Wednesday [December 3] of last week. While driving cattle into a corral, riding at a full gallop, his horse stumbled and fell. Mr. Hill was thrown violently to the ground and received internal injuries from which he died within an hour."[22]

Pete Spence, according to modern writers, so feared the wrath of Wyatt Earp that he surrendered himself to the law and was sent to the Yuma penitentiary. Traywick, for instance, states, "Terrified at these events, Spencer fled to Tucson where a territorial court sentenced him to a long term in the Territorial Prison at Yuma."[23] There, according to these authors, he would be safe from Earp. Contemporary documents do not support that story. Spence did enter Yuma, as convict 885, but not until June 10, 1893. He gave his age as forty and his occupation as teamster. The charge was aggravated assault. The *Yuma Times* commented, "Pete Spence, who was sentenced to five years in the Yuma Penitentiary, is a well-known character in Arizona; a man that never knew what danger meant, and during the early days of Tombstone was disliked and feared by the famous Earp gang. Pete is a generous man and his great fault lies in the too ready use of his gun."[24] Spence was unconditionally pardoned on November 29, 1894. He died of natural causes on January 13, 1914.

Fate was less kind to Ike Clanton. On June 1, 1887, J.V. Brighton was attempting to arrest Clanton for cattle rustling. Brighton later claimed that Clanton drew his Winchester from its saddle scabbard and tried to flee. Why Clanton would attempt to draw a rifle when his pistol was readily at hand is unknown. Brighton shot him in the back, fatally. Ike's brother, Phin, was charged at the same time was. Phin was sent to Yuma but pardoned when authorities learned he had been convicted by perjured testimony.

John Ringo's life ended at about three o'clock in the afternoon on July 13, 1882. His journey into folklore had begun.

CHAPTER
TWENTY-THREE

═══◄►◄═══

"...bitter and conspiratorial silence..."

In recent years historians have questioned John Ringo's character as evidenced by his relations with his immediate family. The controversy is largely due to two men, the first of whom was Charles Ringo. Charles informed author Jack Burrows that John's sisters denied him entry to their home in 1881.[1] In the same letter, however, Charles contradicted himself: "In 1881 he [John Ringo] came home and went back to sell his cattle and then come back." Neither version is necessarily more believable than the other. Burrows accepts the former. Traywick, too, accepts the first account, but as he offers no footnotes, his source is unknown.[2]

Of Charles Ringo, friend and family member David Leer Ringo would write that he was neither a genealogist nor a historian. "He loved a good story, whether factual or not..."[3] Building on letters provided by Charles, Burrows alleged that John's sisters never forgave his escapades.[4] Mary Enna Ringo, portrayed as an "angry and sanctimonious spinster," appears as the driving force among his sisters.[5] "The bitter and conspiratorial silence," Burrows asserts, "endured."[6] It did not, however, endure more than a few days after Ringo's death. On July 25, 1882, the *Epitaph* reported that it "yesterday received a letter from Miss Emma [sic: Enna] Ringo, sister of the late John Ringo, in which she says that John was born in Indiana, in 1850, and was thirty-two years old at the time of his death. Col. Younger was an uncle by marriage, and consequently Ringo was no relative of the Younger boys."[7]

That article shatters the illusion of a family shamed and disgraced by their brother. Indeed, Enna had provided biographical information to a newspaper which she undoubtedly knew could, and probably would, publish it. Obviously she had neither disowned him nor attempted to conceal their relation.

Yet, in later years, the Ringo family would lapse into silence. Why? According to Burrows, Charles Ringo informed him in 1971 that Enna had destroyed everything she could find linking John to Texas and Arizona. Burrows also references Charles' alleged conversation with Frank Cushing, in which Cushing, at Enna's direction, threatened to take legal action against a Florida relative who wished to publish an article on John.[8] Based on that information, Burrows determined that John's sisters appeared "humorless and lacking in introspective powers."[9]

Actually, John's sisters knew little of his activities in Texas and Arizona beyond the fact that he was in the cattle business. Little, that is, until 1934, when the Ringo research group was being founded. One of the group's earliest members was Minerva Letton, of Valrico, Florida. On September 15, 1934, Mrs. Letton wrote to David L. Ringo, "You ask me to write about 'John Ringo of Tombstone.' Do you know that Charles Ringo (of San Fran - and NJ) *found him*? I did not know a thing about 'the big brave bandit' until Charles wrote me all about him, and told me to read Walter Noble Burns' book."[10]

At David Ringo's request, Mrs. Letton drafted a short monograph titled "One Honorable Outlaw":

> John Ringo of Tombstone Arizona was one of the greatest and most colorful outlaws of the Southwest. Numerous books written on that section call him 'the honorable outlaw,' 'the gentleman outlaw,' and the 'intellectual outlaw.' So really 'Cousin John' is not a bad fellow to read about.
>
> 'Cousin John'…yes, his descent has been proven, and he was really and truly one of our Ringo family, one of whom we are not ashambed [sic]. Even tho fate tossed him into a

regrettable role, he lived it as a gentleman, and died with the respect of all who knew him.

When merely a boy, John Ringo's only brother was killed in a 'cattle war' in a western state. John avenged his death in the way such things were done, and left home to escape the law. For a while he was a vagabond, but soon formed a close friendship with the bold and jovial 'Curly Bill,' which lasted as long as he lived. 'Curly Bill' was something of a mediaeval robber baron, and could call a hundred men to arms in a day. He 'rustled cattle' from Mexican ranches across the border where a thousand head would not be missed when taken at a time. John Ringo became 'Curly Bill's' right-hand-man, and some say 'the brains.' Of course John Ringo took part in the raids, drank and gambled with his associates, but he remained a man apart, preserving something of the dignity of his inheritance.

He was a tall, dark, straight, commanding figure and always had two ivory handled six-shooters at his side. He was absolutely fearless, afraid of no man, but had the highest reverence for womankind. If any man made an unkind remark about any woman, good or bad, in his presence, he had to 'eat his words, or fight, that was John Ringo's way.'

He was the trusted friend of high officials. When he gave his word, they knew he would live up to it, or die trying. He thought nothing of riding horseback all night long over dangerous roads to aid someone who had befriended him.

John Ringo was miserably ashambed [sic] of the life he led, but found no way out of it. He felt that he had disgraced his family, and did not want them to know. In that he misjudged us. Knowing the facts, we his kinsmen feel no shame in calling him 'our cousin.'

The manner in which he met death remains a mystery. His grave is high on the bank of Turkey Creek Canon. Up this steep embankment his friends carried enough smooth stones and boulders from the creek bed to form a giant mound twelve feet long, four feet wide and four feet high. This is eloquent proof of the love and respect they had for him. I know of no other grave in that section marked in like manner, it was their silent, impressive way of giving honor where honor was due.

Shortly afterwards, one of John Ringo's associates lost his life while trying to avenge Ringo's death.

Even now, John Ringo's ghost is frequently seen in that valley...so the natives say.

> John Ringo was born May 3, 1850, died July 14, 1883
> [sic] and in between…he lived….[11]

With the notation that, as is clearly evident, she had drawn upon Burns, Mrs. Letton sent a copy of the monograph to John's sisters, Mattie and Enna, for comments. A response was quickly forthcoming. On October 5, 1934, they wrote:

> We protest very strongly against what you have written about our brother. In the first place we don't consider that he was an outlaw, he was a cowboy and had stock ranches in Texas for several years. He did not leave San Jose on account of any crime he had committed, he went to Southern California with a harvesting outfit and from there wandered into Arizona and Texas. The story of his only brother being killed is entirely false. Albert lived at home and helped his mother until he was taken with tuberculosis and after a lingering illness died at the age of nineteen years.
>
> When we know and can prove that the statement about his having to leave the country was false how do we know but that the other statements are false also? No doubt he lived a cowboy life for several years—gambled and carried firearms as all men did in those frontier towns—but we don't think he was half as bad as he was painted, but if he was why bring it up when he has been dead for 52 years and cannot refute any of your statements. He visited us in San Jose in 1880 and was a fine upright gentleman.
>
> I thought this society of the Ringo Clan was formed to promote a friendly feeling among the members. How can that be done if in the first issue of your paper you publish something detrimental about one of the family! [I]t isn't pleasant for us to contemplate and many people would know nothing about him if you hadn't taken the trouble to look it up.
>
> I think it would be better to give an account of some prominent man who has led a good life and left a good example to follow.
>
> We sincerely hope you will see this matter in the same light that we do and write something else that will not cause the unhappiness that this will.
>
> We cannot understand how any one in a friendly society would go back 52 years to hunt up something to write against a person—you had better spend your time finding

out good things to say about them.[12]

Mattie and Enna sent David Ringo a copy of their letter. Mrs. Letton agreed to withhold the monograph, and David did not publish it. In a letter to David, Mrs. Letton lamented, "I regret it as much as you—but *we* did *not 'hunt up'* the data and publish the book. It has been *public* property in all libraries of any size for 7 years. If it wronged them, they should have settled it with the publishers years ago and had the book withdrawn....I am so thankful I sent them a copy 'before it was published'—if I hadn't, I wonder what they would have *done to us*....Honestly, I am almost afraid to write to Mrs. Cushing and Miss Ringo fearing my apology will be worse than the offense."[13]

Clearly, although Mrs. Letton feared a legal action, none was threatened. The clash effected her greatly, but not nearly as much as it did Mattie and Enna, who began their own search for the truth. On November 5 they wrote a second letter to David Ringo and Mrs. Letton:

> We must apologize for holding up the printing of your paper but we did not receive the letter. Miss Ringo had moved and the letter was missent so we did not receive it until the day before we wrote to you.
>
> We want to thank you both for withholding the article about our brother. We still feel it would just be spreading the stories about him. After receiving Mrs. Letton's letter we read the book 'Tombstone' and found even more untruthful things about him, he was not related to the Younger boys at all, an aunt of ours married Mr. Coleman Younger but that did not make him a relative. The book stated that he was John's grandfather.
>
> We went to Tombstone to investigate for ourselves, we talked with several men who had known John although they were younger than he. They all spoke very well of him, said he was not as bad as he was painted and that when he was sober was a perfect gentleman but when he was drinking he was ugly. No doubt he felt remorseful for neglecting his family.
>
> The men to whom we talked said Mr. Walter Burns was around there for several days asking questions about early days then went away and wrote the book. If the rest of the book is as untruthful as the chapters about John it is a mere fiction founded on a few facts.

> We took quite a long trip this summer returning a few days ago when we found the letters from both of you. We want to thank you both for your kindly letters and thank Mr. D.L. Ringo for the efforts he made to get his letter to us quickly. [14]

They closed the letter cordially, "Wishing the Ringo Society every success."

Yet the rumor of a threatening letter spread through the family. May Ringo King would write to Joanna Green, "One reason you never see any stories about his parentage was because he never talked about his family who were ashamed of him. During the late '20's and '30's some of the family researchers wrote his sisters in San Jose, Ca. and they wouldn't admit that he was their brother."[15] Mrs. King later clarified her intent: "This letter was mostly about [Joanna Green's] ancestor Malinda Humbert who married John Ringo a brother to Martin Ringo, Johnny's father....In the above quote I was referring mainly to Mrs. Letton...."[16]

Nor was May King the only researcher whom Minerva Letton contacted. Dr. William K. Hall, Ringo researcher and coauthor of the *Simms Family of Stafford County, Virginia*, recalled, "In one of her letters [Mrs. Letton] warned me to be extremely careful what I said about Johnny Ringo if I wrote to his sisters as they were extremely sensitive on the subject. She had apparently made some careless remark and the sisters took offense and stopped writing Mrs. Letton although I think they later patched things up."[17]

Burns' book was not the end of it. Stuart N. Lake's fictionalized glorification, *Wyatt Earp, Frontier Marshal*, published in 1931, inspired movies about Earp, and the handwriting was on the wall. John's sisters realized not only that they could not compete with Burns and Lake, but that any rebuttal they made would meet with skepticism on the one hand and draw a horde of researchers and news people on the other. They resolved to keep silent. Even when Wyatt Earp attained legendary status via television in the 1950s, the Ringo family remained mute. They might well have never spoken had it not been for a dogged researcher named Allen Erwin.

Erwin first contacted Frank Cushing around 1958. How Erwin located Cushing is unknown, but the two men corresponded over the next several years. Erwin also visited Cushing several times "in connection with his research on Johnny Ringo."[18] Cushing's sister, Zana

Cushing Batchelder, and his cousin, Frank Jackson, also maintained contact with Erwin and provided information.

Erwin was a thorough researcher, and he was determined to be the first to write a full-length book on Ringo. In 1973 Erwin wrote to historian Chuck Parsons, "Once my book is out, I am in hopes others then will follow the Ringo trail, as there should be plenty of data that they can pursue. It has cost me a small fortune and many years of time."[19] Parsons was only one of dozens of people that Erwin contacted in his search for Ringo. Cushing thought highly of him, writing that "he has always appeared to be a fine gentleman."[20] But Erwin was determined to defend his claim, and from others another portrait of him emerges.

David Leer Ringo wrote Charles in 1970 that Erwin had refused to return papers to him dealing with Martin Ringo's Mexican War experiences.[21] Other complaints are recorded. "I will attempt to find out about your copy of the Virginia City Enterprise," Cushing wrote Charles. "I hate to thing [sic: think] that he [Erwin] would stoop so low as to steal.…"[22] Another wrote, "You may not know this either, but a man in California can sure lead you astray so be Careful—he wanted to write a book on John Ringo—he's very dishonest. His name, I believe, is Erwin."[23]

Erwin played cat and mouse with those who sought information on Ringo from him, fearful perhaps that they would get a Ringo book into print before him. He voiced that concern in a letter to Chuck Parsons, "Unfortunately a couple of others have also gotten the Ringo writing fever, which some of the Ringo's [sic] have leaked information to. This always is a factor which is part of researching, which is a hindrance."[24] Erwin, however, had hit upon a scheme to keep other researchers away from what he regarded as his personal preserve. In another letter to Parsons he complained, "Two of the Ringo family are still living, a niece and a nephew of John Ringo. But they have threatened to bring a suit against me, if I mention Ringo's parents, sisters and brother."[25] This bold-faced lie, obviously at variance with Cushing's impression of Erwin as a "fine gentleman" was repeated widely in Erwin's correspondence with others. Researchers knowing the Letton story in garbled form were ready to accept it as truth. Ironically Erwin died before he could write his book.

In 1970 Charles Ringo contacted Frank Cushing. His initial letter illustrates what he knew of John Ringo.

> I have been corresponding with Dr. Hall, my cousin, about his book and what it says about John Ringo. I am very much interested in early Western history. My family knew your family in San Jose and I have heard a great deal about 'Cousin Mattie' and 'Cousin Enna'. *I did not know anything about 'Cousin John'* (emphasis added). I am enclosing a copy of a letter from him enclosing your letter of Nov. 11, 1969.
>
> Today I received my copy of the magazine 'American West' for January 1970. I am enclosing a copy of an article about 'Ringo.' I wrote to the author and sent him data from Dr. Hall's book.
>
> I checked with the Calif. Hist. Soc. and they do not have a copy of the Diary kept by your grandmother nor of your miniature. Is there any possibility of getting a copy of same. [26]

Cushing's thoughts on the article would have been evident. In one part the author noted that Ringo was a partner in Curly Bill Brocius' gang, "as miserable a gaggle of backshooters as was ever known to the western frontier...."[27] Such sentiments could hardly have inspired Cushing's confidence in the author's impartiality. He would write of the piece, "The last article I have seen about him was written by a history professor in San Jose College in 1970 [who] was not sure whether his name was Ring, Ringold or Ringo. He has spent several summers in Arizona checking on the history of that territory but could find but a few facts with which to substantiate some of the stories written about him."[28]

For Ringo's sisters life remained as it had been prior to the publication of Burns' book. The family remained close to the Youngers and attended celebrations at Coleman Younger's home.[29] Fanny never lived to see the stories of her beloved brother unfold. She died on May 13, 1932. Her husband, Frank Moses Jackson, had died on September 6, 1917. Mary Enna died on June 27, 1941. She had served as a teacher in the San Jose, California, schools for fifty years. Mattie Bell Ringo died on May 20, 1942. Her husband, William LeBaron Cushing had died on August 5, 1935. During their lifetimes the family gave no word of John's origins to outsiders.

John Ringo remains today as Burns described him, a tragic figure.

From his youth, death stalked his family. His efforts to help them drew him into the violence of the Mason County War and, later, into the notoriety of Tombstone. He has been branded a cattle thief—a charge for which not a single indictment has been located. Since his suicide in 1882 his family have been victimized, first by the unscrupulous Erwin and later by writers who have tarnished their names. Yet in the end we are left with the recollections of those contemporaries who knew him best. "Friends and foes are unanimous in the opinion that he was a strictly honorable man in his dealings, and that his word was as good as his bond."

It is a fitting epitaph for a man.

APPENDIX
The "Apocryphal" Ringo

Much has been written about John Ringo since he first attracted Walter Noble Burns' notice so many years ago. Of those vast volumes of material, a great deal paraphrases Burns. In some cases the stories were made up out of whole cloth. Although I considered all of the sources available, I have not attempted to refute all of that apocryphal literature in this work. To do so would have resulted in a book three or more times the length of the present volume. Some cases, however, do merit consideration as examples of the literature and speculation in print. One such instance is the accusation that the Town Lot Company employed Ringo either to jump claims in Tombstone or to protect already jumped claims from their rightful owners. That allegation has been stated as a fact, without the benefit of any contemporary reference. No contemporary source yet located indicates Ringo was in any way involved in the Town Lot episode. Indeed, he appears to have spent most of that period in southwestern New Mexico.

In the years when Ringo's life held more mystery than it does today, a number of historians and authors speculated on incidents in which Ringo might have been involved, based on various historical information that surfaced during their own research. Ed Bartholomew, for example, located the account of a gunfight in Wittsburg, Arkansas, in which two brothers named Williams came hunting one John Runge. Unfortunately for them they found him. The *Memphis Appeal* of March 2, 1876, under the headline "Grit To The Last" reported:

> WITTSBURG, ARK., February 29—I give you an account of a shooting affray which happened ten miles from Wittsburg in Arkansas. I was sitting on my horse talking with a young man from Illinois by the name of John C. Runge when two men, well-mounted, rode up, drew their pistols and fired at young Runge, at the same time remarking to him that he had killed their two brothers some two or three months ago, but d——d if he could kill them. Such rapid shooting with as deadly effect I never witnessed, although I served in the army four years. Both of the

strangers were killed. Runge's horse went down at the first fire, when he placed himself behind the dead animal, and two shots from his pistols killed both of his enemies. Runge then came to where I was, and told me that he had had three different shooting scrapes with this same crew, and he was getting d——d tired of the life he had to lead. He took one of the dead men's horses, gave one good look at his victims, handed me twenty dollars to bury them, and rode off. He has been pursued but has not been heard from since. I have learned that the two men killed were named Williams, from Tennessee. I hope you will publish this so that they may know what became of them.

This shooting apparently took place on February 29, and Bartholomew speculates that the man may have been Ringo due to the similarity in the names. He was not. At the time both Ringo and Cooley were in jail in Austin.

Similarly, Bartholomew also uncovered the killing of a deputy sheriff named Stokes in Cimarron, New Mexico, on March 27, 1879. Stokes and Sheriff Pete Burleson heard gunfire and traced it to the back of the Masonic Hall where they found H. Gordon, John Hill, George Hill, and Robert Leigh. Burleson demanded their weapons, some of which were delivered up, but George Hill pulled a pocket pistol and began firing. Stokes was killed. Both Hill and Leigh were wounded. John Hill fled but was captured according to the story which appeared in the Santa Fe *New Mexican* of April 5, 1879. Bartholomew theorizes that John Hill might have been Ringo.

That George Hill might have been an Olney is a valid theory. The 1886 *Fugitives From Justice* lists on "Jennings, E.T., alias Olney, alias Hillbrother, now in New Mexico; theft of a horse." The crime was committed in Blanco County. However, if Jennings was indeed one of the Olney brothers, he is more likely to have been Ed rather than George. Here the theory of John Hill's identity being Ringo unravels. George Hill's case files indicate he was still in Colfax County in late August, apparently serving time in jail while waiting for his trial. The court records from this case indicate the Hills were both charged in the shooting. Neither of the men was John Ringo, and the George Hill noted was not Joe Olney's brother.

Of more recent vintage is the speculation that John Ringo was involved in the attempt to lynch (or free) Johnny-Behind-The-Deuce on January 14, 1881, following the killing of Henry Schneider, a mining engineer. The killer, Michael O'Rourke, was taken from Charleston to Tombstone where, according to Stuart N. Lake, Wyatt Earp saved him from a lynch mob. Historian Jack DeMattos concludes that the crowd was simply a group of miners who had concluded their shift. That there was no lynch mob, concludes DeMattos, "seems to say all that is necessary about Ringo's participation in this highly overblown affair."

NOTES

Preface

1 Walter Noble Burns, *Tombstone: An Iliad of the Southwest* (1927; rpt. New York: Ballantine Books, 1974), p. 94.

2 Jeffrey J. Morey, "The Curious Vendetta of Glenn G. Boyer," *National Association of Outlaw and Lawman History Quarterly* 18, No. 4 (1994): 22. Hereafter cited as NOLA *Quarterly.*

3 Gary L. Roberts, "The West's Gunmen: II," *The American West,* March 1971, p. 20.

4 Ellsworth (Kansas) *Reporter,* August 21, 1873; Ed Bartholomew, *Wyatt Earp: The Untold Story* (Toyahvale, Texas: Frontier Book Company, 1963), pp. 64–74; Stuart N. Lake, *Wyatt Earp, Frontier Marshal* (New York: Houghton Mifflin Company, 1931), pp. 81–93. Billy Thompson shot Whitney in Ellsworth, Kansas, on August 14, 1873. No one has ever located a contemporary source mentioning Wyatt Earp's presence at the event.

5 Jack Burrows, "Ringo," *The American West* (January 1970), p. 21. Hereafter cited as Burrows, "Ringo."

6 Burns, p. 95.

7 Grace McCool to the author, October 4, 1982.

8 Jack Burrows, *John Ringo—The Gunfighter Who Never Was* (Tucson: University of Arizona Press, 1987), p. 202. Hereafter cited as Burrows, *Gunfighter.*

9 The late Al Turner authored two books dealing with the Earps, *The Earps Talk* and *The O. K. Corral Inquest.*

10 Steve Gatto, "Johnny Ringo: Land and Cattle Speculator?" NOLA *Quarterly* 18, No. 4 (1994): 9–10.

Chapter 1

1 Ben F. Traywick, *John Peters Ringo—Mythical Gunfighter* (Tombstone, Arizona: Red Marie's Bookstore, 1987), p. 2. Allen Erwin also believes that Burtis Ringo was John's ancestor. In a letter to Thos. C. Ferguson dated November 27, 1970, Erwin wrote, "The first to make any noticeable strides under the name of Ringo was Burtis Ringo, soldier of the American Revolutionary War. All the Ringo's [sic] related to John Ringo (our subject) are descendants of Burtis Ringo." Courtesy Pete Rose, who received the information from Mr. Ferguson. Copy in author's files.

2 Hannah Rector, born January 26, 1771, was the daughter of John Rector and Jane Grace Glascock. She married Burtis Ringo on February 22, 1790, in Fauquier County, Virginia. Hannah died in Fleming County, Kentucky, on July 26, 1845. See Larry King, *Rector Records* (Hendersonville, Tennessee: Privately printed, 1986), p. 8.

3 As noted in the text, the name Ringo has been spelled various ways over the centuries. For simplicity, *Ringo* has been used consistently throughout the text except where old variants are discussed. Nowhere in the old archives has the spelling Ringgold been found. This spelling was sometimes used incorrectly by the contemporary press instead of Ringo. Most recently the untenable theory has been advanced that John

Ringo of Arizona was not the John Ringgold of Texas. See C.F. Eckhardt, "The Real Johnny Ringo Legend Not Square with the Facts," *Tombstone Epitaph* (National Edition), August 1994.

[4] David Leer Ringo, *The Ringos in Europe*, Ringo Family History Series [RFHS], Vol. I, Part 1 (Alhambra, California: The Freeborn Family Organization, Inc., 1984), p. 39.

[5] Ibid., pp. 56–57.

[6] Ibid.

[7] Ibid., p. 1.

[8] The word *Walloon* has its origins in the Flemish words *wal* (foreign) and *oon* (one)—literally "foreign one." The term was used to differentiate the French speaking residents of Flanders from Flemish speakers.

[9] Joe C. Hill to the author, undated letter. The story was written by Jenna V. Ownbey and included in a two volume history of the Stephenson family.

[10] During the Napoleonic Wars, the French occupied Vlissingen in 1795. On August 13, 1809, British forces subjected the town to a naval bombardment which lasted nearly twenty-four hours. The town hall, together with all its archives, was destroyed.

[11] David L. Ringo to Charles R. Ringo, July 13, 1970. Philip made two wills in America in 1644 and 1646 but noted no family in Europe in either of them.

[12] David Leer Ringo, *The First Five Generations of the Ringo Family in America*, RFHS, Vol. II. (Alhambra, California: The Freeborn Family Organization, Inc., 1982), p. 5. Hereafter cited as Ringo, *Generations*.

[13] Ibid., p. 11. Manuel remained a captive until February 17, 1648, when he was freed for the sum of three hundred guilders.

[14] Ringo, *The Ringos in Europe*. Vol I, Part 1. The entry comes from *Collections of the New York Genealogical and Biographical Society*, Vol. IX, p. 14.

[15] Ringo, *Generations*, p. 17. Philip's death left the family in debt, and his wife later forfeited their estate. The date of Geertje Ringo's death is unknown. She was still living in 1680.

[16] Albertus and Jannetje Ringo had eight children, two of whom were named Aefje. The first, baptized on May 8, 1680, apparently died in infancy. Her namesake was the couple's third child who was baptized on February 28, 1685.

[17] Ringo, *Generations*, p. 67. Philip's godparents were his uncle, Jan Philipszen Ringo, and his aunt, Engeltie Stoutenburg.

[18] Ibid.

[19] Ibid., p. 69.

[20] Ibid., p. 71.

[21] Ibid., p. 72. Jane Cook, born June 13, 1701, was a daughter of Henry Cook and Wyntje Franse Klauw.

[22] Ibid., p. 75.

[23] Ibid., p. 85.

[24] Ibid., p. 89.

[25] Ibid., p. 93. Philip's will, dated April 21, 1757, indicates he owned two slaves, a woman named Noane and a boy named Patrick.

[26] Margaret Major was born on June 21, 1732. Her parents' names are unknown at present.

27 Ringo, *Generations*, pp. 113–17.

28 Ibid., p. 119.

29 Henry and Margaret Ringo had eight children. Of them, Philip, the eldest, (born August 23, 1750) died on March 10, 1785. Frances, the youngest child, was born on August 14, 1766. She died on June 16, 1796. The remaining children were Peter, Cornelius, Major, John, Samuel H., and Joseph.

30 Ringo, *Generations*, p. 241.

31 Ibid., pp. 245–47. One of the slaves was named Jefferson, a young man aged seventeen or eighteen for whom Major Ringo paid $450. The second, James, was age thirteen or fourteen. Major Ringo paid $320 for the youth.

32 *The Line of Descent from Major Ringo*, RFHS, Vol. V. (Alhambra, California: The Freeborn Family Organization, Inc., 1981), p. 5. Hereafter cited as *Major Ringo*. Margaret Henderson was born on March 20, 1794.

33 Wayne County, Indiana, deed records, Vol. A, p. 426.

34 Wayne County, Indiana, 1820 Census. The age ranges given indicate three male children under age ten—Joel, William, and Martin—and one female, Elvira, under age ten. Peter is clearly noted as being between twenty-six and forty-four. However, the older female, listed as between ten and fifteen, does not appear to be Margaret, who was twenty-six in 1820. Possibly it was Peter's sister, Lucinda, who was born March 23, 1810. Lucinda lived a number of years with Peter. Margaret was either away from home at the time or, perhaps, either missed or entered incorrectly.

35 *1884 History of Wayne County, Indiana*. Vol. II, (Chicago: Inter-State Publishing Co., 1884), p. 320. Andrew White Young's *History of Wayne County, Indiana*, dates this church's formation in 1823. See Young, page 171. Centerville was originally known as "Centreville." The spelling of *Centerville* has been used throughout the text.

36 Ibid., Vol. I, p. 448.

37 Wayne County, Indiana, deed records, Vol. F, p. 168.

38 Ibid., Vol. F, p. 179.

39 The family referred to Melissa as "Manica." Her birthdate is alternatively listed as January 27, 1826. She married twice. Her first husband was Elias F. Halliday (born January 17, 1824), whom she married in Wayne County on March 31, 1846. Following his death she wed W.M. Halliday. The 1880 Census for Indiana indicates that she was living in Randolph County. Pugh Ringo was the only child of Peter and Margaret Ringo who did not survive childhood. He died on April 12, 1828.

40 Wayne County, Indiana, 1830 Census. The family's age grouping notes two children, a boy and a girl, less than five years old. There were two boys between five and ten, two boys and a girl between ten and fifteen, one male between fifteen and twenty, and one male and one female between thirty and forty.

41 Wayne County, Indiana, 1840 Census. W.F. Brown made several errors in recording the ages. Hamilton Ringo is noted between the age of ten and fifteen when in fact he was sixteen. Similarly Martin, then twenty-one, was noted as less than twenty.

42 Daniel Ringo was born October 27, 1803, to Major Ringo and Elizabeth Hazelrigg. By the 1820s he had moved to Arkansas where, on June 19, 1834, he married Mary Ann Cocke. Daniel served as chief justice of the Arkansas Supreme Court from 1836 to 1844. Following that he served as a United States district judge. He died at Little Rock, Arkansas, on September 3, 1873.

[43] Pulaski County, Arkansas, will records, Book C, pp. 131–35.

[44] John R. Funk was born August 3, 1808, in Virginia. The couple had eleven children, of whom Joel H., Martha I., and Margaret R. were all born prior to the 1840 census.

[45] *Major Ringo*, p. 11.

[46] *Indiana True Republican*, April 12, 1860.

[47] Lucinda was the second of Peter's siblings to predecease him. The first was William Ringo, born July 26, 1793, who served during the War of 1812. William enlisted as a private in Captain Samuel L. Willliams' Company, Fifth Regiment, Kentucky Volunteers. He was among the men sent to capture Frenchtown, Michigan, from the British. He was captured by the British on January 22, 1813, during the Raisin River massacre. His health never recovered from the experience, and he died on August 17, 1817.

[48] The families of both Major and Samuel Ringo remained very close for several generations.

[49] Prince William County, Virginia, deed records, Vol. W, p. 297.

[50] *The Line of Descent from Samuel H. Ringo*, RFHS, Vol. VII (Alhambra, California: The Freeborn Family Organization, Inc., 1980), p. 3. Hereafter cited as *Samuel Ringo*.

[51] Ibid., p. 4. Samuel Ringo's wife was named Catherine, but her surname is unknown. They had fourteen children.

[52] Traywick, p. 3.

[53] Burrows, *Gunfighter*, p. 119.

[54] Tombstone *Epitaph,* July 22, 1882.

[55] Liberty (Missouri) *Tribune,* August 17, 1860. The date on Peters' tombstone is February 15, 1792. In this case the *Tribune* was undoubtedly correct, for the Clay County, Missouri, census records noted him as fifty-four in 1850 and sixty-four in 1860.

[56] Wilma Chappell and William K. Hall, *The Simms Family of Stafford County, Virginia* (St. Louis, Missouri: n.p., 1969), p. 38. Hereafter cited as *Simms Family*.

[57] *Samuel Ringo*, p. 9.

[58] *Simms Family*, p. 38. The authors reference *Missouri Democracy—A History*, Vol. III, which notes, "John R. Peters, brother of Ira Peters, was an early settler of Liberty and served as sheriff of Clay country [sic]. Another brother was Ashby Peters, father of Mason S. Peters, who was a member of congress, and still another brother was William Peters, who settled in St. Joseph, Missouri" (p. 627).

[59] Liberty *Tribune,* July 27, 1860.

[60] *Simms Family*, p. 18.

[61] Ibid., p. 39.

[62] Ibid., p. 65.

[63] Henry Washington Younger and Bursheba Leighton Fristoe had fourteen children, of whom Cole, Jim, John, and Bob are the best known. Henry, born February 22, 1810, was killed by Missouri militia on July 20, 1862. His wife, born June 6, 1816, in McMinnville, Tennessee, was the daughter of Richard Marshall Fristoe and Mary L. (Polly) Sullivan. She died on June 6, 1870.

[64] Adeline Lee Younger was born in 1836 to Charles Lee Younger and his common-law wife, Parmelia Dorcus Wilson, a daughter of Thomas and Malinda Wilson.

Adeline married James Lewis Dalton, Jr., on March 12, 1851. The couple had thirteen children, of whom Gratton, Robert, and Emmett are best known.

65 Benjamin A. Simms Pension File, National Archives, Washington, DC. Simms was drafted around July 1814 and served through December as a private.

66 *Simms Family*, p. 41.

67 William A. Settle, *Jesse James Was His Name* (Columbia: University of Missouri Press, 1966), p. 8.

68 Liberty *Tribune*, January 6, 1854.

69 Military Record of Martin Ringo, National Archives, Washington, DC.

70 Mary Ringo, *The Journal of Mrs. Mary Ringo* (Santa Ana, California: privately printed by Frank Myrle Cushing, 1956), Foreword. Hereafter cited as *Ringo Journal*.

71 Military Record of Martin Ringo.

72 Ibid.

73 Clay County, Missouri, marriage records.

74 Liberty *Tribune*, September 8, 1848.

Chapter 2

1 Emma Lou Thornbrough, *Indiana in the Civil War Era, 1850–1880*, Vol. III (Indianapolis, Indiana: Indiana Historical Bureau and Indiana Historical Society, 1965), p. 13.

2 Ibid.

3 Ibid., p. 35.

4 Frederick J. Jobsson, *America and American Methodism*, quoted in Thornbrough, p. 38.

5 *History of Wayne County, Indiana*, Vol. I (Chicago: Inter-State Publishing Co., 1884), p. 419.

6 Henry Clay Fox, ed., *Memoirs of Wayne County and the City of Richmond, Indiana* (Madison, Wisconsin: Western Historical Association, 1912), p. 234.

7 Burrows, *Ringo*, p. 106.

8 Traywick, p. 2.

9 Allen Erwin to Thos. C. Ferguson, November 27, 1970. Courtesy Pete Rose, copy in author's files.

10 Richmond (Indiana) *Palladium-Item*, September 23, 1968.

11 Ibid., November 11, 1978.

12 Ibid., May 23, 1976. This article gives the name as John Morgan.

13 Ibid.

14 Ibid., November 11, 1978.

15 Luther Feeger, "Described Building of Forts to which Early Families Fled." Undated clipping from the *Palladium-Item* in a historical scrapbook at the Morrison-Reeves Library, Richmond, Indiana.

16 *Major Ringo*, p. 23. John's birthdate was confirmed by his nephew Frank M. Cushing, who published it in his mother's diary.

17 1850 Census, Wayne County, Indiana.

18 1850 Productions of Agriculture, Wayne County, Indiana.

19 1850 Productions of Industry, Wayne County, Indiana.

20 As noted throughout, a number of deeds were located for Peter Ringo but none

for Martin. It appears that Martin did not use his bounty land grant while he was in Indiana.

[21] Centerville (Indiana) *Free Territorial Sentinel*, October 11, 1848.

[22] Liberty *Tribune*, September 16, 1864.

[23] Ibid., August 17, 1860.

[24] Ibid.

[25] Traywick, p. 3; Erwin to Ferguson, November 27, 1970.

[26] *Samuel Ringo*, p. 11.

[27] Ibid.

[28] Ibid.

[29] 1850 Census, Red River County, Texas.

[30] Clarksville (Texas) *Northern Standard*, June 14, 1845.

[31] Ibid., July 15, 1846.

[32] Peter Ringo's second wife was named Elizabeth, but to date her maiden name has not been determined. A Mary Elizabeth Ringo married Mathew James Nealy on October 28, 1855, but it is uncertain if this was the same woman.

[33] Texas Court of Appeals Records. Courtesy Texas State Archives, Austin, Texas.

[34] Era Fay Huff to the author, May 24, 1983.

[35] *Northern Standard*, October 21, 1854. Peter had ten children by his first wife: James, Abraham, Benjamin, Samuel, Robert, Elizabeth, Elias, Marinda, Amanda, and Mary.

[36] Ibid.

[37] Ibid.

[38] Ibid.

[39] 1850 Census, Wayne County, Indiana.

[40] Major Ringo, p. 5.

[41] *Indiana True Republican*, September 15, 1859.

[42] Helena (Arkansas) *Southern Shield*, July 26, 1851.

[43] Major Ringo, p. 12. Hamilton's marriage to Mary Ann Martin on February 16, 1843, is noted in Book D, p. 169, of the Wayne County marriage records. Their children were James Monroe, Margaret, John Wesley, Sarah Jane, and William, born between 1843 and 1851. Mary Ann later married Isaac Crittenberger.

[44] Ibid., p. 11. William H. Ringo married Prudence L. Lewis on November 20, 1844. The 1850 census for Helena Township, Phillips County, Arkansas, notes that he was a lawyer and that, in addition to his wife and two children, his brother Albert and sister Martha were living with him. One Samuella Peniston, an eighteen-year-old female born in Kentucky, was also in residence. Prudence was born December 30, 1821, and died July 17, 1861. Their sons were Willie Jo and Richard.

[45] Ibid., p. 12.

[46] Ibid. Traywick states that Martin Albert Ringo was named for his father, Martin Albert Ringo, Sr. Despite extensive research, no evidence has been found to support the claim that the senior Martin's middle name was Albert, or even that he had a middle name. Most probably the younger Ringo's middle name was in remembrance of his Uncle Albert. See Traywick, p. 2. Erwin makes a similar comment in his letter to Thos. C. Ferguson.

[47] Burrows, *Gunfighter*, p. 118.

[48] Ibid., p. 107.

49 Thornbrough, p. 6.

50 Ibid.

51 Richmond *Palladium*, April 25, 1850. The mayor of Richmond at the time was John Sailor. The city council had elected William A. Bickle prosecuting attorney. Bickle was to receive two dollars for every conviction of a defendant who retailed or otherwise disposed of "spiritous liquors contrary to the law."

52 *Ringo Journal*, Foreword.

53 George W. Ewing to Allen Hamilton, March 31, 1850, Hamilton papers, Indiana State Archives.

54 Indianapolis *Daily Journal*, February 28, 1856.

Chapter 3

1 *Liberty Tribune*, September 12, 1856.

2 *Major Ringo*, p. 25.

3 *Samuel Ringo*, p. 9; *Simms Family*, pp. 53–54. A letter from Samuel Ringo to his wife dated March 26, 1828, notes that he had reached Pittsburgh, Pennsylvania, on March 25. In Pittsburgh he purchased $1,300 worth of tin ware, glassware and iron castings.

4 1850 Census, Clay County, Missouri.

5 Richmond *Missourian*, April 13, 1934; Liberty *Tribune*, July 7, 1854.

6 *Samuel Ringo*, p. 13; *Simms Family*, p. 56.

7 1850 Census, Ray County, Missouri.

8 1860 Census, Ray County, Missouri.

9 *Simms Family*, p. 55. Elizabeth died on April 28, 1889, in Parkville, Missouri. The Richmond *Missourian* of April 19, 1934, reprinted her obituary from the Liberty *Advance* of 1889. Margaret died on February 19, 1874, at Richmond, Missouri.

10 Clay County, Missouri, Deed Records, Vol. G, p. 463.

11 *Liberty Tribune*, April 25, 1851.

12 Daviess County Deed Records, Vol. I, p. 133.

13 Ibid., Vol. H, p. 236.

14 David Stark to the author, July 1992; Gallatin *North Missourian*, July 22, 1992.

15 Erwin to Ferguson, November 27, 1970.

16 Gallatin *North Missourian*, April 8, 1926.

17 Daviess County Deed Records, Vol. I, p. 133.

18 1860 Census, Daviess County, Missouri.

19 *Ringo Journal*, p. 38.

20 Daviess County Deed Records, Vol. J, p. 551.

21 *Major Ringo*, p. 25.

22 David B. Stark, "Skirmish at Cravensville" (unpublished manuscript, 1992), p. 1. Copy in author's files.

23 Ibid., pp. 2–3.

24 Ibid., p. 4.

25 Gallatin *Democrat*, June 18, 1936.

26 Daviess County Deed Records, Vol. K, p. 218.

[1] *Ringo Journal*, Foreword by Mattie Bell Ringo Cushing. Mrs. Cushing wrote the foreword to her mother's journal in February 1942. She died on May 20, 1942. Mattie had married William LeBaron Cushing on April 23, 1890, in San Jose, California. Cushing, born January 1, 1859, in Coloma, Illinois, died on April 5, 1935. They had two children: Zana Cushing, born April 23, 1891, and Frank Myrle Cushing, born January 10, 1893. Frank Cushing, a noted printer, privately printed the diary for limited distribution in 1956.

[2] Ibid.

[3] Burrows, *Gunfighter*, pp. 108–109.

[4] Dr. William K. Hall to Charles R. Ringo, February 21, 1970. Copy in author's files.

[5] *Ringo Journal*, Note.

[6] Ibid., May 18, 1864. Mary's entries hereafter are cited in the text.

[7] Mary obviously spelled the names as she heard them. The families in question probably should have been Kirby and Moore or Morris.

[8] Efforts to learn the identities of the dead child and man have proven fruitless.

[9] Vienna Strother Simms Peters, the eldest child of John R. Peters, was born May 26, 1822, in Anderson County, Kentucky. She married William H. McCoun in November 1842. After McCoun's death while serving with General Crabb's expedition at Caborca, Mexico, on April 7, 1847, Vienna taught school at Liberty, Missouri. The 1860 Census for Clay County lists her among her father's household. She died at Liberty on May 2, 1868. The couple had four children, two of whom survived childhood.

[10] Liberty *Tribune*, September 16, 1864. William H. Davenport, writing three days after the shooting, identified the man as one "Davis of Kansas."

[11] Ibid.

[12] Traywick, p. 4.

[13] Ed Bartholomew, "John Ringo" (unpublished manuscript). Copy in author's collection. The second grave was that of J.P. Parker, who died there in 1860.

[14] Mary Enna Ringo to David Leer Ringo, January 4, 1935. Copy in author's collection.

[15] *Ringo Journal*, p. 37. Mattie placed this event at Fort Laramie, but it more probably occurred at Platte Bridge Station. See Randy Brown, "The Death of Martin Ringo," *Overland Journal* 7, No. 1 (1989): 22.

[16] Burrows, *Gunfighter*, p. 115.

[17] Ibid., p. 108. With Martin's death as his basis, Burrows diagnoses John as suffering some form of psychological trauma. That anything can be inferred from John's driving the second wagon is extremely speculative. Nothing in Mary's journal or in family correspondence gives any indication that John suffered such a trauma from his father's death.

[18] Erwin to Ferguson, November 27, 1970.

[19] Burrows, *Gunfighter*, p. 115.

Chapter 5

1 *Ringo Journal*, p. 37. Burrows stated that Mattie's testimony suggests a profound belief in "divine retribution or intervention" which would later prevent John's sisters from forgiving his sins (*Gunfighter*, p. 118). When she transcribed her mother's journal in February 1942, however, the seventy-nine-year-old Mary relied on her secondhand recollections of events that occurred when she was two years old: "I will have to finish as best I can from things she [Mary Ringo] told us at different times" (p. 37). Her oblique reference to an old wives' tale hardly confirms that she—or anyone else in the family—believed devoutly in divine intervention.

2 Traywick, p. 4.

3 Erwin to Ferguson, November 27, 1970.

4 *Ringo Journal*, pp. 37–38.

5 Traywick, p. 4.

6 *Ringo Journal*, p. 38.

7 Letter received from James Chase, undated.

8 Chappell and Hall, p. 63.

9 Santa Clara County, California, probate records, courtesy of Marley Brant.

10 Ibid. Charles Bruce Younger was the eldest son of Thomas Coleman Younger by Elinor Murray. He was born in 1832.

11 Ringo Journal, p. 38.

12 Burrows, *Gunfighter*, p. 120.

13 Ibid.

14 San Jose City Directory, 1870, p. 115.

15 1870 Census, Santa Clara County, California.

16 Marley Brant, *The Outlaw Youngers—A Confederate Brotherhood* (Lanham, Maryland: Madison Books, 1992), pp. 13–14.

17 San Jose City Directory, 1871–1872, p. 299.

18 Mattie B. Cushing and M. Enna Ringo, letter to Mrs. J.H. Letton, October 5, 1934. Courtesy David L. Ringo, copy in author's files.

19 Burrows, *Gunfighter*, p. 137.

20 Major Ringo, p. 23

21 Ibid., p. 34. Burrows himself criticized Burns' work as "a view without the refraction of mature historical research…with no responsibility or respect for history and incisive scruple" (*Gunfighter*, p. 4).

22 Letter received from Dr. William K. Hall, September 14, 1992.

23 Letter received from May King, August 27, 1992.

24 David Leer Ringo, review of *John Ringo: The Gunfighter Who Never Was*, by Jack Burrows, *Ringo Researcher* 3, No. 3 (1987): 126.

Chapter 6

1 Jack DeMattos, "Johnny Ringo," *Real West* (April 1985), p. 38. Hereafter cited as DeMattos, "Johnny Ringo."

2 Burrows, *Gunfighter*, pp. 130–31, 136.

3 Ibid., p. 137.

4 Chuck Parsons, rev. of *John Ringo: The Gunfighter Who Never Was*, by Jack

Burrows, *New Mexico Historical Review* 64 (1989): 468.

5 Traywick, p. 4. Traywick further notes that when Ringo left Indiana he went on to both Gallatin and Liberty, Missouri.

6 Cushing and Ringo to Letton.

7 Letter received from Era Fay Huff, February 17, 1983.

8 Santa Clara County, California, probate records. Courtesy Marley Brant.

9 Telephone interview with Ed Bartholomew, Spring 1993. Neither Bartholomew nor the author could locate the newspaper containing the exact date.

10 Jack DeMattos, "Johnny Ringo! The Elusive Man Behind the Myth," NOLA *Quarterly* 13, No. 2 (1977): 8.

11 *Samuel H. Ringo*, p. 10.

12 George Kobayashi, Senior Librarian, San Jose Public Library, letter to the author, October 26, 1982; 1874 San Jose City Directory.

13 Allen A. Erwin to Charles [Chuck] N. Parsons, January 19, 1973. Copy in author's files.

14 Era Fay Huff, "Ringo Genealogy," letter to the editor, *True West* (July 1988), p. 6.

15 Clarke Thomas and Jack Glendenning, *The Slicker War* (Aldrich, Missouri: Bona Publishing Company, 1984), p. 10.

16 Ibid., p. 11.

17 Ibid., p. 26.

18 Clarksville *Northern Standard*, July 31, 1844.

19 Blanco County, Texas, deed abstract. Courtesy Pete Rose.

20 Allen Erwin to Charles Parsons, January 19, 1973.

21 James H. Olney, *A Genealogy of the Descendants of Thomas Olney* (Providence, Rhode Island: E.L. Freeman & Son, 1889), p. 92.

22 1840 Census, Yalobusha County, Mississippi.

23 The Lordsburg *Liberal* of March 4, 1920, stated, probably incorrectly, that Samuel was born in Bastrop County, Texas.

24 Sophie Olney Haynes, a daughter of John T. Olney, recorded in her compilation of Olney genealogical material that "The middle names borne by descendants of Joseph and Mary Katherine Tanner Olney were the surnames of Mary's family and friends. Haynes manuscript. Courtesy Iru Zeller.

25 Burleson County, Texas, Deed Records, Volume AP, p. 96.

26 1850 Census, Burleson County, Texas.

27 1840 Census, Yalobusha County, Mississippi.

28 1850 Census, Burleson County, Texas.

29 1860 Census, Burleson County, Texas. Besides John, Johnathan, and Alice, the children included Samuel, age seven; Lucy, six; and Allen, four.

30 "Ranger of the Sixties," *Frontier Times* (October 1923), p. 27.

31 John T. Olney, Soldier's Application for Pension, Number 40122. In a letter to the comptroller of the State of Texas dated March 17, 1924, the adjutant general's office advised that Olney had enlisted at Dallas, Texas. That notwithstanding, both J.W. Hodges and Hiram Casner swore in separate statements that John had enlisted at Georgetown, Texas. Courtesy Texas State Archives, Austin, Texas.

32 Samuel Olney War Record, Texas State Archives, Austin, Texas.

33 1860 Census, Burleson County, Texas. The family name is often misspelled as

Beard. Documents signed by family members indicate that they consistently used the Baird spelling.

34 Burnet County, Texas, Deed Records, Vol. G, p. 155.

35 1870 Census, Burnet County, Texas.

36 Modern descendants of the family use the spelling Faris, while early court records and newspapers refer to the family as Farris. The latter spelling has been used for consistency.

37 Ina Davis to the author, April 10, 1986.

38 John Wesley Hardin, *The Life of John Wesley Hardin, as Written by Himself* (rpt., Norman: University of Oklahoma Press, 1980), p. 24.

39 Burnet (Texas) *Bulletin*, July 19, 1881.

40 Burnet County District Court Records, Cause 854.

Chapter 7

1 The term Hoo-Doo is of uncertain origin. The epithet was applied to the mob in Mason County. Freedmen in other parts of Texas often referred to the Ku Klux Klan as Hoo-Doos, and Lee Hall's rangers earned the same nickname along the Rio Grande.

2 DeMattos, "Johnny Ringo," p. 38.

3 Traywick, p. 5.

4 Burrows, *Gunfighter*, pp. 131–33.

5 Jack Burrows, "John Ringo: The Story of a Western Myth," *Montana: The Magazine of Western History* 30, No. 4 (October 1980): 8. Hereafter cited as "Ringo Myth."

6 C.L. Sonnichsen, *Ten Texas Feuds* (Albuquerque: University of New Mexico Press, 1971), pp. 92–93. In addition to his primary sources, Sonnichsen relied on the oral traditions of Henry Doell, Jr., and Ernest Lehmberg. His files indicate that he was unable to locate any descendants of the "American" faction.

7 Irene Marschall King, *John O. Meusebach* (Austin: University of Texas Press, 1987), p. 34.

8 Ibid., pp. 5–6.

9 Ibid., pp. 102–103.

10 Ibid., pp. 106–107.

11 Don H. Biggers, *German Pioneers in Texas* (Austin, Texas: Eakin Publications, Inc., 1983), pp. 57–61; R.H. Williams, *With the Border Ruffians* (Lincoln: University of Nebraska Press, 1982), pp. 242–43.

12 Biggers, p. 60.

13 Minnie Gandy Schmidt, "Schmidt Hereford Ranch, Inc.," *Edwards Plateau Historian* 8 (1978–82): 70.

14 Julius E. DeVos, "Mason County's Unsettled Years 1860–1880," *Edwards Plateau Historian* 7 (n.d.): 20.

15 Gilbert J. Jordan, *Yesterday in the Texas Hill Country* (College Station: Texas A&M University Press, 1979), p. 100.

16 Austin *Weekly Statesman*, November 18, 1875. Dreux was one of several correspondents who wrote letters concerning the feud. Others included "Peter," "Otho," and Henry M. Holmes.

17 Burrows, *Gunfighter*, p. 132.

[18] DeVos, p. 21.

[19] Austin *Daily Statesman*, October 17, 1875.

[20] Max Amadeus Paulus Krueger, *Second Fatherland* (College Station: Texas A&M University Press, 1976), p. 78.

[21] Ibid., p. 99.

[22] Sonnichsen, pp. 90–91.

[23] Drive Book of M.L. Hayes, ca. 1874–75. Courtesy Mason County Historical Society. Copy in author's files.

[24] Sonnichsen, p. 91.

[25] Burnet *Bulletin*, May 23, 1874.

[26] Austin *Daily Statesman*, October 17, 1875.

[27] Dan W. Roberts, *Rangers and Sovereignty* (Austin, Texas: State House Press, 1987), p. 92.

[28] Telephone interviews with George M. Taft, July 1988; December 7, 1990.

[29] 1860 Census, Burnet County, Texas.

[30] Ranger Muster Rolls, Texas State Archives, Austin, Texas.

[31] *Burnet Bulletin*, September 5, 1874.

[32] Ibid.

[33] *San Antonio Daily Herald*, August 24, 1874.

[34] Gilbert J. Jordan, *A Biographical Sketch of Ernst and Lizette Jordan* (n.p.: n.p., circa 1931), p. 23. Hereafter cited as *Ernst Jordan*.

[35] Jordan, *Ernst Jordan*, p. 23; Burnet *Bulletin*, September 5, 1874.

[36] 1860 Census, Burnet County, Texas.

[37] 1870 Census, Burnet County, Texas.

[38] Burnet County, Texas, District Court Records, Cause 311.

[39] Confederate Muster Rolls, TSA.

[40] 1870 Census, Burnet County, Texas.

[41] State Police Muster Rolls, TSA.

[42] 1880 Census, Maverick County, Texas.

[43] Hayes, Drive Book.

[44] 1850 Census, Bastrop County, Texas.

[45] Interview with LaVoy Taylor, July 29, 1983.

[46] 1860 Census, Burnet County, Texas.

[47] Burnet County, Texas, District Court Records, Cause Number 390: Daniel Hoerster v. A.T. Taylor.

[48] [Adjutant General William Steele], *A List of Fugitives from Justice* (Austin, Texas: Adjutant General's Office, 1878), p. 77. Hereafter cited as *1878 Fugitives*.

[49] Burnet *Bulletin*, September 5, 1874.

[50] Ibid.

Chapter 8

[1] Lieutenant Daniel Webster Roberts to Major John B. Jones, January 15, 1875. Adjutant General's Records, Texas State Archives. Hereafter cited as AGR.

[2] Several family sources, including H.V. "Todd" Faris and Foster Casner, both deceased, attested that Ringo drove cattle to Kansas in the early 1870s. Stuart N. Lake, who is generally unreliable, stated, "That galaxy of shooting stars which reddened the

cowtown firmament in the eighteen-seventies included...John Ringo." Lake also notes, "...[Brocius] and Ringo—family name, Ringgold—were fearless gunmen of the first order, professional killers, trained in the wars of the Texas cattle barons. Each had encountered Wyatt Earp as marshal in Wichita and Dodge City" (Stuart N. Lake, *Wyatt Earp, Frontier Marshal* (Boston: Houghton Mifflin Company, 1931], pp. 72 and 235). Earp served as a policeman in both of those towns during the 1870s. If Ringo did encounter him during 1875, it would have been in Wichita, where Earp was appointed a policeman on April 21, 1875.

3 Roberts to Jones, February 14, 1875, AGR.

4 Thomas W. Gamel, *The Life of Thomas W. Gamel* (Mason, Texas: Privately printed, circa 1932), p. 18; Lucia M. Holmes, *Diary of Lucia M. Holmes* (Mason, Texas: Mason County Historical Commission, 1985), entry for February 13, 1875. Hereafter cited as Holmes Diary.

5 J. Marvin Hunter, "Brief History of Early Days in Mason County," *Frontier Times* (January 1929), p. 162.

6 1875 Mason County, Texas, Tax Roll.

7 Burrows, *Gunfighter*, p. 132.

8 Letter received from Johnie-Lee Reeves, August 1994.

9 Betty Hennig, "'Frank' Francis Johnson and Related Families" (unpublished manuscript, n.d). Hereafter cited as Hennig Manuscript.

10 Ibid.

11 Holmes Diary, February 17, 1875.

12 Hunter, pp. 161–62.

13 Gamel, p. 18.

14 Ibid., p. 20.

15 Gamel, pp. 20–21; Roberts, pp. 87–89; Holmes Diary, February 18, 1875; Sonnichsen, p. 87.

16 Ibid.

17 Holmes Diary, February 19, 1875.

18 In New Mexico Hall was poisoned by a woman, one of his victims. He survived the experience, but it left his health broken. Hall eventually moved to Colorado. He died at Cripple Creek on March 12, 1935.

19 Gamel, p. 4.

20 Roster of the State Police, AGR.

21 Holmes Diary, February 25, 1875.

22 Sonnichsen, p. 89.

23 John Anton Wohrle military record, National Archives.

24 State Police Arrests ledger, AGR.

25 Nelson Geistweidt, *Geistweidt Family History* (Doss, Texas: Privately printed, 1971), p. 7.

26 Roberts to Jones, March 1, 1875.

27 Miles Barler, *Early Days in Llano* (Llano, Texas: The Llano Times, n.d.), p. 32.

28 Holmes Diary, March 6, 1875 and March 7, 1875.

29 Ibid., March 13, 1875.

30 Ibid., March 19, 1875.

31 Ibid., March 22, 1875.

32 San Antonio *Daily Herald*, August 30, 1875.

[33] Holmes Diary, March 27, 1875.

[34] Roberts to Jones, April 1, 1875.

[35] Holmes Diary, April 8, 1875.

[36] Burnet County, Texas, District Court Records, Cause 854.

[37] Joan DeKorte, personal interview, October 28, 1993.

[38] 1875 Mason County, Texas, Tax Rolls.

[39] Gamel, p. 23.

[40] Austin *Daily Statesman*, October 17, 1875.

[41] Ibid.

[42] Ibid., May 18, 1875; Gamel, pp. 23–24.

[43] Holmes Diary, May 17, 1875.

Chapter 9

[1] 1850 Census, Izard County, Arkansas, and 1860 Census, Jack County, Texas.

[2] Dallas *Herald*, February 10, 1872.

[3] Galveston *Christian Advocate*, May 29, 1872. The sheriff was George W. Stevens, who was originally appointed June 9, 1869, by General J.J. Reynolds' Special Order Number 136. Stevens was elected on December 3, 1869, and served until December 2, 1873.

[4] 1870 Mortality Schedule, Jack County, Texas.

[5] Gillett, p. 47.

[6] Texas Ranger Muster Roll, TSA.

[7] Austin *Daily Statesman*, November 28, 1874.

[8] Gamel, p. 24.

[9] San Antonio *Daily Herald*, August 30, 1875.

[10] Ibid.

[11] Austin *Daily Statesman*, July 31, 1875.

[12] The topic of Doell's killing is discussed in the author's "The Doell Killing: Feudal Vengeance or Private Murder?" NOLA *Quarterly* 9, No. 1 (Summer 1986).

[13] Burnet County, Texas, District Court Records. Cause 854.

[14] 1860 Census, Burnet County, Texas.

[15] 1870 Census, Burnet County, Texas.

[16] Burnet County, Texas, District Court Records, Cause 854.

[17] Gamel, p. 24.

[18] Ibid., pp. 24–25.

[19] San Antonio *Daily Herald*, August 30, 1875.

[20] Julius E. De Vos, editor, *One Hundred Years of the Hilda (Bethel) Methodist Church and Parent Organizations* (Hilda, Texas: Hilda United Methodist Church, 1973), p. 47.

[21] Gamel, p. 30.

[22] Burrows, "Ringo Myth," p. 8. Burrows made the same claim in *Gunfighter*, p. 135.

[23] Traywick, p. 7.

[24] For a complete analysis of who killed Karl Bader see the author's "Revenge in Mason County, Texas," NOLA *Quarterly* 10, No. 1 (1985): 7–8, 12.

[25] Austin *Daily Statesman*, August 24, 1875.

26 San Antonio *Daily Herald*, August 30, 1875.

27 Gamel, p. 25.

28 Roberts, pp. 97–98.

29 Gamel, p. 25.

30 San Antonio *Daily Herald*, September 14, 1875.

31 Henry M. Holmes to Richard Coke, September 8, 1875. TSA.

Chapter 10

1 Personal interview with Jane Hoerster, March 8, 1994.

2 Personal interview with H.V. "Todd" Faris, June 24, 1983.

3 Personal interviews with Foster Casner, September 14, 1982, and Todd Faris, June 24, 1983. Foster Casner, John Olney's grandson, heard the story both from his grandfather and from Sam Tanner.

4 Gamel, p. 26.

5 Ibid.

6 Ibid.

7 San Antonio *Daily Herald*, September 20, 1875.

8 Letter received from Nina Legge, May 3, 1986.

9 Gamel, p. 27.

10 Frank Tinker, "No One Called Him Johnny," *Tucson Citizen*, October 30, 1982.

11 Holmes Diary, October 4, 1875.

12 Austin *Daily Statesman*, December 4, 1875.

13 James B. O'Neil, *They Die But Once* (New York: Knight Publications, 1935), p. 95. These recollections of Jeff Ake, taken down near the end of his life, must be used with caution. Ake proves accurate in many cases, but not all; moreover, he omitted a great deal of his own life.

14 Galveston *Daily News*, November 25, 1875.

15 Ibid., December 3, 1875. Alazan's letter was dated November 26, 1875, from San Antonio. The error of calling John Ringo "Ringgold" proved common in ensuing years. Ringo never used it as an alias.

16 Monthly Return, Company A, November 1875. TSA.

17 Austin *Daily Statesman*, January 2, 1876, and reprinted in the San Antonio *Daily Express*, January 5, 1876.

18 Austin *Daily Statesman*, January 4, 1876.

19 Galveston *Daily News*, January 28, 1876.

20 Austin *Daily Statesman*, February 1, 1876.

21 Burnet County, Texas, District Court Records, Causes 925 and 926.

22 Ibid., Cause 854.

23 Ibid., Causes 925 and 926.

24 Ibid.

25 Darrell Debo, *Burnet County History*, vol. II (Burnet, Texas: Eakin Press, 1979), p. 41.

26 Galveston *Daily News*, February 9, 1876.

27 H.V. "Todd" Faris interview, June 24, 1983.

28 *Fayette County New Era*, May 12, 1876.

[29] San Antonio *Daily Express*, May 19, 1876.

[30] Testimony of J. T. Walker, Lampasas, Texas, District Court Records.

[31] Personal interview with Foster Casner, Summer 1983.

[32] Lampasas, Texas, District Court Records, Testimony of W.P. Hoskins. Courtesy of Jeff Jackson.

[33] Ibid.

[34] Holmes Diary, May 8, 1876.

[35] Ibid., May 9, 1876.

[36] Galveston *Daily News*, May 23, 1876.

[37] Personal interview with H.V. "Todd" Faris, June 24, 1983.

[38] Gamel, p. 30.

[39] Houston *Daily Telegraph*, June 14, 1876.

[40] Personal interview with Max Gipson, caretaker of Miller Creek Cemetery where Scott Cooley is buried, summer 1988.

[41] Austin *Daily Statesman*, June 9, 1876.

Chapter 11

[1] 1876 San Jose, California, City Directory.

[2] Santa Clara County, California, probate record 983.

[3] Liberty *Tribune*, August 4, 1876.

[4] Burnet County, Texas, District Court Records. Cause 977.

[5] Burnet *Bulletin*, July 14, 1876.

[6] Galveston *Daily News*, August 18, 1876.

[7] Burnet *Bulletin*, August 25, 1876.

[8] Ibid., September 1, 1876.

[9] Holmes Diary, September 5, 1876.

[10] Barler, p. 32.

[11] Burnet *Bulletin*, September 8 and 15, 1876; Austin *Daily Statesman*, September 15, 1876.

[12] Personal interviews with Foster Casner and Jim McFarland, August 1982. Mr. Casner heard his version of the story from posseman Clint Breazeale.

[13] Burnet *Bulletin*, September 15, 1876.

[14] Barler, pp. 43–44.

[15] J.J. Bozarth became sheriff of Llano County after the forced resignation of William P. Hoskins in the fall of 1876. Barler alleged that Bozarth was operating with the mob in Llano. He died on November 20, 1880, while in office.

[16] Austin *Daily Statesman*, November 7, 1876.

[17] Ibid., December 1, 1876. These arrests proved to be very important in determining who was stealing cattle in Mason. Frank Enoch was overtaken with Clark's posseman, Caleb Hall, while running another stolen herd in Uvalde County. Enoch attempted to escape and was shot. He died on February 6, 1877, of his wounds. The San Antonio *Daily Express* carried the news of his death on February 13, 1877. Cain survived until 1879 when he was assassinated at his home at Taylorville, Texas. According to the Austin *Daily Statesman* of April 23, 1879, Cain was shot in his home and died on the morning of April 22.

[18] Ibid.

19 Burnet *Bulletin*, November 14, 1876. Alex Erwin was a cousin of Joe Olney. Mob member A. J. Mackey dragged Alex's brother, Ben, to death because the mob believed he had overheard them making plans.

20 Ibid., December 22, 1876.

21 Ibid., December 8, 1876.

22 Ibid., December 15, 1876.

23 O'Neil, pp. 135-36.

24 Galveston *Daily News*, May 11, 1877. This Bill Clements appears to have been William Clements, a son of Emanuel Clements and Martha Balch Hardin, born 1839. Clements was a brother of the more famous Mannen Clements. His mother was a sister of James G. Hardin, Wes Hardin's father.

25 Burnet *Bulletin*, January 26, 1877.

26 Mason County, Texas, District Court Records, Cause 21.

27 *Cases Argued and Ajuded in the Court of Appeals*, Soule, Thomas & Wentworth, 1878, II, p. 292.

28 Lampasas County, Texas, District Court Records.

29 Mason County, Texas, District Court Records, Cause 21.

30 Austin *Daily Statesman*, July 15, 1877.

31 Lampasas County, Texas, District Court Records; John Wesley Hardin to Jane Bowen Hardin, April 13, 1879. The latter courtesy Chuck Parsons.

32 Monthly Return, Company D, November, 1877. TSA.

33 Hardin, p. 126.

34 Burrows, *Gunfighter*, p. 135.

35 William P. Longley to Milton Mast, October 29, 1877. Courtesy Chuck Parsons.

36 Mason County, Texas, District Court Records, Cause 21.

37 Galveston *Daily News*, January 17, 1878.

Chapter 12

1 Traywick, p. 6.

2 Lampasas *Dispatch*, February 7, 1878; Galveston *Weekly News*, February 18, 1878.

3 Mason County, Texas, District Clerk Records, Cause 21.

4 Monthly Returns, Company D, February 1878, TSA.

5 Ibid.

6 Ibid.

7 Ibid.

8 Ibid.; Galveston *Daily News*, May 31, 1878.

9 Lampasas County, Texas, District Court Records, Causes 380 and 381.

10 Mason County, Texas, Election Records.

11 Mason County, Texas, Records of Marks and Brands.

12 Letter received from Janaloo Hill, December 22, 1982. Hill and her husband, Manny Hough, live in and preserve the historic ghost town of Shakespeare, New Mexico.

13 Personal interview with Jane Hoerster, Summer 1984.

14 Traywick, p. 8.

15 "Fifty-two Years in West Texas," *Frontier Times* 5, No. 8 (February 1928): 341–42. Reprinted from the Junction (Texas) *Eagle* of February 23, 1928. Patterson places the incident in the summer, which would have been far too early for Ringo's departure in late 1878 or early 1879. The discrepancy is probably due to a faulty memory. When Ringo left Texas for the second time during 1879 he was traveling with the three Olney brothers.

16 Interviews with John Olney, June 1, 1983, and January 10, 1985.

17 Governor Lew Wallace to Captain Henry Carroll, March 11, 1879. This and the other documents cited are in the Lew Wallace Collection of the Indiana State Library, Indianapolis, Indiana. Hereafter cited as Wallace Collection.

18 Undated list, Wallace Collection.

19 "Statements made by the Kid," March 23, 1879, Wallace Collection. The Gist Hardin referred to is probably "West" Hardin—John Wesley Hardin—with whom Joe Olney's name had been linked in the Brownwood, Texas, jail break in May 1877.

20 Lampasas County, Texas, District Court Records.

21 Tombstone *Epitaph*, July 22, 1882.

22 John Olney interviews.

23 Jennie Parks Ringgold, *Frontier Days in the Old Southwest* (San Antonio, Texas: The Naylor Company, 1952), pp. 1–15.

24 Ibid., p. 15.

25 Jennie Parks Ringgold to Ben Olney, December 12, 1953. Courtesy Annie May Durrant. Copy in author's files.

26 Ringgold. pp. 1–15. See also Daniel Aranda's excellent account of the incident, "An Episode from Victorio's War," *Real West* (February 1984).

27 J.C. Hancock File, Arizona Pioneers' Historical Society, Tucson, Arizona. Hereafter cited as Hancock.

28 Ibid.

29 Personal interview with Frank and John Stark by Emil Schaaf, Audio 400, University of Arizona, Special Collections.

30 Tombstone *Epitaph*, July 22, 1882.

31 Erwin to Ferguson, November 27, 1970.

32 Personal interview with Walker W. "Bud" Jordan, July 7, 1989.

33 Letter received from Jim Peterson, March 30, 1984.

34 Santa Fe *New Mexican*, January 19, 1880.

35 *Arizona Star*, December 14, 1879.

36 Traywick, p. 8.

Chapter 13

1 Hancock.

2 Larry D. Ball, *The United States Marshals of New Mexico and Arizona Territories, 1846–1912* (Albuquerque: University of New Mexico Press, 1978), p. 108.

3 Tucson *Weekly Citizen*, September 4, 1880.

4 John J. Gosper to Secretary of State James G. Blaine, September 30, 1881. Record Group 60, National Archives, Washington, D.C.

5 Britton Davis, *The Truth About Geronimo* (Lincoln: University of Nebraska Press, 1976), p. 31.

6 Glenn G. Boyer, "Curly Bill Has Been Killed at Last," *Real West* (June 1984), p. 32.

7 Ed Bartholomew, *Wyatt Earp: The Man and the Myth* (Toyahvale, Texas: Frontier Book Company, 1964), passim.

8 Ball, p. 116.

9 Pima County, Arizona, District Court Records. Courtesy Steve Gatto. The "R" in Ringo's name looks like a G, making the name appear to be Gingo. Gatto commented that "it could be a bad copy, or they may have made a mistake. Possibly, he gave that name. (Remember Collins' letter.)"

10 Robert N. Mullin Collection, Nita Stewart Haley Memorial Library, Midland, Texas.

11 Traywick, p. 9.

12 "Reminiscences of a Stranger," monograph dated July 29, 1927, Arizona Pioneer's Historical Society, Tucson, Arizona.

13 Grant County, New Mexico, Deed Records.

14 Ibid.

15 Janaloo Hill, "Yours Until Death, William Grounds," *True West* (March-April 1973), p. 55.

16 J.B. Collins B.M. Jacobs, July 17, 1880, University of Arizona Special Collections, Tucson, Arizona.

17 William A. Duffen. "'Jollification'—Arizona Style: A Description of Gunplay in 1880," *Arizona and the West* 1 (1959): 282.

18 Alford E. Turner, "The Clantons of Apache County," *Real West Annual* (1980).

19 Bartholomew, p. 81.

20 Philip Ashton Rollins, *The Cowboy* (1922; rpt. New York: Ballantine Books, 1973), p. 293.

21 "Reminiscences of A.M. Franklin," undated manuscript, Arizona Pioneers' Historical Society, Tucson, Arizona.

Chapter 14

1 Douglas D. Martin, *Tombstone's Epitaph* (Albuquerque: University of New Mexico Press, 1951), p. 146.

2 *Epitaph*, October 20, 1880.

3 Ibid.

4 Ball, pp. 115–16.

5 *Arizona Star*, January 22, 1881.

6 E.B. Pomroy to Wayne MacVeagh, June 23, 1881, Record Group 60, "Materials relating to the COWBOY troubles and to the investigation of Marshal C.P. Dake." National Archives, Washington, DC. Hereafter cited as RG60.

7 C.M. Chase, *The Editor's Run in New Mexico and Colorado* (Fort Davis, Texas: Frontier Book Company, 1968), p [?].

8 *The New Southwest and Grant County* (New Mexico) *Herald*, October 1, 1881.

9 George W. Parsons, *The Private Journal of George W. Parsons* (Tombstone, Arizona: Tombstone Epitaph, 1972), entry for May 22, 1880. Hereafter cited as Parsons Journal.

10 Ball, p. 108.

11 *Arizona Citizen*, November 4, 1871.

12 Ibid., August 23, 1880.

13 Parsons Journal, entry for August 31, 1880.

14 *Nugget*, September 2, 1880.

15 *Arizona Citizen*, September 4, 1880.

16 *Arizona Star*, September 2, 1880.

17 Hancock.

18 John P. Gray Manuscript, Arizona Pioneers' Historical Society, Tucson, Arizona; Reminiscences of Henry Morgan, Arizona Pioneers' Historical Society, Tucson, Arizona.

19 *Arizona Star*, January 22, 1881.

20 Ibid.

21 Richard Van Valkenburgh, "Who Was Elected Sheriff?" [Arizona] *Sheriffs Magazine* (February 1949).

22 *Arizona Star*, April 28, 1881.

23 Tombstone *Daily Nugget*, October 19, 1880.

Chapter 15

1 Grant County, New Mexico, Land Records. Courtesy Steve Gatto.

2 Some recent writers have tried to establish that Alonzo Clanton was Peter Alonzo Clanton; however, no contemporary evidence establishes the existence of a Peter Alonzo Clanton. A Peter Blanton, whose name was given erroneously in some newspaper accounts as Clanton, was killed by a posse in 1877. For a full discussion of this see Sue C. Van Slyke and Dave Johnson, "Pete Clanton—What's in a Name?" NOLA *Quarterly* 18, No. 2 (1994).

3 Confederate Muster Rolls. TSA.

4 Ibid.

5 Ibid.; and Record Group 109, "Proceedings of the Court Martial in the Case of John W. Clanton, Company B, Parson's Regt. Cavalry." National Archives.

6 Confederate Muster Rolls.

7 Van Slyke and Johnson, p. 17.

8 Tucson *Citizen*, December 13, 1873.

9 Ibid., September 12, 1874.

10 To date three major articles have dealt with the Clantons in addition to that cited: Alford E. Turner, "The Clantons of Apache County," *Real West Annual* (1980); Sue C. Van Slyke, "The Truth About the Clantons of Tombstone," NOLA *Quarterly* 7, No. 1 (Spring 1982); and Sue C. Van Slyke and Dave Johnson, "Kin to the Clantons," NOLA *Quarterly* 14, No. 2 (Summer 1990). Turner focuses on the period from 1881 to Phin Clanton's death in the early 1900s and omitted information favorable to the Clantons. Van Slyke provided a a more even-handed and relatively complete account of the family. The third article dealt with Medal of Honor winner Eben Stanley, who married Mary E. Clanton, Ike Clanton's sister.

11 *Arizona Weekly Star*, December 2, 1880.

12 William M. Breakenridge, *Helldorado* (Lincoln: University of Nebraska Press, 1992. Breakenridge referred to Turner as "the banker for the rustlers," p. 226.

13 Dodge City *Times*, August 17, 1878.

14 Las Vegas (New Mexico) *Gazette*, March 20, 1881.

15 Philip J. Rasch, "'Six Shooter' and 'Three Shooter Smith,'" NOLA *Quarterly*, 9, No. 4 (Spring 1985), p. 9. Rasch also points out that Smith was linked not only to Holliday but to J.J. Harlan, alias "the Off Wheeler," who had served time in prison for a rape committed in Kansas. See also Chuck Parsons and Gary P. Fitterer, *Captain C.B. McKinney: The Law in South Texas* (Wolfe City, Texas: Henington Publishing Company, 1993), pp. 51–52.

16 *Denver Tribune*, May 16, 1882.

17 Phillip J. Rasch, "Adios, Dick Lloyd!" NOLA *Quarterly* 8, No. 1 (Spring-Summer 1983).

18 Burns, pp. 55–58.

19 Lily Klasner, *My Girlhood Among Outlaws*, ed. Eve Ball (Tucson: University of Arizona Press, 1972), p. 60.

20 Ibid.

21 Melvin W. Jones file, Arizona Pioneers' Historical Society, Tucson, Arizona. James C. Hancock disputed this identification. Brocius and Graham were probably two separate individuals.

22 *Epitaph*, October 28, 1880.

23 Ibid., October 29, 1880.

24 Breakenridge, pp. 192–94.

25 Jones file.

26 *Arizona Weekly Citizen*, March 13, 1881.

27 *Epitaph*, March 10, 1881.

28 Bartholomew, p. 270.

Chapter 16

1 *Epitaph*, March 16, 1881.

2 Parsons Journal, entry for March 16, 1881.

3 Ibid., entry for March 20, 1881.

4 Fred J. Dodge to Stuart N. Lake, September 18, 1930, in Fred Dodge, *Under Cover for Wells Fargo: The Unvarnished Recollections of Fred Dodge*, ed. Carolyn Lake (Boston: Houghton Mifflin, 1969), p. 246. Fred J. Dodge was born August 29, 1854, at Spring Valley, California. According to his own account he arrived in Tombstone on December 7, 1879. Dodge assisted Stuart N. Lake, who first contacted him in September 1928, in preparing Lake's book on Wyatt Earp. Dodge was initially cautious of Lake, writing in part on September 18 that he would be happy to help him, "But first I must know that it is for Wyatt, and that it will benefit him from a pecuniary standpoint. Have him write me or give me his ad[d]ress and I will write him." Lake complied. Curiously enough Dodge himself appears to have contacted Earp some six days *before* Lake initiated his contact with Dodge. He died on December 16, 1938, at Boerne, Texas.

5 Dodge, p. 24. Dodge claimed to have been an undercover Wells, Fargo agent during the Earp years in Tombstone, but that cannot be verified due to the destruction of the early Wells, Fargo records. Earp himself stated in 1885 that the special agent was John N. Thacker. See Chalmers to Garland, August 13, 1885, and September 3, 1885, RG60. Dodge did work for Wells, Fargo at a much later date. Dodge's unsupported

statement is the only indication of Barnes' involvement in the holdup.

6 Las Vegas *Daily Optic*, July 20, 1881.

7 Gray manuscript, p. 54.

8 Joe Chisholm. *Brewery Gulch* (San Antonio: The Naylor Company, 1949), p. 98.

9 Wyatt S. Earp, *Wyatt Earp* (Sierra Vista, Arizona: Yuma Bissette, 1981), p. 202. Earp here stated that Behan let King talk to Len Redfield. Paula Mitchell Marks and Lake indicated that Earp was incensed that Behan allowed Redfield to engage King in secret conversation.

10 *Nugget*, March 29, 1881.

11 Parsons Journal, March 28, 1881.

12 *Epitaph*, April 1, 1881.

13 "Wells Spicer Hearing," District Court Records, Cochise County, Arizona, Document 94, quoted in Alford E. Turner, *The O.K. Corral Inquest* (College Station, Texas: Creative Publishing Company, 1981), pp. 52–226.

14 *Epitaph*, March 17, 1881.

15 Robert Todd Lincoln to Wayne MacVeagh, April 12, 1881, RG60.

16 Wayne MacVeagh to E.B. Pomroy, April 14, 1881, RG60.

17 E.B. Pomroy to Mulliken, April 21, 1881, RG60.

18 Austin *Daily Statesman*, May 3, 1881. Historian Jack DeMattos discovered this item and graciously called it to the author's attention.

19 Record of Arrests, Austin History Center, Austin, Texas.

20 *Nugget*, June 9, 1881.

21 Bowyer to Gosper, September 17, 1881, RG60.

22 Joe Evans to C.P. Dake, June 30, 1881, RG60. Joe Evans was stationed in Tucson. Available information indicates this relatively unknown lawman pursued outlaws such as Brigido Reyes on both sides of the border. Governor Luis Torres knew and respected Evans. Notwithstanding that Virgil Earp had received his commission as a deputy United States marshal in 1879, Record Group 60 indicates clearly that Earp did nothing to resolve the border problems and is first mentioned after the O.K. Corral gunfight.

23 Orlando B. Willcox to Adjutant General, Military Division of the Pacific, June 9, 1881, RG60.

24 Chuck Parsons, *"Pidge," A Texas Ranger From Virginia* (Wolfe City, Texas: Henington Publishing Co., 1985), pp. 87–91, 135–36. McNelly's "invasion" of Mexico was lauded by the Texas press. The *Galveston Daily News* of December 12, 1875, reported in part "The policy of retaliation, swift and vigorous, is the only one that promises relief to the citizens of a long suffering frontier — the only one which will purchase immunity from further outrages. Through a long series of years the citizens of the border have suffered from predatory bands, until forbearance has ceased to be a virtue. . . . This can be done only by following the bands to their strongholds, wherever they may be, and teaching them that American citizens are not to be robbed and murdered with impunity by thieving cut-throats, who believe (and with good reason) that the Rio Grande is a rubicon beyond whose waters none dare pass; that once on the Mexican bank, they are safe from pursuit, and even from inquiry."

Chapter 17

1 *Weekly Arizona Star*, June 16, 1881.

2 Las Vegas *Daily Optic*, June 21, 1881.

3 J.W. Evans to C.P. Dake, June 18, 1881, RG60.

4 Luis Torres to J.W. Evans, June 24, 1881, RG60.

5 *Star*, June 23, 1881.

6 Orlando B.Willcox to the Adjutant General, Military Division of the Pacific, June 28, 1881, RG60.

7 *Weekly Star*, June 23, 1881.

8 *Daily Star*, June 23, 1881.

9 Traywick, p. 9; DeMattos, "Johnny Ringo," p. 41; Burrows, *Gunfighter*, p. 145.

10 *Daily Nugget*, July 12, 1881.

11 E.B. Pomroy to Wayne MacVeagh, June 23, 1881, RG60. Apparently Pomroy was not aware that Virgil Earp held an appointment as a United States deputy marshal at the time.

12 C.P. Dake to Wayne MacVeagh, May 30, 1881, RG60.

13 Leigh Chalmers to A. H. Garland, United States Attorney General, September 3, 1885, RG60.

14 Hancock.

15 Gray manuscript, pp. 139–40.

16 Burns, pp. 88–90.

17 *Nugget*, August 3, 1881.

18 Ibid. The *Epitaph* reported substantially the same story under the headline "An Interrupted Breakfast" on August 5, 1881, two days after the *Nugget's* story.

19 J.W. Evans to C.P. Dake, August 4, 1881, RG60.

20 C.P. Dake to Wayne MacVeagh, August 5, 1881, RG60.

21 J.W. Evans to C.P. Dake, August 10, 1881, RG60.

22 Hancock.

23 *Epitaph*, August 13, 1881.

24 Ibid., August 14, 1881.

25 *Nugget*, August 11, 1881.

26 Breakenridge, p. 231.

Chapter 18

1 Cochise County, Arizona, District Court Records.

2 Dan L. Thrapp, *The Conquest of Apacheria* (Norman: University of Oklahoma Press, 1967). Carr's expedition ended in disaster when gunfire erupted. The Prophet was killed along with a number of others, and the Apaches went on the war path.

3 Gray manuscript, p. 36.

4 Ibid.

5 Ibid.

6 This is not the only link the Earp brothers had with accused stage robbers. In July of 1881 the stage running from Arizona Territory to Hermosilla, Mexico, had been held up. Virgil Earp dispatched two men to trail the robbers, Dan Tipton and Sherm MacMasters. MacMasters was then wanted in connection with yet another stage rob-

bery that occurred near Globe in February 1881 along with Charles Ray, better known as Pony Diehl. MacMasters was also wanted for stealing some mules from Camp Rucker.

[7] Traywick states that Clanton "had bought a herd of stolen cattle (Mexican) from Curly Bill, Ringo, and their rustler friends" (p. 11). If this statement refers to the herd that Milt Hicks and his cronies stole from the Mexicans, it is provably incorrect.

[8] *Star*, September 1, 1881.

[9] Glenn Boyer, "Welcome to Wyatt Earp Country," *Arizona Highways* (November 1982).

[10] Glenn G. Boyer, *Wyatt Earp's Tombstone Vendetta* (Honolulu, Hawaii: Talei Publishers, Inc., 1993), p. 121. Boyer based this "nonfiction novel" on the pseudonymous account of "Theodore Ten Eyck."

[11] Boyer, *Vendetta*, p. 120.

[12] *Star*, September 1, 1881.

[13] *Citizen*, August 21, 1881.

[14] *Star*, August 25, 1881.

[15] *The New Southwest and Grant County Herald*, August 20, 1881.

[16] Kelton to Adjutant General, August 22, 1881, RG60.

[17] Parsons Journal, entry for August 17, 1881.

[18] Letter received from Chuck Parsons, June 28, 1994. Chuck Parsons is no relation to George W. Parsons.

[19] A.M. Franklin, "Story of Ringo and the Cattle Thieves" (unpublished manuscript, Arizona State Archives). Franklin narrated the story in 1925 to a Mr. Widdowsen.

[20] Ibid.

[21] Ibid.

[22] Ibid.

[23] Ibid.

Chapter 19

[1] *Nugget*, September 10, 1881.

[2] *Epitaph*, September 13, 1881.

[3] *Daily Nugget*, September 10, 1881; Bartholomew, pp. 206–207.

[4] *Nugget*, November 17, 1881. Even at this late date, the newspapers did not know the correct spellings of either Ringo's or the McLaury brothers' names.

[5] C.P. Dake to Wayne MacVeagh, September 14, 1881, RG60.

[6] John Gosper to James G. Blaine, September 30, 1881, RG60.

[7] Parsons Journal, October 5, 1881.

[8] Ibid.

[9] Turner, p. 99. The two major documents relating to the O. K. Corral gunfight are the coroner's inquest, Document 48, and the Spicer hearing, Document 94 which now exist only in the manuscript of Hal L. Hayhurst. To simplify access for the reader interested in learning more about this fight, the footnotes and text have generally been drawn from Turner. A word of caution: in his foreword, Turner remarked that Hayhurst "also was thoroughly anti-Earp in his viewpoint and footnoted his work accordingly....Hayhurst's prejudiced footnotes have been deleted and replaced" (p.

16); Turner might have added, "with prejudiced footnotes of my own." A remark concerning the testimony of J. H. Allman and Andrew Mehan that Tom McLaury and Ike Clanton had checked their weapons is typical: "Allman and Mehan's testimony regarding the checking of Ike Clanton and Tom McLaury's weapons appears to be real enough on the surface, but the weapons in question could easily be a plant by the prosecution to help convict the Earps" (p. 89). Readers should disregard all notes, both Hayhurst's and Turner's, and form their own opinion.

10 Ibid., Testimony of Joseph I. Clanton, p. 97.

11 Ibid., Statement of Wyatt S. Earp, pp. 159–60. Wells Spicer permitted Earp was to read his statement in court. Cross examination was not allowed.

12 Ibid., Testimony of E. F. Boyle, p. 174.

13 Ibid., Testimony of Julius Kelley, p. 203.

14 Ibid., Testimony of R. F. Hafford, p. 62.

15 Ibid., Testimony of Joseph I. Clanton, pp. 98–99.

16 Ibid., Statement of Wyatt S. Earp, p. 161.

17 Ibid., Testimony of A. Bauer, p. 122.

18 Ibid., Testimony of J. H. Batcher, p. 126.

19 Ibid., Testimony of Thomas Keefe, p. 127.

20 Ibid., Testimony of William Allen, p. 55.

21 Turner, p. 61.

22 Ibid., Testimony of Martha J. King, p. 40.

23 Ibid.,Testimony of H. M. Matthews, p. 134.

24 Ibid., Testimony of James Kehoe, p. 69.

25 Ibid.,Testimony of Thomas Keefe, p. 130.

26 Ibid., Testimony of Andrew Mehan, p. 75; Testimony of J. H. Allman, p. 88.

27 Ibid., Testimony of E. F. Boyle, pp. 174–75.

28 Tombstone *Epitaph*, October 28, 1881.

29 *Nugget*, September 14, 1881.

30 Ibid., November 26, 1881.

31 Ibid., November 29, 1881.

32 Ibid., November 30, 1881.

33 Ibid., December 1, 1881.

34 Prescott *Miner*, November 10 and 24, 1881, quoted in Ball, p. 121.

Chapter 20

1 John J. Gosper, to Chester A. Arthur, December 12, 1881, RG60.

2 *Epitaph*, December 15, 1881.

3 Ibid., December 16, 1881.

4 Ibid.

5 Traywick, p. 13.

6 Parsons Journal, December 17, 1881.

7 Tombstone *Epitaph*, December 18, 1881. "Fight is not my racket" is a clear reference to Ike Clanton, who Spicer may have felt was behind the letter.

8 C.P. Dake to Phillips, December 8, 1881, RG60.

9 J.J. Gosper to Samuel F. Phillips, acting attorney general December 8, 1881, RG60.

[10] Parsons Journal, December 29, 1881. The McLaury referred to is William Rowland McLaury, a brother of Tom and Frank, born December 6, 1844. McLaury had a legal practice in Fort Worth, Texas, but went to Tombstone and assisted the prosecution during the Earp hearings. October 1881 was a tragic month for McLaury, for on the thirty-first his wife, Lona DeWitt, died. Disillusioned with Arizona justice, McLaury returned to his home shortly after Earp's shooting. He may well have been implicated in the ambush, for on April 13, 1884, he wrote to his father, "My expense out there has been very unfortunate—as to my health and badly injured me as to money matters—and none of the results have been satisfactory. The only result is the death of Morgan and crippling of Virgil Earp and death of McMasters."

[11] DeMattos, "Johnnny Ringo," p. 41.

[12] Traywick, p. 13.

[13] Epitaph, January 9, 1882. The Mexican wood hauler's identity is intriguing. Some writers have identified him as Florentino Cruz, a Mexican wood hauler whom the Earps later killed. If Cruz was at the holdup, their motivation for killing him could have been to silence a witness. However, no contemporary evidence indicates that Cruz was the man in question.

[14] DeMattos, "Johnny Ringo," p. 41.

[15] Epitaph, January 9, 1882.

[16] Epitaph, July 22, 1882.

[17] Parsons Journal, January 17, 1881.

[18] Hancock.

[19] Ibid.

[20] Personal interview with Ben Olney, undated, in author's collection.

[21] Breakenridge, pp. 266–67.

[22] Affidavit of James C. Earp, Arizona Pioneer's Historical Society.

[23] Parsons Journal, January 25, 1881.

[24] Epitaph, January 25, 1882.

[25] Ibid.

[26] Nugget, February 1, 1882.

[27] Epitaph, January 25, 1882. The telegram also appeared in the Nugget.

[28] Optic, January 31, 1882.

[29] Parsons Journal, January 30, 1881.

[30] Ibid., September 1, 1880.

[31] Cochise County, Arizona, District Court Records, Cause 81.

Chapter 21

[1] Parsons Journal, February 15, 1882. Dan "Big Tip" Tipton was a close adherent of the Earps.

[2] Grace McCool, So Said the Coroner (Tombstone, Arizona: The Tombstone Epitaph, 1968), p. 84.

[3] Epitaph, March 20, 1882.

[4] Traywick, p. 15.

[5] Epitaph, March 22, 1882.

[6] Ibid.

[7] Glenn G. Boyer, "Wyatt Earp, Legendary American," True West (August 1994),

p. 18.

8 *Epitaph,* March 22, 1882.

9 Parsons Journal, March 21, 1882.

10 Ibid., March 22, 1882.

11 *Epitaph,* March 23, 1882. Sherman MacMasters was then under indictment for stage robbery and rustling.

12 Ibid.

13 Parsons Journal, March 23, 1882.

14 *Epitaph,* March 27, 1882.

15 Ibid., April 3, 1882.

16 Breakenridge, p. 175.

17 *Nugget,* March 31, 1882.

18 Hancock.

19 *Rocky Mountain News,* May 21, 1882.

20 *Epitaph,* March 27, 1882.

21 Philip J. Rasch, "The Brief Careers of Billy Grounds and Zwing Hunt," *Real West* (February 1985).

22 *Epitaph,* August 19, 1882.

Chapter 22

1 Cochise County, Arizona, District Court Records, Cause No. 53. This cause was noted as Territory of Arizona v. John Ringgold.

2 1882 Great Register of Cochise County, Arizona.

3 Ibid., Causes 53 and 81.

4 Ibid.

5 Emma M. Muir, *Old Shakespeare* (Lordsburg, New Mexico: John T. Muir Ranch, n.d.), p. 16.

6 *Daily Epitaph,* July 18, 1882. The same article appeared in the *Weekly Epitaph* of July 22, 1882.

7 Ibid.

8 Breakenridge, p. 313.

9 *Epitaph,* July 18, 1882.

10 See Appendix 1 for more on the Johnny-behind-the-Deuce theory.

11 Burrows, *Gunfighter,* p. 188.

12 Ibid., p. 141.

13 Ibid., pp. 142–43.

14 Tucson *Weekly Citizen,* July 30, 1882. Joe Olney may have accompanied Ringo on this trip. One of the existing photographs of Joe was taken at John A. Todd's studio in Sacramento, California.

15 *Weekly Star,* July 20, 1882.

16 Phoenix *Gazette,* July 18, 1882. Accounts of Ringo's death appeared in many newspapers including the *Los Angeles Times,* July 18, 1882.

17 Reminiscences of Robert M. Boller. Arizona Historical Society.

18 Ibid.

19 Hancock.

20 Boller.

[21] Tucson *Weekly Citizen*, July 30, 1882.

[22] *Arizona Silver Belt*, December 13, 1884. The *Arizona Weekly Citizen* of December 13, 1884, also published an obituary of Joe "Hill" Olney.

[23] Traywick, p. 16.

[24] Yuma Penitentiary Prison Records; Yuma (Arizona) *Times,* June 14, 1893.

Chapter 23

[1] Burrows, *Gunfighter*, p. 141.

[2] Traywick, p. 5.

[3] David Leer Ringo, rev. of Jack Burrows, *John Ringo: The Gunfighter Who Never Was* in *Ringo Researcher* 3, No. 3 (1987): 127.

[4] Burrows, "Ringo Myth," p. 6.

[5] Burrows, *Gunfighter*, p. 147.

[6] Burrows, "Ringo Myth," p. 6.

[7] *Daily Epitaph*, July 25, 1882.

[8] Burrows, *Gunfighter*, p. 138.

[9] Ibid., p. 139.

[10] Minerva Hamblin Letton to David L. Ringo, September 15, 1934.

[11] Letton monograph. Courtesy David L. Ringo.

[12] Mattie B. Cushing and M. Enna Ringo to Mrs. J.H. [Minerva] Letton, October 5, 1934.

[13] Minerva H. Letton to David L. Ringo, October 12, 1934.

[14] Mattie B. Cushing and M. Enna Ringo to David Leer Ringo and Mrs. J.H. Letton, November 5, 1934.

[15] Burrows, *Gunfighter*, p. 141, quoting May Ringo King to Joanna.

[16] Letter received from May King, August 27, 1992.

[17] Letter received from Dr. William K. Hall, September 14, 1992.

[18] Frank Cushing to Charles R. Ringo, August 12, 1970. Cushing noted that he had "known him [Erwin] for twelve or more years…"

[19] Allen Erwin to Charles Parsons, January 19, 1973.

[20] Frank Cushing to Charles Ringo, August 12, 1970.

[21] Burrows, *Gunfighter*, p. 214.

[22] Frank Cushing to Charles Ringo, August 12, 1970.

[23] Letter received from Era Fay Huff, February 17, 1983.

[24] Allen Erwin to Charles Parsons, January 19, 1973.

[25] Allen Erwin to Charles Parsons, May 9, 1971.

[26] Charles Ringo to Frank Cushing, January 8, 1970.

[27] Burrows, "Ringo," p. 17.

[28] Frank Cushing to May King, March 2, 1971.

[29] San Jose (California) *Pioneer*, December 13, 1879, and April 23, 1881.

SELECTED BIBLIOGRAPHY

The following represents an abbreviated bibliography of sources used in preparing this biography for publication. While it does not pretend to be an all inclusive listing of all the sources consulted, it should provide interested readers with enough information to pursue their own research.

Books and Pamphlets

Ball, Larry D. *The United States Marshals of New Mexico and Arizona Territories 1846–1912.* Albuquerque: University of New Mexico Press, 1978.

Barler, Miles. *Early Days In Llano.* Llano, Texas:The Llano Times, [c. 1900].

Bartholomew, Ed. *Western Hard-Cases or, Gunfighters Named Smith.* Frontier Book Company, Ruidoso, New Mexico. 1960.

————. *Wyatt Earp: The Man and the Myth.* Toyahvale, Texas: Frontier Book Company, 1964.

————. *Wyatt Earp: The Untold Story.* Toyahvale, Texas: Frontier Book Company, 1963.

Biggers, Don H. *German Pioneers in Texas.* Austin: Eakin Publications, Inc., 1983.

Boyer, Glenn G. *Wyatt Earp's Tombstone Vendetta.* Honolulu: Talei Publishers, Inc., 1993.

Brant, Marley. *The Outlaw Youngers—A Confederate Brotherhood.* Lanham, Maryland: Madison Books, 1992.

Breakenridge, William M. *Helldorado.* Boston, 1928; rpt. Lincoln: University of Nebraska Press, 1992.

Burns, Walter Noble. *Tombstone: An Iliad of the Southwest.* Garden City, NY, 1927; rpt. New York: Ballantine Books, 1974.

Burrows, Jack. *John Ringo—The Gunfighter Who Never Was.* Tucson, Arizona: University of Arizona Press, 1987.

Chappell, Wilma and William K. Hall. *The Simms Family of Stafford County, Virginia.* St. Louis: n.p., 1969.

Chase, C. M. *The Editor's Run in New Mexico and Colorado.* Fort Davis, Texas: Frontier Book Company, 1968.

Chisholm, Joe. *Brewery Gulch.* San Antonio: The Naylor Company, 1949.

Davis, Britton. *The Truth About Geronimo.* Lincoln: University of Nebraska Press, 1976.

Debo, Darrell. *Burnet County History.* Vol. 2. Burnet, Texas: Eakin Press, 1979.

De Vos, Julius E., ed. *One Hundred Years of the Hilda (Bethel) Methodist Church and Parent Organizations, 1856–1955.* Hilda, Texas: Hilda United Methodist Church, 1973.

Dodge, Fred. *Under Cover For Wells Fargo.* Edited by Carolyn Lake. New York: Houghton-Mifflin Company, 1969.

Earp, Wyatt S. *Wyatt Earp.* Foreword by Glenn G. Boyer. Sierra Vista, Arizona: Yuma Bissette, 1981.

1884 History of Wayne County, Indiana. Vol. 2. Chicago: Inter-State Publishing Co., 1884.

Fox, Henry Clay, ed. *Memoirs of Wayne County and the City of Richmond, Indiana.* Madison, Wisconsin: Western Historical Association, 1912.

Gamel, Thomas W. *The Life of Thomas W. Gamel.* Mason, Texas: privately printed, [c. 1932].

Geistweidt, Nelson. *Geistweidt Family History.* Doss, Texas: n.p., 1971.

Hardin, John Wesley. *The Life of John Wesley Hardin.* Seguin, Texas, 1896; rpt. Norman, Oklahoma: University of Oklahoma Press, 1980.

Holmes, Lucia M. *Diary of Lucia M. Holmes.* Mason, Texas: Mason County Historical Commission, 1985.

Jordan, Gilbert J. *A Biographical Sketch of Ernst and Lizette Jordan.* N.p.: n.p., [c. 1931].

_____. *Yesterday in the Texas Hill Country.* College Station: Texas A&M University Press, 1979.

Gillett James B. *Six Years with the Texas Rangers.* Austin, 1921; rpt., Lincoln: University of Nebraska Press, 1976.

Jacobsen, Joel. *Such Men as Billy the Kid.* Lincoln, Nebraska: University of Nebraska Press, 1994.

King, Irene Marschall. *John O. Meusebach.* Austin: University of Texas Press, 1987.

King, Larry. *Rector Records.* Hendersonville, Tennessee: Privately printed, 1986.

Klasner, Lily. *My Girlhood Among Outlaws.* Edited by Eve Ball. Tucson: University of Arizona Press, 1972.

Krueger, Max Amadeus Paulus. *Second Fatherland.* Texas College Station: Texas A&M University Press, 1976.

Lake, Stuart N. *Wyatt Earp, Frontier Marshal.* New York: Houghton Mifflin Company, 1931.

McCool, Grace. *So Said the Coroner.* Tombstone, Arizona: The Tombstone Epitaph, 1968.

Martin, Douglas D. *Tombstone's Epitaph.* Albuquerque: University of New Mexico Press, 1951.

Muir, Emma M. *Old Shakespeare.* Lordsburg, New Mexico: John T. Muir Ranch, n.d.

Nolan, Frederick. *The Lincoln County War: A Documentary History.* Norman: University of Oklahoma Press, 1992.

Olney, Thomas. *A Genealogy of the Descendants of Thomas Olney.* Providence, Rhode Island: E.L. Freeman & Son, 1889.

O'Neil, James B. *They Die But Once.* New York: Knight Publications, Inc., 1935.

Parsons, Chuck. *"Pidge": A Texas Ranger from Virginia.* Wolfe City, Texas: Henington Publishing Company, 1985.

_____, and Gary P. Fitterer. *Captain C. B. McKinney: The Law In South Texas.* Wolfe City, Texas: Henington Publishing Company, 1993.

Parsons, George W. *The Private Journal of George W. Parsons.* Tombstone, Arizona: Tombstone Epitaph, 1972.

Ringo, David Leer. *The First Five Generations of the Ringo Family in America.* RFHS, Vol. 2. Alhambra, California: The Freeborn Family Organization, Inc., 1982.

_____, ed. *The Line of Descent from Major Ringo.* RFHS, Vol. 5. Alhambra, California: The Freeborn Family Organization, Inc., 1981.

_____, ed. *The Line of Descent from Samuel H. Ringo.* RFHS, Vol. 7. Alhambra, California: The Freeborn Family Organization, Inc., 1980.

_____. *The Ringos in Europe.* Ringo Family History Series [RFHS], Vol. 1, Part 1. Alhambra, California: The Freeborn Family Organization, Inc., 1981.

Ringo, Mary. *The Journal of Mrs. Mary Ringo.* Santa Ana, California: Privately printed, 1956.

Ringgold, Jennie Parks. *Frontier Days in the Old Southwest.* San Antonio: The Naylor Company, 1952.

Roberts, Dan W. *Rangers and Sovereignty.* Austin: State House Press, 1987.

Rollins, Philip Ashton. *The Cowboy.* New York: Ballantine Books, 1973.

San Jose (California) *City Directory,* 1870.

San Jose (California) *City Directory,* 1872–3.

San Jose (California) *City Directory,* 1876.

Secrest, William B. *Lawmen & Desperadoes.* Spokane, Washington: The Arthur H. Clark Company, 1994.

Settle, William A. *Jesse James Was His Name.* Columbia: University of Missouri Press, 1966.

Sonnichsen, C. L.. *I'll Die Before I'll Run.* New York, 1951; rpt., Lincoln: University of Nebraska Press, 1988.

_____. *Ten Texas Feuds.* Albuquerque: University of New Mexico Press, 1971.

Thomas, Clarke and Jack Glendenning. *The Slicker War.* Aldrich, Missouri: Bona Publishing Company, 1984.

Thornbrough, Emma Lou. *Indiana in the Civil War Era, 1850–1880.* Vol. 3. Indianapolis: Indiana Historical Bureau and Indiana Historical Society, 1965.

Thrapp, Dan L. *The Conquest of Apacheria.* Norman: University of Oklahoma Press, 1967.

Tise, Sammy. *Texas County Sheriffs*. Albuquerque, New Mexico: privately printed, 1989.

Traywick, Ben F. *John Peters Ringo: Mythical Gunfighter*. Tombstone, Arizona: Red Marie's Bookstore, 1987.

Turner, Alford E.. *The O. K. Corral Inquest*. College Station, Texas: Creative Publishing Company, 1981.

Utley, Robert. *High Noon in Lincoln: Violence on the Western Frontier*. Albuquerque: University of New Mexico Press, 1987.

Williams, R.H. *With the Border Ruffians*. Lincoln, Nebraska: University of Nebraska Press, 1982.

Young, Andrew White. *History of Wayne County, Indiana*. Cincinnati: Robert Clarke & Co., 1872.

Magazines and Periodicals

Aranda, Daniel. "An Episode From Victorio's War." *Real West*, February 1984, pp. 14–19.

Boyer, Glenn G. "Curly Bill Has Been Killed at Last." *Real West*, June 1984, pp. 32-49.

_____. "Welcome to Wyatt Earp Country." *Arizona Highways*, November 1982, pp. 4–15.

_____. "Wyatt Earp Legendary American." *True West*, August 1994, pp. 14–20.

Brown, Randy. "The Death of Martin Ringo." *Overland Journal*, 7, No. 1 (1989), pp. 20–23.

Burrows, Jack. "John Ringo: The Story of a Western Myth." *Montana*, October 1980, pp. 2–15.

_____. "Ringo." *The American West*, January 1970, pp. 17–21.

_____. "Johnny Ringo." *Real West*, April 1985, pp. 38–42, 51.

_____. "Johnny Ringo! The Elusive Man Behind the Myth." NOLA *Quarterly* 3, No 2. (1977): 1–5, 10.

DeVos, Julius. "Mason County's Unsettled Years 1860–1880." *Edwards Plateau Historian* 7 (1978–82): 18–25.

Duffen. William A. "'Jollification'—Arizona Style: A Description of Gunplay in 1880." *Arizona and the West* 1, No. (1959): 281–84.

Eckhardt, C. F. "The Real Johnny Ringo Legend Not Square with the Facts." *Tombstone Epitaph* (National Edition), August 1994, pp. 12–13.

"Fifty-two Years in West Texas." *Frontier Times*, May 1928, pp. 340–43.

Gatto, Steve. "Johnny Ringo: Land and Cattle Speculator." NOLA *Quarterly* 18, No. 4. (1994): 9–10.

Hill, Janaloo. "Yours Until Death, William Grounds." *True West*, March-April 1973, pp. 14–15, 54–59.

Hunter, J. Marvin. "Brief History of Early Days In Mason County." *Frontier*

Times, January 1929, pp. 153–66.

Johnson, Dave. "The Doell Killing: Feudal Vengeance or Private Murder?" NOLA *Quarterly* 11, No. 1 (1986): 8–10.

———. "Revenge In Mason County, Texas." NOLA *Quarterly* 10, No. 1 (1985): 7–8, 12.

Morey, Jeffrey J. "The Curious Vendetta of Glenn G. Boyer." NOLA *Quarterly* 18, No. 4 (1994): 22–28.

Parsons, Chuck. Review of *John Ringo: The Gunfighter Who Never Was,* by Jack Burrows. In *New Mexico Historical Review* 64, (1989): 468.

Rasch, Phillip J. "Adios, Dick Lloyd!" NOLA *Quarterly* 8, No. 1(1983): 7.

———. "'Six Shooter' and 'Three Shooter Smith.'" NOLA *Quarterly* 9, No. 4 (1985): 9–10.

———. "The Brief Careers of Billy Grounds and Zwing Hunt." *Real West,* February 1985, pp. 12–15.

Ringo, David Leer. Review of *John Ringo: The Gunfighter Who Never Was,* by Jack Burrows. In *Ringo Researcher* 3, No. 3 (1987): 125–26 .

Roberts, Gary L. "The West's Gunmen." Part 2. *The American West,* March 1971, pp. 18–23, 61–62.

Schmidt, Minnie Gandy. "Schmidt Hereford Ranch, Inc." *Edwards Plateau Historian* 8 (1983–89): 57–69.

Shirley, John. "The Real Clantons: A Consensus." NOLA *Quarterly* 16, No. 1 (1992): 20–24.

Turner, Alford E. "The Clantons of Apache County." *Real West Annual* (1980), pp. 38–41, 73.

Van Slyke, Sue C. "The Truth About the Clantons of Tombstone." NOLA *Quarterly* 7, No. 1. (1982): 12–17.

——— and Dave Johnson. "Kin to the Clantons." NOLA *Quarterly* 14, No. 2, (1990), pp. 8, 21–23.

———. "Pete Clanton—What's in a Name?" NOLA *Quarterly* 18, No. 2 (1994): 17–22.

Van Valkenburgh, Richard. "Who Was Elected Sheriff?" [Arizona] *Sheriff's Magazine,* February 1949, p.11.

Newspapers

ARIZONA

Globe *Arizona Silver Belt.*

Phoenix *Gazette.*

Tombstone *Daily Epitaph.*

Tombstone *Daily Nugget.*

Tombstone *Weekly Epitaph.*

Tombstone *Weekly Nugget.*

Tucson *Arizona Daily Star.*

Tucson *Arizona Weekly Star.*

Tucson *Daily Citizen.*
Tucson *Weekly Citizen.*
ARKANSAS
Helena *Southern Shield.*
COLORADO
Denver *Tribune*
Denver *Rocky Mountain News.*
INDIANA
Centerville *Indiana True Republican.*
Centerville *Free Territorial Sentinel.*
Indianapolis *Daily Journal.*
Richmond *Palladium.*
Richmond *Palladium–Item.*
KANSAS
Dodge City *Times.*
Ellsworth *Reporter.*
MISSOURI
Gallatin *Democrat.*
Gallatin *North Missourian.*
Liberty *Advance Tribune.*
Liberty *Tribune.*
Richmond *Missourian.*
MONTANA
Conrad *Independent Observer.*
Great Falls *Tribune.*
NEW MEXICO
Cimarron *News and Press.*
Las Vegas *Daily Optic.*
Las Vegas *Gazette.*
Lordsburg *Liberal.*
Santa Fe *New Mexican.*
Silver City *The New Southwest and Grant County Herald.*
TENNESSEE
Memphis *Appeal.*
TEXAS
Austin *Daily Statesman.*
Austin *Weekly Statesman.*
Burnet *Bulletin.*
Clarksville *Northern Standard.*
Dallas *Herald.*
Fayette County New Era.
Galveston *Christian Advocate.*
Galveston *Daily News.*

Galveston *Weekly News.*
Houston *Daily Telegraph.*
Lampasas *Dispatch.*
San Antonio *Daily Express.*
San Antonio Daily Herald.

Adjutant General of Texas Files

These files include monthly reports of Ranger commanders, Muster Rolls, Pay Rolls, State Police Muster Rolls and related documents. The originals are located in the Texas State Archives, Lorenzo de Zavala State Archives & Library Building, P.O. Box 12927, Austin, Texas 78711. Donaly E. Brice, research specialist, has been consistently helpful in my research efforts.

Documents of Texas Rangers utilized in this study include reports and letters from Dan W. Roberts, Henry M. Holmes, John B. Jones, and William Steele.

[Kirk, John P.]. *A List of Fugitives from Justice*, Austin, Texas. 1886.

[Steele, William]. *A List of Fugitives from Justice*, Austin, Texas. 1878.

Documents and Records

Cochise County Arizona. Great Register, 1882.
Confederate Army. Muster Rolls. Texas State Archives.
Confederate Army. Military Record of Samuel Olney. Texas State Archives.
Confederate Army. Military Record of Allen G. Roberts. Texas State Archives.
Mullin (Robert N.) Collection. Nita Stewart Haley Memorial Library.
State of Texas. Pension Application File. John T. Olney. Texas State Archives.
U.S. Army. Military Record of Martin Ringo. National Archives.
U.S. Army. Military Record of John Anton Wohrle. National Archives.
U.S. Army. Proceedings of the Court Martial in the Case of John W. Clanton, Company B, Parson's Regt. Cavalry. Record Group 109. National Archives.

Legal Sources

Arizona Territorial Penitentiary (Yuma). Prison Records.
Blanco County, Texas. Deed Records.
Burleson County, Texas. Deed Records.
Burnet County, Texas.
    Deed Records.
    District Court Records.
Cases Argued and Adjuded in the Court of Appeals. Vol. 2. n.p.: Soule, Thomas

& Wentworth, 1878.
Clay County, Missouri.
>Deed Records
>Marriage Records.
Cochise County, Arizona.
>Coroner's Inquests
>District Clerk Records.
Colfax County, New Mexico. District Court Records.
Daviess County, Missouri. Deed Records.
Grant County, New Mexico.
>Deed Records
>District Court Records.
Lampasas County, Texas. District Court Records.
Pima County, Arizona. District Court Records.
Mason County, Texas.
>District Court Records.
>Election Records.
>Records of Marks and Brands.
Pima County, Arizona. District Court Records.
Prince William County, Virgina. Deed Records.
Pulaski County, Arkansas. Will Records.
Record Group 60. National Archives.
Santa Clara County, California. Probate Records.
Travis County, Texas. Record of Arrests [Austin].
Texas Court of Appeal Records. Texas State Archives.
Texas Tax Rolls 1872–1875. Texas State Archives.
Wayne County, Indiana (Richmond).
>Deed Records.
>Administrators, Executors and Guardians Docket.

Unpublished Source Material

Bartholomew, Ed. Unpublished manuscript. Author's files.
_____. Archival collection.
Collins, Jerome B. Correspondence. University of Arizona.
Cushing, Mattie B. Correspondence. Author's files.
Boller, Robert. "Reminiscences of Robert Boller." Arizona Pioneers' Historical Society.
Erwin, Allen. Correspondence. Author's files.
Franklin, A.M. "Reminiscences of A. M. Franklin." Arizona Pioneers' Historical Society.
_____. "Story of Ringo and the Cattle Thieves." 1925. Arizona State Archives.

Gray, John P. Unpublished manuscript. Arizona Pioneers' Historical Society.

Hancock (J. C.) File. Arizona Pioneers' Historical Society.

Hardin, John Wesley. Correspondence.

Hayes, M.L. Drive Book. Mason County, Texas, Historical Society.

Hennig, Betty. "'Frank' Francis Johnson and Related Families." Unpublished manuscript. c. 1988. Author's files.

Letton, Minerva Hamblin. Correspondence. Author's files.

_____. "One Honorable Outlaw." Unpublished manuscript. 1934. Author's files.

Longley, William P. Correspondence. Author's files.

Lower Willow Creek Methodist Church Records. Lower Willow Creek, Texas.

Morgan, Henry. "Reminiscences of Henry Morgan." Arizona Pioneers' Historical Society.

Olney, Sophie Haynes. Unpublished manuscript. No date. Author's files.

"Reminiscences of a Stranger." July 29, 1927. Arizona Pioneers' Historical Society.

Ringo, Charles R. Correspondence. Author's files.

Ringo, Mary Enna. Correspondence. Author's files.

Ringgold, Jennie Parks. Correspondence.

Schaaf, Emil. Interview of Frank and John Stark. Undated. University of Arizona.

Stark. David. "Skirmish at Cravensville." Unpublished manuscript. 1992. Author's files.

Interviews, Letters, Research Notes

In compiling the research for this book a number of interviews and significant correspondence has taken place. Those of particular help include, but are not limited to: Janet Baccus, Ed Bartholomew, Hiram Foster Casner, James Chase, Joan DeKorte, Ina Davis, Sherry Davis, Annie May Durrant, H. V. "Todd" Faris, Steve Gatto, Dr. William K. Hall, Carolyn Harsh, Janaloo Hill, Joe C. Hill, Jane Hoerster, Era Fay Huff, Walker W. "Bud" Jordan, May Ringo King, George Kobayashi, Nina Legge, Grace McCool, Jim McFarland, Rick Miller, Ben Olney, John Olney, Chuck Parsons, Jim Peterson, Johnie-Lee Reeves, David L. Ringo, David Stark, George M. Tagg, LaVoy Taylor, Sue C. Van Slyke.

Feeger, Luther. Scrapbook. This is a scrapbook of undated newspaper clippings compiled by the Morrison–Reeves Library.

Parsons, Chuck. Archival Collection.

Rose, Pete. Archival Collection.

INDEX

Getty, D.: 31
Gibson, Nathan: 16
Gillespie, John: 194
Gillett, James B.: 71
Gladden, George W.: 60, 74–76, 79–82, 84, 94–99
Gooch, Ben: 56, 92
Goodfellow, George: 135
Goodrich, Briggs: 183, 187, 196
Gosper, John J.: 113–114, 139, 141, 170, 177, 180
Graff, Leopold: 155
Graham, Bill: 131–132
Graham, George: 131–132
Gray (judge): 132
Gray, Alice: 50
Gray, Dixie Lee: 149, 151, 157–161, 163
Gray, John P.: 123, 137, 149, 151, 157, 159–160
Gray, Mike: 161
Green, Charlie: 151
Green, John (Indiana pioneer): 14–15
Green, John (Arizona pioneer): 151
Green's Fork, Indiana, confusion over name of John Ringo's birthplace: 14
Grounds, William: 115, 194

Hafford, R.F.: 171
Hall, Caleb: 65
Hall, Caleb "Kale": 64–66
Hall, Lucy: 65
Halliday (acquaintance of Martin Ringo): 38
Hancock, James C.: 108, 111, 123, 149, 151, 154, 182, 193, 202
Hancock, Louis: 109–110
Hankins, John Henry: see Smith, Six-Shooter
Hannah, Henry: 16
Harcourt, Charles: 72–73
Hardin, John Wesley: xvi, 51, 97–99, 104
Harding, Elijah: 10
Harpon (Harpin), James: 6
Harrington, Jimmy: 178
Harris, George W.: 67
Harrison, John: 116
Hase (Hays[?]; wagon master): 31
Haslett, Bill: 148
Haslett, Ike: 148

Hatch, Bob: 187
Hatfield, Jonas, Sr.: 14
Hatfield, Thomas: 14
Hayes, M.L.: 56
Haynes, John: 94
Head, Harry: 135, 138, 148, 173
Henry (slave): 26
Herndon (member of Bass gang): 98
Hey, Wilson: 67, 101
Hickey, N.L.: 106
Hicklin, Thomas: 28
Hicks, Bill: 123, 169
Hicks, Milt: 123, 149, 151, 154, 169
Hill, Joe: see Olney, Joseph Graves
Hinds, Benjamin: 51
Hinds, Benjamin J.: 51
Hinds, J.B.: 106
Hinds, Laurinda: 51
Hinds, Levi: 51
Hinds, Margery: 51
Hinds, William: 51
Hoerster, Daniel: 60, 64, 68, 74–75, 80, 82
Hoerster, Heinrich: 54
Hoerster, Katherine: 74
Hole, Daniel: 28
Holliday, John Henry "Doc": 130, 136–138, 157, 170–174, 181, 184, 188–189, 193, 195, 201
Holmes, Lucia: 64–67, 82, 88, 92
Holmes, Henry M.: 67, 69, 76–78, 92
Hoo-Doo War: 53; see also Mason County War
Hooker, H.C.: 192–193
Hopkins, Mark: 101
Horton, Joseph: 71
Hoskins, William P.: 87
Howard, Ulysses: 59
Hughes, Jim: 132, 151, 154, 197
Hughes, Mary: 197
Hughes, Nick: 108, 132
Hugo, Charles: 120
Hume, James B.: 181
Humphries, William: 18
Hunt, F.F.: 194
Hunt, Zwing: 194

Indian Charlie: 188–189
Indiana: influences of, on Ringo family:

O'Rourke, Michael: 201

Parks, Jennie: 104
Parks, John: 104, 106
Parsons, George W.: 114, 121–122, 135, 137, 162, 170, 179, 181–182, 184, 186, 189
Patrick, W.J.: 126
Patterson, Frank: 131
Patterson, N.C.: 102
Paul, Bob: 119, 123–125, 134, 137, 168, 188, 193
Peck, Fred: 85
Peel, B.L.: 194
Peel, M.R.: 194
Pesqueira (Mexican general): 154
"Peter" (newspaper correspondent): 56
Peters, Ashby: 10
Peters, Augusta: 10–11, 40,
Peters, Charley: 38–39
Peters, Enfield S. "Enna": 10, 22, 31
Peters, John R.: 10–11, 17, 23
Peters, Martha "Mattie": 10, 33, 38
Peters, Vienna Strother: 10, 31
Peters, William: 10
Phillips, John R.: 115
Phillips, Samuel F.: 180
Philpott, Eli "Bud": 134–136, 157, 160, 190
Pipes (member of Bass gang): 98
Pluenneke, Henry: 82
Pomroy, E.B.: 120, 140, 148
Powers, William: 18–19
Price, James B.: 115
Price, Sterling: 27
Pritchet, John: 16
Pryor, Bennett B.: 24, 28
Pryor, James: 24
Pryor, Lavinia: 26–27
Pryor, Silas H.: 26–27
Purcell, Sarah Sullivan: 40
Pursley, James: 194
Pyle, John F.: 41

Ranck, J.E.: 100
Randall, Bill: 92
Ray, Loudrich "Loud": 48
Raymond (San Simon ranchman): 129
Rector, Hannah: 3

Redding, J.M.: 59
Redding, John: 91
Redding, William R.: 59
Redding, William Z.: 48, 56, 59
Redfield, Len: 135, 137
Reingodus: 4
Reyes, Brigido: 112–113, 121–122, 146
Reynolds, N.O.: 100
Richards (land owner): 16
Richildis, countess of Hainaut: 4
Ringo surname: patronymic origins of, 3–4; family origin of, 4–5
Ringo I the Bald: 3–4
Ringo, lord of Dendermonde: 4
Ringo, Aefje (daughter of Albertus): 6
Ringo, Albert H.: 8, 19
Ringo, Albertus: 5
Ringo, Alburtis "Burtis": 3
Ringo, Alburtus: 6
Ringo, Andrew Hodge: 22–23
Ringo, Catherine: 7, 17
Ringo, Charles R.: 4, 42–43, 201
Ringo, Cornelis: 5
Ringo, Cornelius (son of Henry): 3, 6
Ringo, Cornelius (son of Philip): 6–7
Ringo, Cornelius (son of Samuel H.): 17
Ringo, Daniel: 9
Ringo, Elias: 18
Ringo, Elizabeth Hazelrigg: 7
Ringo, Elvira: 8–9, 45
Ringo, Fanny Fern: 25, 36, 41–42, 90, 196
Ringo, Geertje Cornelis Philipszen: 5
Ringo, Hamilton: 8–9, 19
Ringo, Lucinda: 9
Ringo, Henry: 3, 6–7
Ringo, Jacques: 4
Ringo, Jan: 5
Ringo, Janneken: 5
Ringo, Jane Cook: 6–7
Ringo, Jean (Jan): 4
Ringo, Joel: 8–9
Ringo, John (son of Peter): 19
Ringo, John (son of Philip): 6–7
Ringo, John Peters: 3–4, 8, 10, 14, 18, 22, 25, 27, 30–31, 36, 38–42, 45–54, 59, 62, 67, 72, 74, 78–79, 100- 106, 108, 111–112, 114–117, 119, 123, 125, 129–130, 134, 138,

140, 144, 148, 151, 153–156, 168–169, 173, 175, 177–179, 180–189, 193, 195, 204; ancestors of, 3–11; arrest and escape from Lampasas jail, 83–89; arrest and trial in Mason, 90–99; attitude to mob law, 20, 28, 65; birth, 15; Burns' portrait of, xv–xvii; California influence on, 39–44; challenges Wyatt Earp, 182; death, 196–203; emigration to California, 29–38; Indiana influence on, 12–20 passim; killing of Dick Lloyd, 132–133; kills Jim Cheyney, 80; plans retaliation against Mexicans, 162–166; ranch partner with Ike Clanton, 126–127; shoots Louis Hancock, 109–110; suffers from post traumatic stress syndrome, 109

Ringo, Major: 3, 7
Ringo, Margaret Henderson: 8, 19
Ringo, Margaret Major: 3, 7
Ringo, Marshall C.: 8
Ringo, Martha Elizabeth: 8, 19, 24, 46
Ringo, Martin: 8–11, 15, 20–29, 31–33, 41; death of, 35–36, 38; description of, 17; suffers from tuberculosis, 22, 28–29
Ringo, Martin Albert: 20, 25, 31, 36, 41–42, 47, 90
Ringo, Mary Enna: 25, 41–42, 90
Ringo, Mary Peters: 10–11, 15, 20, 22-23, 25, 29–33, 35–36, 39–43, 46; death of, 90–91; description of, 17, 33, 37–38; grammatical skills of, 29–30
Ringo, Mattie Bell: 26–27, 29, 39–42, 90
Ringo, Melissa: 8
Ringo, Peter (son of Henry): 7, 9
Ringo, Peter (son of Major): 7–9, 19–20, 24–25
Ringo, Peter (son of Philip): 6–7
Ringo, Peter (son of Samuel H.): confused with John Ringo's grandfather, 17–19, 22, 47–48, 64–65
Ringo, Philip: 3, 6–7
Ringo, Philip Janszen: 3–5
Ringo, Pieter: 5
Ringo, Pugh: 8–9
Ringo, Robert William: 47

Ringo, Samantha V.: 47
Ringo, Samuel: 9–10, 22–23, 46
Ringo, Samuel H.: 7, 9
Ringo, Waldo P.: 8, 19
Ringo, William: 48
Ringo, William H.: 8–9, 19
Roberts, Allen G.: 50–52, 57, 59–60, 66
Roberts, Daniel Webster: 57, 62, 64, 66–67, 71
Roberts, Kate: 59
Roberts, Louisa: 59
Roberts, William: 59
Robinson, A.W.: 95–96
Robinson, J.S.: 196
Roerig, Peter: 135
Rountree, Bob: 94
Rountree, Wilson: 94
Russey, William: 15
Ryland, C.T.: 41

Sabins, Thomas B.: 24–25
Sanches, Cleto: 106
Saxon, W.W.: 60
Schofield, John M.: 27
Schubert (New Braunfels colonist): 54
Selman, John: 65
Selyns, Hendricus: 6
Sheets, Henry: 24
Sheets, John W.: 24
Shibbel, Charles: 114, 122–125
Shortridge, John: 14–15
Simmers (prospector): 16
Simmons (posse member): 18
Simms, Benjamin: 23
Simms, Benjamin A.: 10–11
Simms, Elizabeth Ashby: 10
Simms, Frances A.: 10
Simms, John: 23
Simms, Joseph S.: 23
Simms, Margaret: 23
Simms, Mary Augusta: 23
Simms, Richard: 10, 23
Simms, Terissa: 23
Singer, Sarah: 15
Slaughter, John H.: 136
Smith, B.F.: 200, 203
Smith, Charley: 169
Smith, Six-Shooter: xvi, 129–130, 194–195

Wiggins, Abe: 63, 65
Wilbur (Arivaca rancher): 121
Wilkes, F.D.: 97
Wilkinson, William: 149
Willard, Ashbel P.: 20
Willcox, Orlando B.: 141, 147
Williams (companion of John Ringo): 80
Williams, Jim: 60, 94–95
Williams, John M.: 16
Williams, Marshall: 124, 135–137, 167, 169, 178–179
Williams, T.S.: 146
Williamson, Cyrus: 68
Williamson, Frederick: 51–52
Williamson, Hannah: 68
Williamson, Lee: 68
Williamson, Timothy P. 51–53, 60, 67–69, 71–74, 144
Wills, Bill: 87
Wilson, R.B.: 97
Wingfield, C.W.: 99, 101
Winn, Rufus: 66–67
Winter, "Old Man": 169
Wirt, Elizabeth Ashby: 23, 46
Wirt, John R.: 23
Wirt, Margaret Simms: 23
Wirt, Philip: 23
Witzleben, Ernestine von: 54
Wohrle, Charles J.: 66
Wohrle, Helene: 65–66
Wohrle, John A.: 64–66, 68, 71–74, 84
Wohrle, John C.: 66
Woods, Daniel T.: 16
Woods, David B.: 16
Woods, Harry: 137–138, 167, 191–193
Woolf, Robert: 194
Wright, John W.: 21
Wright, Joseph A.: 12
Wright, "Whistling Dick": 178, 191
Wynn, Polk: 100
Yost, John: 198–202
Young, Jack: 194
Young, Mrs. (passerby): 200
Young, William: 16
Younger, Adeline Lee: 10
Younger, Bruce: 46
Younger, C.B.: 42
Younger, Charles Lee: 40

Younger, Coleman Purcell: 10, 40–42, 47, 91
Younger, Henry W.: 42
Younger, Thomas "Cole": 42
Younger brothers: 26, 40